BROKEN to *Beautiful*

Robin Rehbein

Trilogy Christian Publishers
A Wholly Owned Subsidiary of Trinity Broadcasting Network
2442 Michelle Drive
Tustin, CA 92780

For information, address Trilogy Christian Publishing
Rights Department, 2442 Michelle Drive, Tustin, Ca 92780.
Trilogy Christian Publishing/ TBN and colophon are trademarks of Trinity Broadcasting Network.

For information about special discounts for bulk purchases, please contact Trilogy Christian Publishing.

Manufactured in the United States of America

10 9 8 7 6 5 4 3 2 1

Library of Congress Cataloging-in-Publication Data is available.

ISBN 978-1-64088-519-6 (Print Book)
ISBN 978-1-64088-520-2 (ebook)

Dedication

It is my prayer that this book enriches your life as it has mine. Now may the Lord's hand bless it and may it do what the Father has created it to do: bring solace and healing. He wrote the book; I was merely his scribe. All glory to him in Jesus's name.

Contents

Preface

I am inviting you to join me on a journey from *Broken to Beautiful.* Come, walk with me through the trauma and fragmenting of my very soul as the Godhead delivers me and brings me through. Witness how my Father in heaven heard my hearts cries day and night. See how Jesus Christ, my Messiah my Savior, petitioned the courtroom of heaven on my behalf for answers to my prayers. Feel how the Holy Spirit, my Counselor, my Comforter held me close and sheltered me in the night hours as the enemy of my soul tried to rob me of any hope for my sanity. The Holy Spirit enveloped my soul to keep my thoughts captive to the obedience of his Word.

Journey with me as the Holy Spirit caught each piece of my heart as it broke into fragments, as my very life threatened to leave my body. My Comforter, my life preserver, my very breath at times. He never left me, never removed his presence from me, never once was he not surrounding me with his strength. He pulled me from the deep waters as they threatened to overtake me. Holy Spirit sustained my very life as my Savior stood in the gap for me, petitioning the Father on my behalf. The Father heard my cries, heard the petitions of Jesus.

The Father sent forth his Word and answered me.

Let us walk together from *Broken to Beautiful*, hand in hand, with the one who created us, the one who loved us more than life, and the one that promised never to leave us. Beautiful waits! Beautiful becomes! Beautiful is yours!

Broken

Having been fractured or damaged and no
longer in one piece or in working order.
(*Online Dictionary*)

Heart's Cry

Oh, so broken! Fragments of me scattered by the relentless winds that assault me. When will this ever end, Father? Oh, my God! My Father! What is left of me? Where do I go to find all the pieces of me? Show me the way back. I must live and not die.

Father Speaks

The road you have been called to walk has been a rough road, and I have been with you every step. I have seen the pain you have suffered. I have felt it. I have felt the anguish of your heart. The terror in your spirit, the hopelessness of your soul. Yet I say to you, I have been with you. I have never left you. The enemy of your soul desires to drain you of any hope, of any strength. He desires to bring you to the point of believing I am not watching over you. That I am not hearing your prayers, your calls of despair. That I have no time for you. Child, THAT IS NOT TRUE! I have been at your side. I have loved you with an everlasting love. I will never fail you! Speak my name out loud, over and over, until the demons flee and you have peace within. Then begin to praise me, for I will be found in your praise. This season will come to an end. You will make it through. Hold on to me, the lover of your soul. For I am a jealous God. I will not allow Satan to have you. He will no longer sift you. I have declared that you are coming up, you are coming out! Keep your eyes upon ME.

Scripture

W hy, my soul, are you downcast? Why so disturbed within me? Put your hope in God, for I will yet praise him, my Savior and my God. (Psalm 42:5, 11, NIV)

It shall come to pass, that before they call, I will answer; and while they are yet speaking, I will hear. (Isaiah 65:24, KJV)

God is our refuge and strength, always ready to help in times of trouble. (Psalm 46:1, NLT)

The name of the LORD is a strong tower; the righteous man runs into it and is safe. (Proverbs 18:10, ESV)

Do not grieve, for the joy of the LORD is your strength. (Nehemiah 8:10b, NIV)

Don't be afraid, for I am with you. Don't be discouraged, for I am your God. I will strengthen you and help you. I will hold you up with my victorious right hand. (Isaiah 41:10, NLT)

The LORD is my strength and my song; he has given me victory. This is my God, and I will praise him—my father's God, and I will exalt him! (Exodus 15:2, NLT)

Let's Make It Personal

1. Do you remember a time you were broken? Perhaps you are broken right now. What does that look like to you? Get a journal and write.
2. Your feelings have a voice, and you have a right to express them. Nothing will take your Father by surprise. He knows. Now you can tell him how you feel. Allow him to speak to you.
3. Journal your thoughts, tell the Lord about it. Listen for his Word to you. Record what he has to say. In Scripture he tells you (Isaiah 28:23, NLT), "Listen to me; listen, and pay close attention."
4. He is a loving and kind Father; he will never turn away from you.

Scripture

All those the Father gives me will come to me, and whoever comes to me I will never drive away. (John 6:37, NIV)
The Lord is close to the brokenhearted and saves those who are crushed in spirit. (Psalm 34:18, AMP)
And I will make an everlasting covenant with them: I will never stop doing good for them. I will put a desire in their hearts to worship me, and they will never leave me. (Jeremiah 32:40, NLT)

Confession

Oh, my soul, why are you in such despair within me, and why is my heart so sad? My hope is in my God. He is my salvation. I will again praise him. As I seek him, I will find him because he loves me. He is my hope, my Savior, and my God. (Scripture reference: Psalm 42:11, NLT; Proverbs 8:17, NIV)

Abandoned

Left without needed protection, care, or support.
(*Merriam-Webster Dictionary*)

Heart's Cry

Where are you, Father? I have searched for you, yet you are not to be found. Come to my rescue! I am so alone.

Father Speaks

I always desire—no, long—for time, quiet time, when your heart and mind is stayed on me. During the turbulent times you must tighten your faith belt and lean into me. I am the rescue you are looking for. Rescue from the storms in your life that would toss you to and fro. Never allowing you to be settled. When you are not settled, you cannot hear my voice or feel my touch. My touch, child. In a still slight breeze is where you will hear and feel me. For some this will be enough of a reminder that I am close; for others, they will, NO! They must! Sharpen their spiritual abilities. For to walk in step with me, you must be able to heed my voice, to feel my touch. Oh, child, there is so much I desire to show you. So much I delight in giving to you. Your Father has many joyous moments for you. Yes, you! The one who feels as though I have abandoned you. I say to you, it is not me who has moved. Examine yourself, child.

Scripture

Therefore, My people shall know My name; therefore, they shall know in that day that I am He who does speak: Here I AM. (Isaiah 52:6, MEV)

Then they cried out to the LORD in their trouble, and he brought them out of their distress. He still the storm to a whisper; the waves of the sea were hushed. (Psalm 107: 28–29, NIV)

You will keep in perfect peace whose mind is stayed on you, because he trusts in you. (Isaiah 26:3, NLT)

He says, "Be still, and know that I am God." (Psalm 46:1a, NIV)

Listen and hear my voice; pay attention and hear what I say. (Isaiah 28:23, NIV)

For the LORD will not abandon His people, nor will He forsake His inheritance. (Psalm 94:14, NASB)

He will not fail you or forsake you. (Deuteronomy 31:6b, NASB)

I will be with you; I will not fail you or forsake you. (Joshua 1:5a, NASB)

Let's Make It Personal

1. You must believe that God loves you. He has not abandoned you. He will never ever abandon you.
2. Life can be difficult. You can be reassured that God is not in a hurry, but he is never too late.
3. If you are in a storm right now, believe that God did not bring you this far to abandon you. Hebrews 13:6 (ESV), So we can confidently say, "The Lord is my helper; I will not fear; what can man do to me?"
4. Seek his face and his answers. He is eager and able to show you his will and direction. Be sure to journal.

Scripture

I will never leave you nor forsake you. (Hebrews 13:5b, ESV)
Have I not commanded you? Be strong and courageous!
Do not tremble or be dismayed, for the LORD your God
is with you wherever you go. (Joshua 1:9, NASB)
For God is working in you, giving you the desire
and the power to do what pleases him.
(Philippians 2:13, NLT)
It is the LORD who goes before you. He will be with
you; he will not leave you or forsake you. Do not fear
or be dismayed. (Deuteronomy 31:8, ESV)

Confession

Father, you love the just and will not abandon your heritage. You make everything beautiful in its time, and you will never forsake your people. (Scripture references: Psalm 37:28a, NLT; Ecclesiastes 3:11, NKJV)

Acceleration

The act or process of moving faster or happening more quickly.
(*Merriam-Webster Dictionary*)

Heart's Cry

I sense it! Father, I sense that things are moving along much quicker than before. The darkness is beginning to clear. I can see the light breaking forth.

Father Speaks

This is a new season, my child. Old has passed away; a new beginning is here. Do you not perceive it? I will put my Word in your mouth. I will level hills before you. You will speak to mountains, and they must move, because you see, child, it is I who go before you. It is I who walk behind you. I am he who has called you. It is I who will bring it to pass.

Scripture

Therefore, if anyone is in Christ, the new creation has come: The old has gone, the new is here! (2 Corinthians 5:17, NIV)

There is a time for everything, and a season for every activity under the heavens. (Ecclesiastes 3:1, NIV)

I will go before you and will level the mountains; I will break down gates of bronze and cut through bars of iron. (Isaiah 45:2, NIV)

What I tell you in the darkness, speak in the light; and what you hear whispered in your ear proclaim upon the housetops. (Matthew 10:27, NKJV)

Let's Make It Personal

1. What are you sensing that the Spirit of God is doing in you? Can you feel the acceleration in the Spirit? Journal about it.
2. Take that to the Father, and seek to understand what he is doing. He is bringing order to the chaos and peace to the craziness around you. He is going to move swiftly in your life.
3. List out the direction you feel he has set forth for you.
4. Find scriptures to verify what he is doing and write them down on three-by-five cards.

Scripture

Show me the right path, O LORD; point out the road for me to follow. Lead me by your truth and teach me, for you are the God who saves me. All day long I put my hope in you. (Psalms 25:4–5, NLT)

I am the LORD; I have called you in righteousness; I will take you by the hand and keep you. (Isaiah 42:6a, ESV)

Confession

You, my Lord, go before me, and you will never leave me or forsake me. I will not be discouraged, because the darkness has passed and your light now shines upon me. (Scripture references: Deuteronomy 31:8, NIV; 1 John 2:8, KJV)

Adversary

One that contends with, opposes, or resists: an enemy or opponent.
(*Merriam-Webster Dictionary*)

Heart's Cry

Father, you tell me that you chose me before the foundation of the world. That it is your pleasure to give me the kingdom. Yet my adversary seeks to overtake me. He lost the battle before it began. You have given me the kingdom, and you are going to completely rout out my enemies and cause complete surrender. You have placed my foot on the neck of my adversary. I will NOT be shaken. Thank you, Father.

Father Speaks

The demons in hell are very angry. Why? Because you, my child, are coming into what I created you for! This is your time with me! Let us go together and conquer the enemies together. For I go before you. I level the mountains. I create a way through the waters. I will lead you, child. Nothing, NO thing, NO THING shall stand in your way. For it is I who go before you. I am your shield and buckler. I am your Father! Not one hair on your head will be harmed. Child! Child! Come run into my arms. I have so much for us to do. Trust me, child. Let me take you by the hand and lead you on to and within the path of righteousness. Come, child.

Scripture

Behold, I give unto you power to tread on serpents and scorpions, and over all the power of the enemy: and nothing shall by any means hurt you. (Luke 10:19, KJV)

I will go before you and will level the mountains; I will break down gates of bronze and cut through bars of iron. (Isaiah 45:2, NIV)

Be sober-minded; be watchful. Your adversary the devil prowls around like a roaring lion, seeking someone to devour. (1 Peter 5:8, ESV)

Your hand shall be lifted up over your adversaries, and all your enemies shall be cut off. (Micah 5:9, ESV)

Let's Make It Personal

1. Are you in a battle with your adversary? Do you know what his goal is? Journal your thoughts. He wants to rob you of rest. Your Father wants you to rest; rest in him. Mine out scriptures regarding rest.
2. Are there areas in your life that you have not been resisting Satan?
3. Get into the Word and study the scriptures that give you examples on how to fight.
4. Scripture talks about casting anxieties, being sober-minded and watchful. We are told to resist Satan. Find scriptures that you can speak over yourself. You will have victory over your adversary! Put on your armor! (Ephesians 6:10–18, NIV).

Scripture

Casting all your anxieties on him, because he cares for you. Be sober-minded; be watchful. Your adversary the devil prowls around like a roaring lion, seeking someone to devour. Resist him, firm in your faith, knowing that the same kinds of suffering are being experienced by your brotherhood throughout the world. (1 Peter 5:7–9, ESV)

Put on all of God's armor so that you will be able to stand firm against all the strategies of the devil. (Ephesians 6:11, NLT)

Confession

No one can stop my Lord from doing anything he wants to do. He has made everything for his purposes, even the wicked for a day of disaster. His hand will lift up against my adversaries, and all my enemies shall be cut off. (Scripture references: Job 42:2, NLT; Proverbs 16:4, NLT; Micah 5:9, ESV)

Adversity

A condition marked by misfortune, calamity, or distress.
(*Dictionary.com*)

Heart's Cry

Disappointment, distress, misfortune everywhere I look in my life. This is not surprising to you, Father. I know you have seen it all and you have the way through this for me. For in the pain, you are doing a work in me; you are preparing me and equipping me for your service. You are not punishing me; you are strengthening me. I must not listen to the voice of others skepticism. I do not deserve this. I did nothing to deserve this treatment. Show me your ways, and I will walk in them. Help me, Holy Spirit, to keep my eyes upon Jesus. Help me to stand strong in the face of others disbelief. I am called by you to be your child, to reflect Jesus to others. I will continue to do that, Father. You will bring me through. This time is strengthening me. I will make it.

Father Speaks

My sweet, sweet child. Please stay seated in MY rest until I say, "Rise up, child." I am doing a deep work in you and preparing you for this next season. Bringing to remembrance there is a time and season for everything. Trust me! Let go and place yourself on my altar, and I will finish my work in you before this next season. I am working on your behalf. Keep walking forward, step by step. I have this. The snare has been set. You will hear me tell you which way to walk and what to speak. Victory is in sight. TRUST!

Scripture

Dear friend, I hope all is well with you and that you are as healthy in body as you are strong in spirit. (3 John 1:2, NLT)
The LORD has taken away your punishment, he has turned back your enemy. The LORD, the King of Israel, is with you; never again will you fear any harm. (Zephaniah 3:15, NIV)
Answer me when I call, O God of my righteousness! You have given me relief when I was in distress. Be gracious to me and hear my prayer! (Psalm 4:1, ESV)
You, dear children, are from God and have overcome the, because the one who is in you is greater than the one who is in the world. (1 John 4:4, NIV)

Let's Make It Personal

1. If the suffering you are going through is because of your belief in Jesus Christ, then you are actually participating in God's will for your life. You can be guaranteed that he will walk with you through whatever trouble comes your way. He will bring you out the other side in victory.
2. Do you think it is possible that knowing that you are suffering for Christ's sake will give you the determination to rise above what you are experiencing? That his peace will surround you? Strength will be found in the joy of the Lord. Journal your thoughts.
3. Your Father will give you the words to speak when called upon by others to give an account for what you believe. His Spirit will rise up inside of you, and you will tell about your trust and faith in God.
4. He will honor you and will answer you swiftly.

Scripture

For what credit is it if, when you sin and are beaten for it, you endure? But if when you do good and suffer for it you endure; this is a gracious thing in the sight of God. (1 Peter 2:20, ESV)
Have I not commanded you? Be strong and courageous. Do not be afraid; do not be discouraged, for the LORD your God will be with you wherever you go. (Joshua 1:9, NIV)

Confession

Thank you, God, that you are my refuge and strength; you are a very present help in trouble. The grace you give is sufficient for me; your power is made perfect in my weakness.
(Scripture references: 2 Corinthians 12:9a NIV; Psalm 46:1, ESV)

Alone

Without people that you know or that usually are with you: feeling unhappy because of being separated from other people. (*Merriam-Webster Dictionary*)

Heart's Cry

I am so alone. My family and I are not on the same page. We have not been able to communicate for a long time. I do not know how to heal inside when others will not even consider that they hurt me so badly. I don't have trust in my heart. Will I live my life coexisting? If necessary, I can. I never want to walk out of your will or hurt you. I do not ever want to grieve the Holy Spirit. I am sorry that I do not handle things well. It is a daily walk for me to lay down that which so would beset me, pick up my cross, and follow you. I am gaining strength. I must trust you, Father, when nothing around me is trustworthy. I will have someone I can trust, you, Father. You will help me.

Father Speaks

Bear no unforgiveness in your heart, child. That will stop up the perfect and powerful flow of my Spirit within you. It is your contrite spirit toward those that hurt you that pleases me, child. I have heard your heart's prayer. I will help you overcome the deep, deep wounds and pain. I am your Healer. You have asked; I will do it.

Scripture

I will be glad and rejoice in your love, for you saw my affliction and knew the anguish of my soul. You have not given me into the hands of the enemy but have set my feet in a spacious place. (Psalm 31:7–8, NIV)

Be kind to one another, tenderhearted, forgiving one another, as God in Christ forgave you. (Ephesians 4:32, ESV)

Not that I have already attained, or am already perfected; but I press on, that I may lay hold of that for which Christ Jesus has also laid hold of me. (Philippians 3:12, NKJV)

Let's Make It Personal

1. What do you think the phrase "pick up your cross and follow me" means? Is it something that is difficult? It is something that has to be done in your mind.
2. When your thoughts are not pleasing to the Father, you must deal with them; put them to death, using scripture as your weapon to do just that.
3. Judgmental thoughts, sinful thoughts, etc. are "suggestions" from Satan that must be dealt with swiftly and consistently by putting them to death. Do not dwell on those thoughts.
4. As you choose to deny those thoughts access to your mind, you will be denying them access to your heart. The thought(s) must meet with a firm "NO" in your mind. As you are doing this, you are taking up your cross daily. It is a daily picking up your cross. However, you will see progress. As you take up your cross daily, putting to death sinful thoughts, you will be ceasing from sin. (See 1 Peter 4:1, NKJV, below.)

Scripture

Do not rejoice when your enemy falls, an let not your heart be glad when he stumbles. (Proverbs 24:17, ESV)

Then He said to them all, "If anyone desire to come after Me, let him deny himself; and take up his cross daily, and follow Me. (Luke 9:23, NKJV)

Therefore, since Christ suffered for us in the flesh, arm yourselves also with the same mind, for he who has suffered in the flesh has ceased from sin. (1 Peter 4:1, NKJV)

Know this, my beloved brothers: let every person be quick to hear, slow to speak, slow to anger; for the anger of man does not produce the righteousness of God. (James 1:19–20, ESV)

Confession

Thank you, Father, that you have forgiven me as I purpose to forgive others. I will strive for peace with everyone, and for holiness, because without that I will not see you. (Scripture references: Matthew 6:12, ESV; Hebrews 12:14, ESV)

Amazing

Causing astonishment, great wonder, or surprise.
(*Merriam-Webster Dictionary*)

Heart's Cry

You say you choose me. That you gave me the kingdom. You are going to completely rout the enemy and cause complete surrender. You are putting my foot on the neck of my adversary. You give the kingdom to whoever you choose; today you choose me. I will be astonished at what you are doing! Those around me will see your hand moving in behalf of me, your daughter. No longer will tongues wag against me for you are stopping the chatter. Things will happen quickly for me. You are a God of the miraculous, and you move swiftly when the time is right. Thank you, Father, for now is the time; the time is right for my swift and complete breakthrough.

Father Speaks

My child, my child, pick up your pen and write. For I have a plan for you like none other. People are amazed at what I have done for you so far. They will continue to in their amazement as they watch my hand deliver you and take you places you cannot imagine. Yes, others will want to know what you have, who you know. My daughter, others will inquire about the Lord you serve. A door will be opened, and you will be able to speak of the faith you have in a risen Savior. No man can close the door I am opening for you. Again, I speak, no man can close this door. You have been hurt by "man"; people you trusted. I am no man that I should not tell you the truth. I am not man that I should lie. I am your God, your Father, who watches over you with a jealous love. I shelter you under my wings. No harm will befall you. You shall suffer no lack from this day forward. I have spoken; you must hear what my spirit is speaking within you. There is coming a day that your very thoughts will be answered before you pray them. I am taking you places and doing things with you soon that you cannot even dream about. You have a special gift. You will hear me speak; be quick to obey me, daughter. Now rest and prepare yourself. Doors are even now opening. You will hear a voice behind you saying, "This is the way, walk in it."

Scripture

This is what the LORD, the God of Israel, says: Write in a book all the words I have spoken to you. (Jeremiah 30:2, NIV)

I know your deeds. See, I have placed before you an open door that no one can shut. I know that you have little strength, yet you have kept my word and have not denied my name. (Revelation 3:8, NIV)

God is not man, that he should lie, or a son of man, that he should change his mind. Has he said, and will he not do it? Or has he spoken, and will he not fulfill it? (Numbers 23:19, ESV)

For the Lord you God is a consuming fire, a jealous God. (Deuteronomy 4:24, ESV)

The young lions suffer want and hunger; but those who seek the Lord lack no good thing. (Psalm 34:10, ESV)

Let's Make It Personal

1. If you could create your own life, what would it look like? Do you think that those desires were planted inside of you by God? Journal about this.
2. Is there something you have always wanted to do, but were unsure if it was God's will?
3. Did the pain that "man" caused you hold you back from pursuing what God told you to do? How did you overcome that? Have you overcome that? If not, what do you feel God is telling you to do about it?
4. God chose you. He really did. His plan for you is an awesome plan. Spend time with him and allow him to reveal to you what his plan is. If you know what it is, ask him to increase your vision.

Scripture

Take delight in the Lord, and he will give
you the desires of your heart.
(Psalm 37:4, NIV)

For my thoughts are not your thought, neither are your ways
my ways, declares the Lord. For as the heavens are higher
than the earth, so are my ways higher than your ways and
my thoughts than your thoughts. (Isaiah 55:8–9, ESV)

Confession

I will remain steadfast so that I may be perfect and complete
lacking nothing. I am confident that he who began a good work
in me will carry it on to completion until Jesus Christ returns.
(Scripture references: James 1:4, ESV; Philippians 1:6, NIV)

Anger

A strong feeling of displeasure or annoyance and often of active opposition to an insult, injury, or injustice.
(*Merriam-Webster Dictionary*)

Heart's Cry

Such anger I am dealing with. I am angry, Father! Angry at the way I am treated by those who claim to love me. Angry because I cannot control myself in my pain. Where did kindness and love go? Was it ever a part of me? Has anger swallowed up any good in me? Help me.

Father Speaks

Is help what you desire from me, child? Is it? Have I not provided all for you? My Word is life to your very soul, life to your spirit, life to you, child. Help is found there. Within the pages of my Word you will find life and deliverance in me. Are you seeking me?

Scripture

Therefore, let all the faithful pray to you while you may be found; surely the rising of the mighty waters will not reach them. (Psalm 32:6, NLT)

My child, pay attention to what I say. Listen carefully to my words. Don't lose sight of them. Let them penetrate deep into your heart for they bring life to those who find them, and healing to their whole body. (Proverbs 4:20–22, NLT)

My dear brothers and sisters, take note of this: Everyone should be quick to listen, slow to speak and slow to become angry, because human anger does not produce the righteousness that God desires. (James 1:19–20, NIV)

Let's Make It Personal

1. Are you dealing with anger? Feel like you cannot control yourself? Want help?
2. Your Father has provided the way through that anger: his Word.
3. He is merciful, and he understands just what you are dealing with. He got angry also, but he never sinned. Temptation beckoned to Jesus, and he overcame with the Word.
4. Scripture tells us that he will not give us more than we can handle; he will provide a way through for us. Perhaps he allows "more than we can handle," in the context of anger and relationship issues, because he knows us right well. Just maybe he has a purpose for the pain: so that we find out just how much we need him and stop relying on ourselves. Just some food for thought...
5. Ponder, if you will, what Jesus went through for you. He was ridiculed, mocked, beaten beyond recognition, spit upon, and crucified, yet he NEVER spoke one Word. He did that for you. He knows that with his help, you can overcome this. Let him help you.

Scripture

And "don't sin by letting anger control you." Don't let the sun go down while you are still angry. (Ephesians 4:26, NLT)

No temptation has overtaken you except what is common to mankind. And God is faithful; he will not let you be tempted beyond what you can bear. But when you are tempted, he will also provide a way out so that you can endure it. (1 Corinthians 10:13, NIV)

Confession

I thank you, Father, for being my strength and my song; you bring me victory. This is my God, and I will praise him. He makes everything work out for my good because I love him and I am called according to his purpose. (Scripture references: Exodus 15:2, NLT; Romans 8:28, NIV)

Anguish

Extreme pain, distress, or anxiety cries of anguish, mental anguish. (*Merriam-Webster Dictionary*)

Heart's Cry

You have heard my prayers, haven't you, Father? You hear my deep anguish, my deep sorrow. You have held my tears in your hand. Nothing I am going through will be unnoticed by you.

Father Speaks

I will repay the years the locusts have eaten. I will repay the years of pain and the tears shed. I will repay you, child. You are coming to a place of great faith. For I am granting you the ability to see ME to hear ME and to understand ME. Listen for my voice, child. I delight in speaking to you. I delight in enabling you to hear my voice. For I have a grand plan for you and your family. Things hidden in darkness will begin to be revealed. Justice is coming. I have decreed things that have hurt you, held you back, and scarred you deeply are even now being turned back. Soon, child, you will see the direction I have for you. Do you hear me, child? Listen for that still small voice, the loud voice, the clear voice. Child, I have called you; all is well. Listen for me. Stand back and see the deliverance of the one who loves you. For I delight in you. I am yours, and you are mine. Do you believe this, my child? Guard your heart. For from it flows rivers of life.

Scripture

I will repay for you the years the locust have eaten—the great locust and the young locust. (Joel 2:25, NIV)

He reveals deep and hidden things; he knows what lies in darkness, and light dwells with him. (Daniel 2:22, NIV)

The LORD is near to the brokenhearted
and saves the crushed in spirit.
(Psalm 34:18, ESV)

Whoever believes in me, as Scripture has said, rivers of living water will flow from within them. (John 7:38, NIV)

The Lord replies, "I have seen violence done to the helpless and I have heard the groans of the poor, now I will rise up to rescue them, as they have longed for me to do." (Psalm 15:5, NLT)

Let's Make It Personal

1. As deeply painful as it is, journal a time that you were, or are currently, in anguish. When you get those painful feelings out on paper, somehow they don't have such power. There is healing in journaling.
2. In your journal, ask the Father how he sees or saw that situation.
3. Ask Father who he was to you during that time. Ask him who he wants you to be for him during those times.
4. Be sure to journal all of Father's responses to you. In that process you will find that he was with you, that he loved you and still loves you with an everlasting love.

Scripture

Make me to know your ways, O LORD; teach me your paths. Lead me in your truth and teach me, for you are the God of my salvation; for you I wait all the day long. (Psalm 25:4–5, ESV)

For all that is secret will eventually be brought into the open, and everything that is concealed will be brought to light and made known to all. (Luke 8:17, NLT)

Confession

Father, thank you that you have seen my affliction and you know the anguish of my soul. You have shown me your loving kindness. I will give you thanks because you are such a good God and your loving kindness will never end. (Scripture references: Psalm 31:7, NIV; 1 Chronicles 16:34, NASB)

Anointed

Blessed and called to be great, made with a purpose,
honest and pure; set aside for a unique reason.
Unshakable and strong. (*Urban Dictionary*)

Heart's Cry

People say that I carry an anointing. What is that supposed to mean, Father? I do my very best to walk with you and hear your voice. It is my desire to obey you in all things. Perhaps that is what others see; perhaps that is the anointing they speak of. I must have your Word on this. Walking in your anointing is my heart's desire.

Father Speaks

You do not feel it yet. You do not think it can happen. If I have spoken it, I will bring it to pass. I gifted you many years ago. Now is the time to move out in your gifting. For I will lead you and open all the right doors for you. You will bring glory to me. You will point people to me. You will shower people with my favor and healing touch. Yes, oh yes! I will use you. Move out in the gifts I have given to you. I need you to keep your eyes on me. I am the author and finisher of your faith.

Scripture

Looking unto Jesus the author and finisher
of our faith. (Hebrews 12:2a, KJV)

Commit your way to the LORD; trust in him, and he will act.
(Psalm 37:5, NLT)

As for you, the anointing you received from him remains in you, and you do not need anyone to teach you. But as his anointing teaches you about all things and as that anointing is real, not counterfeit—just as it has taught you, remain in him.
(1 John 2:27, NIV)

Let's Make It Personal

1. You may feel like you cannot live up to what the Father says about you. If he spoke it to you, he will bring it to pass in your life.
2. What is it that he has spoken to you, told you to do?
3. Journal about that. Write anything and everything down that you believe the Father has spoken to you.
4. Take that to him and ask him to quicken to your spirit the things he has called you to.

Scripture

The LORD says, "I will guide you along the best pathway for your life. I will advise you and watch over you." (Psalm 32:8, NLT)
These things I have spoken to you, that my joy may be in you, and that your joy may be full. (John 15:11, ESV)

Confession

You have told me I would see the evidence of things I cannot see now, because I have faith to believe in what I hope for. I believe that your spirit is upon me because you have anointed me to tell this good news to others. (Scripture references: Hebrews 11:1, NLT; Luke 4:18a, NIV)

Answer

An answer is a response to a question, problem, or need.
(*Vocabulary.com*)

Heart's Cry

I have been sobbing for the last hour. My heart is breaking even more than I thought it would do again. I do not see your hand in the land of the living. I do not see you answering my prayers. You hear. You are not answering. I do not understand. You say in your Word that angels are here for me, that you send them to help me. I see no help. What have I done wrong? What have I not done? Help me, Father. Maybe I can correct and you will answer my prayers. Help me find you, Father. It is you that I need, you I must find. Please hear me. Please forgive me for such little faith.

Father Speaks

I hear your cry, my child. All of heaven has heard your cry. All of heaven is at attention and ready to answer your prayers. Angels you have requested, angels you shall have at your bidding. I will say to you that those you are concerned about are under my watchful eye. No breath do they take that I am not aware of. No thought do they have that I do not know. They are protected under my mighty wings. For I have seen your heart, heard your deep, sorrowful prayers, and, my child, I have and will continue to answer you when you call. Daughter, do you not know, do you not perceive that your Father in heaven loves you with an everlasting, powerful, and frightening love? There is nothing too hard for me.

Scripture

Behold, I am going to send an angel before you to guard you along the way and to bring you into the place which I have prepared. (Exodus 23:20, NASB)

Are not all angels ministering spirits sent to serve those who will inherit salvation? (Hebrews 1:14, NIV)

The righteous cry out, and the LORD hears them; he delivers them from all their troubles. (Psalm 34:17, NIV)

Do not be anxious about anything, but in every situation, by prayer and petition, with thanksgiving, present your requests to God. And the peace of God, which transcends all understanding, will guard your hearts and your minds in Christ Jesus. (Philippians 4:6–7, NIV)

Let's Make It Personal

1. It is okay to cry. Many great leaders in scriptures cried out to God in their distress.
2. The best thing you can do when you are sad about anything is to cry out to the Lord and ask him to guide you and to help you. It helps to journal.
3. If you take your sadness to the Father, he will give you a peace and comfort unlike any other feeling. The Holy Spirit is your Comforter.
4. Do not let the enemy bring condemnation on you. There is NO condemnation.

Scripture

So now there is no condemnation for those who belong to Christ Jesus. (Romans 8:1, NLT)

Commit everything you do to the LORD. Trust him, and he will help you. (Psalm 37:5, NLT)

God is our refuge and strength, an ever-present help in trouble. (Psalm 46:1, NIV)

Loudly, I cried to God. Loudly, I cried to God so that he would open his ears to [hear] me. (Psalm 77:1, GW)

Confession

I will cry out to the Lord in my troubles, and he will save me from my distress. My God cares for me, and I will turn all my anxiety over to him. (Scripture references: Psalm 107:19, NIV; 1 Peter 5:7, NIV)

Anticipation

To realize beforehand; foretaste or foresee; to anticipate pleasure. To expect; look forward to; be sure of: to anticipate a favorable decision. (*Dictionary.com*)

Heart's Cry

I know that you are true to your Word! I know the anticipation I feel is real; you are bringing the answers to my prayers. Yet at times I am a bit off guard, spiritually. I purpose to give my thoughts back to you for your control. I feel I am getting stronger. My strength comes from you alone. You, your Word and prayer. The prayers and requests I have brought to you, my Lord; the enemy or my mind has caused me to begin to rationalize. I must give those prayers and needs to you for you delight in blessing me. I have purposed to come to an absolute belief that your Word is true. Every man, every circumstance is a liar. I must see these things through your eyes and your heart. Help me, Father.

Father Speaks

My child, do you believe, really believe, that whatsoever you speak with your mouth and believe in your heart you shall have? Have you come to realize I want to keep no good thing from you? Do you understand to pray my will be done is the perfect prayer for any situation? My will is the perfect will for your life. Perfect will for your health, perfect will for your children, perfect will for your grandchildren. My will be done as it is in heaven. Is this your wish? Your prayer? For I tell you that in heaven everything is in perfect harmony. Everything is beautiful, peaceful, rejoicing at all times because of the goodness of your Lord. There is no sickness, no sadness, no pain, no lack. Can you believe this? I tell you, my child, you are getting closer to that mind-set. Always and in everything remind yourself of who you are, who you belong to, who loves you with an everlasting and perfect love. I am the one who has prepared your way. You will hear that still, small voice behind you saying, "This is the way, walk in it." As I have promised you, I will never leave or forsake you. We have a journey to take together. Yes! It has already begun. Have you not perceived it? Have you not felt the wind of my Spirit envelope you? I say to you that you have already heard the soft, gentle voice guiding you in the way you are to walk. I am proud of you, my child. You have done well. The enemy has tried to destroy you. He has tormented your mind. He has attacked you physically. He has attacked your loved ones. I declare and decree by my power; he is bound away from you. You must always remember Satan is defeated. Your Father, your Savior, your Helper—we have defeated him. All power is yours, daughter. I tell you, it is time. Let's get going! Welcome to our wonderful adventure. A journey of your life! I am so eager and excited. Come! Come! Let us begin!

Scripture

Truly, I say to you, whoever says to this mountain, "Be taken up and thrown into the sea," and does not doubt in his heart, but believe that what he says will come to pass, it will be done for him. (Mark 11:23, ESV)

But, as it is written, "What no eye has seen, nor ear heard, nor the heart of man imagined, what God has prepared for those who love him." (1 Corinthians 2:9, ESV)

Thou shalt also decree a thing, and it shall be established unto thee: and the light shall shine upon thy ways. (Job 22:28, KJV)

Let's Make It Personal

1. Your Father knew that you would struggle at times with unbelief. He has provided you with scripture to encourage you and to strengthen you. Grab your Bible and mine those scriptures out, write them down, and confess them out loud.
2. You must be transformed by his Word. Turn your life into worship so that others may see Jesus in you. This must come from the way you feel and think. If you are consumed by him, your thoughts and the words you speak will reflect that.
3. As you strengthen yourself in the Word of God, you will come to a place where you can confidently stand your ground, resist the enemy, and receive more from God. No matter what happens in your life.
4. Faith is your responsibility; it is not God's, a pastor's or your spouse's. Only you can nurture a relationship with him by spending time with him and in his Word.

Scripture

Blessed is the man who listens to me, watching daily at my gates, waiting at the posts of my doors. For whoever finds me find life, and obtains favor from the Lord. (Proverbs 8:34–35, NKJV)

Do not be conformed to this world, but be transformed by the renewal of your mind, that by testing you may discern what is the will of God, what is good and acceptable and perfect. (Romans 12:2, ESV)

And without faith it is impossible to please God, because anyone who comes to him must believe that he exists and that he rewards those who earnestly seek him. (Hebrews 11:6, NIV)

Hope deferred make the heart sick, but a desire fulfilled is a tree of life. (Proverbs 13:12, ESV)

But seek first the kingdom of God and his righteousness, and all these things will be added to you. (Matthew 6:33, ESV)

Confession

I am able to wait for the Lord as my soul waits because I hope in his Word. Therefore, faith is my assurance of things I hoped for and the guarantee of things not seen. (Scripture references: Psalm 130:5, ESV; Hebrews 11:1, ESV)

Anxious

Experiencing worry, unease, or nervousness, typically about an imminent event or something with an uncertain outcome. (*Online Dictionary*)

Heart's Cry

When will this be over, Father? These people have pursued us for months, demanding from us that which we will never surrender. You see the wickedness in this pursuit of us. You see the dishonestly the all-consuming need to possess something that does not belong to them. Father, come to the rescue of my family, deliver us from this verbal battery. You sit in the heavens, and nothing escapes your sight. I will take comfort knowing that you are in the midst of this and you are vindicating us. You are a just God, and you will bring justice to this situation. Thank you, Father!

Father Speaks

For this day shall be unto you a day of joy and laughter. Child, you have no real idea, yet, how much I love you and how much value I place on you and your love for me. For it has been said, "I will curse those who curse you, and I will bless those who bless you." With my mighty and powerful hand will I protect you. I will build a hedge of awesome protection around you and those you love. I declare this day that those who would reach out to touch my anointed one, to do you harm, shall be dealt with by my mighty arm of justice. Justice is mine, child. I will bring justice to your situation. Quickly I will do a thing and just as quickly will you see the answers to your prayers. I am a just God. My patience is never ending. Yet when my child cries out for justice, I cannot but answer that call. I tell you, daughter, your prayers have not gone unheard. Even now I am bringing my hand of justice into your situation. Those who have harmed you shall no more. Their power is broken.

Scripture

I will bless those who bless you and curse those who treat you with contempt. (Genesis 12:3a, NTL)

But you belong to God, my dear children. You have already won a victory over those people, because the Spirit who lives in you is greater than the spirit who lives in the world. (1 John 4:4, NLT)

For we know the one who said, "I will take revenge. I will pay them back." He also said, "The LORD will judge his own people." (Hebrews 10:30, NLT)

You will only observe with your eyes and see the punishment of the wicked. (Psalm 91:8, NIV)

When I said, "My foot is slipping", your unfailing love, LORD, supported me. When anxiety was great within me, your consolation brought me joy. (Psalm 94:18–19, NIV)

Let's Make It Personal

1. Journal about a time when your anxious mind and meditations of your heart were overwhelming. Did you feel like your situation would never end?
2. Did you think that reaching out to someone was a sign of weakness? We all need help at some point in our life. Share your needs with someone else you trust. Have them come alongside you for prayer and Bible study.
3. He is the answer and has the way through this for you. Journal.
4. Did you call out to Jesus for help? If so, how did he help you? With the help he gives you, you will be equipped to help and strengthen someone else.

Scripture

Do not be anxious about anything, but in every situation, by prayer and petition, with thanksgiving, present your requests to God. And the peace of God, which transcends all understanding, will guard your hearts and your minds in Christ Jesus. (Philippians 4:6–7, NIV)

Let the words of my mouth, and the meditation of my heart, be acceptable in thy sight, O LORD, my strength, and my redeemer. (Psalm 19:14, KJV)

Confession

I thank you, Father! You hear when I cry out to you for help. Your grace is all I need; your power works best in my weakness. You rescue me from all my troubles. (Scripture references: Psalm 34:17, NLT; 2 Corinthians 12:9a, NLT)

Apprehension

Anticipation of adversity or misfortune; suspicion or fear of future trouble or evil. (*Dictionary.com*)

Heart's Cry

What IS IT, Father? This "thing" that presses in on the fringes of my mind and emotions? Only you know, Father! I have cried out to you many times. You do hear me, don't you? Only you can rescue me. I must keep my mind-set on you, your Word. In you alone will I find the peace that I am seeking.

Father Speaks

Yes! Yes! Child, cast your burden upon me! For I do care for you. Is there anything too hard for me? Really? Is there? I created you in your mother's womb! I knew you before the world began. I put my call in and upon your life then. Who are you, oh, child, to think I am not doing just what I said I would do? Peace I leave with you, my child. Do not seek the peace of the world, for you will be sorely disappointed. My peace you are to seek. Look to me. Let me be your goal, let me be your intent. Seek me, and I will be found by you. Do you believe this, my child? There are perilous times coming. There are perilous times now. Hearts will fail within men if it were not for me. I am the anchor in the storm. I calm the waves. Is anything too hard for me? I have asked this before. I ask it again: Is there anything too hard for me? Search yourself, child, find me. You surely will find me, the powerful, almighty ME, when you search yourself and desire to find me. Yes, I am as close as the mention of my name. What does my name mean to you, child? Therein lies the power, the deliverance you seek. What does my name mean to you?

Scripture

This know also, that in the last days perilous times shall come. (2 Timothy 3:1, KJV)

For God alone, O my soul, wait in silence, for my hope is from him. (Psalm 62:5, ESV)

I am the LORD, the God of all mankind. Is anything too hard for me? (Jeremiah 32:27, NIV)

Be strong, and let your heart take courage, all you who wait for the LORD! (Psalm 31:24, ESV)

The LORD is close to all who call on him, yes, to all who call on him in truth. (Psalm 145:18, NLT)

Behold, I am the LORD, the God of all flesh. Is anything too hard for me? (Jeremiah 32:27, ESV)

You will keep in perfect peace those whose minds are steadfast, because they trust in you. (Isaiah 26:3, NIV)

Let's Make It Personal

1. Do you struggle with keeping your mind set on what is good and perfect? Examine your lifestyle. Are you lacking peace simply because you are not following God's pattern for rest?
2. Does apprehension knock on the door of your heart? Try being thankful. "Be thankful in all circumstances, for this is God's will for you who belong to Christ Jesus" (1 Thessalonians 5:18, NLT).
3. Father's Word holds the key to your peace. Look up scriptures on peace. Write them on a three-by-five card. Post those wherever you will see them several times throughout the day.
4. Speak them out loud over yourself. When the Word is spoken, apprehension must leave and peace comes.

Scripture

I am leaving you with a gift—peace of mind and heart. And the peace I give is a gift the world cannot give. So don't be troubled or afraid. (John 14:27, NLT)
In peace I will lie down and sleep, for you alone, O LORD, will keep me safe. (Psalm 4:8, NLT)
Then you will experience God's peace, which exceeds anything we can understand. His peace will guard your hearts and minds as you live in Christ Jesus. (Philippians 4:7, NLT)

Confession

I will not be anxious about anything. In every situation I am faced with I will pray and petition you, Father. I will give thanks to you for what you are doing. Your peace which passes understanding will guard my heart and my mind. I will walk in power and love. I have a sound mind that does not fear.
(Scripture references: Philippians 4:6–7, NIV; 2 Timothy 1:7, NIV)

Audacious

Extremely bold or daring; recklessly brave; fearless. (*Dictionary.com*)

Heart's Cry

You tell me to ask audaciously. It brings your heart joy when your child trusts you enough to ask big, seemingly impossible things of you. For you are a God that does mighty works for your children. You call me your entitled one; what does that look like? Show me, Father.

Father Speaks

Yes, child! One of the entitled ones! Entitled to everything Jesus has, everything Jesus is! I have not called you to sit on the sidelines. No! I have called you into battle. I have called you into peace. I have called you into a deep walk with me. Where you will come to know me better than you ever have. You will come to know me as your heart desires! Child, I have heard your pleas; your heart cries for more of me. More you have and more you shall receive. It is a simple thing, child. Ask and you shall receive. For would a good father, when asked for a good thing, give his child anything less than the best? I AM the best! I AM yours!

Scripture

All I have is yours, and all you have is mine. And glory has come to me through them. (John 17:10, NIV)

I am the LORD, I have called you for a righteous purpose, and I will take hold of your hand. (Isaiah 42:6 NASBa)

This is the confidence we have in approaching God: that if we ask anything according to his will, he hears us. (1 John 5:14, NIV)

Delight yourself in the LORD, and he will give you the desires of your heart. (Psalm 37:4, ESV)

Now suppose one of you fathers is asked by his son for a fish; he will not give him a snake instead of a fish, will he? (Luke 11:11, NASB)

Let's Make It Personal

1. Are you ready to go deeper with the Lord? Do you understand what that may mean?
2. Peter got out of the boat and walked on the water. The other disciples saw Jesus on the water as well. However, Peter chose the deeper experience.
3. Are you able to truly trust God instead of trusting yourself? Journal.
4. Never forget that the path he calls you to walk will not look like someone else's. It is designed specifically for you and the gifts he has given you.

Scripture

Trust in the LORD with all your heart and lean not on your own understanding; in all your ways submit to him, and he will make your paths straight. (Proverbs 3:5–6, NIV)
For we are his workmanship, created in Christ Jesus for good works, which God prepared beforehand, that we should walk in them. (Ephesians 2:10, ESV)

Confession

Father, you have told me to be strong and courageous. I am not to be afraid or discouraged for you are with me wherever I go. Therefore, I will use the spiritual gifts you have given to me to serve others well.
(Scripture references: Joshua 1:9, NIV; 1 Peter 4:10, NLT)

Beaten

Being in a state of exhaustion. (*Merriam-Webster Dictionary*)

Heart's Cry

I am down for the count. Life has given me more that I can handle. I will surely perish if help is not sent to me. Your Word tells me that you never allow more to happen to me than I can handle, but you will provide a way through for me. I must trust you have me in the palm of your hand. I will rest for a time. You will renew my strength, and I will once again stand in your presence, declaring surely you do all things well. Thank you, Father, for being my strength through this.

Father Speaks

My precious child, I called you to this place for this time. I have things for you this day. Child, this day. I delight in blessing you and meeting you every day. You have asked me for something only you and I know. Only you and I know, child. It is deep within your spirit. It resonates within you. I know you can feel my spirit calling you deeper and deeper. Come walk on the water with me child. I will not let you drown. I AM the God that loves you. I AM the God that looks after you. You shall not trip or stumble. I have directed your path. Before time began, I cut out the path you are to walk. Yes, everything in your life was watched by me. I declare to you that nothing—nothing—you have gone through has gone unnoticed by me. I will use everything, yes, everything in your life—past, present, and future—for my glory. Proclaim me, child. Proclaim me. Shout it out. I, your Father, has redeemed you. I am calling you forth. Come forth, child, it is time.

Scripture

But grow in grace, and in the knowledge of our Lord and Savior Jesus Christ. To him be glory both now and for ever. Amen. (2 Peter 3:18, KJV)

Don't be afraid, for I am with you. Don't be discouraged, for I am your God. I will strengthen you and help you. I will hold you up with my victorious right hand. (Isaiah 41:10, NLT)

He brought me out into a broad place; he rescued me, because he delighted in me. (Psalm 18:19, ESV)

And we know that all things work together for good to them that love God, to them who are the called according to his purpose. (Romans 8:28, KJV)

Let's Make It Personal

1. There are many things that cause us to believe something contrary to what scripture tells us. Can you list a few? Journal them. Is what you listed truth?
2. Have you believed that it is easier to avoid problems than to face them? Support your answer with scripture.
3. Just because you "feel" something does not make it true, does it? Have you been fooled by your feelings? Journal about that. Take it to the Father and ask for his truth.
4. The enemy will try to use your weaknesses against you. Do you struggle with unbelief? Are your emotions controlling your daily life?

Scripture

But I did not believe these things until I
came and saw with my own eyes.
(1 Kings 10:7a, NIV)
Stay alert! Watch out for your great enemy, the
devil. He prowls around like a roaring lion, looking
for someone to devour. (1 Peter 5:8, NLT)

Confession

I called to the Lord and have been saved from my enemies.
The peace of God which surpasses all understanding
keeps my heart and my mind safe in Christ Jesus.
(Scripture references: 2 Samuel 22:4, NIV; Philippians 4:7, NIV)

Beauty

The quality or aggregate of qualities in a person or thing that gives pleasure to the senses or pleasurably exalts the mind or spirit. (*Merriam-Webster Dictionary*)

Heart's Cry

Father, you are a good, good Father! You had promised that you would bring beauty for ashes in my life. Now I am beginning to see the beauty you spoke of. Prayers are being answered; peace is being restored; I am finding my way through the chaos. Praise you, Father. How can I ever thank you enough for taking such good care of me?

Father Speaks

My child, my daughter. My beloved one. The one who rests while her daddy fights the battle for her. The one that shines the beauty of her Lord to others. The one that tells others, "Come look what the Lord has done for me! What he has done for me he will do for you." It is okay to show me off to others. Daughter, they will want what they see you have. Now rest...

Scripture

Out of Zion, the perfection of beauty, God shines forth. (Psalm 50:2, ESV)

The LORD will fight for you, and you have only to be silent. (Exodus 14:14, ESV)

Come and see what our God has done, what awesome miracles he performs for people! (Psalm 66:5, NLT)

Let's Make It Personal

1. What does the phrase "beauty for ashes" mean to you? Isaiah 61:3, "Consider the reality that Father is doing just that for you. Journal about what that looks like in your life."
2. Are your prayers being answered? If you do not see any answers, trust that he is at work. Don't step out ahead of him. He WILL bring beauty out of your ashes; trust him.
3. Ask him to reveal to you what he is doing. He will meet you in his Word and give you answers.
4. Remember, faith is the substance we hoped for, the evidence not yet seen.

Scripture

Now faith is confidence in what we hope for and the assurance about what we do not see. (Hebrews 11:1, NIV)
These things God has revealed to us through the Spirit. For the Spirit searches everything, even the depths of God. (1 Corinthians 2:10, ESV)

Confession

As I seek you, I find reassurance that you will answer me. I can make my plans, but you determine my steps. Your Word tells me that everything that is hidden will be brought into the open and secrets will be brought to light. (Scripture references: Mark 4:22, NLT; Proverbs 16:9, NLT)

Belief

A state or habit of mind which trust or confidence is placed in some person or thing; her belief in God. (*Merriam-Webster Dictionary*)

Heart's Cry

I believe. You are a wonder-working God. The God of the miraculous. There is nothing you cannot and will not do for those who are called by your name. As I read your Word, open my eyes to see you, the miracle-working God. My belief gets stronger as I read your Word and speak it out loud over my needs. I praise and thank you, Father, for what you have planned for those who say yes to your call. I say yes!

Father Speaks

Ask and you shall receive. Knock and the door shall be opened to you. Have I not told you I am the God of enough? Have I not told you I am the God of more than enough? You have asked; I have heard. You have waited; I have prepared. You have anticipated; I am delivering. More than you have asked of me. More than enough.

Scripture

Yes, God is more than ready to overwhelm you with every form of grace, so that you will have more than enough of everything—every moment and in every way. He will make you overflow with abundance in every good thing you do.
(2 Corinthians 9:8, TPT)

Keep on asking, and you will receive what you ask for. Keep on seeking, and you will find. Keep on knocking, and the door will be opened to you.
(Matthew 7:7, NLT)

And God is able to make all grace abound toward you, that you, always having all sufficiency in all things, may have an abundance for every good work.
(2 Corinthians 9:8, NKJV)

Let's Make It Personal

1. Good news! If God's Word says it, he can do nothing less. Find scriptures that speak to your need. Journal about them. Speak them over your life.
2. Thank him that his Word say you are healed, you are protected by his blood, you are prosperous.
3. Whatever the need, the answer is in the Word of God. Therefore, you can believe you have received.
4. Do you have an inward conviction that what you are believing for you will, indeed, receive? Journal your thoughts.

Scripture

Therefore I tell you, whatever you ask in prayer, believe that you have received it, and it will be yours. (Mark 11:24, ESV)
And without faith it is impossible to please God, because anyone who comes to him must believe that he exists and that he rewards those who earnestly seek him. (Hebrews 11:6, NIV)

Confession

My heart will not be troubled because I believe in God. Because I believe I will receive whatever I ask for in prayer. (Scripture references: John 14:1, NIV; Matthew 21:22, NIV)

Betrayed

To do something very bad and hurtful to someone that causes a loss of respect. (*Online Dictionary*)

Heart's Cry

Oh, Father, how could I be so betrayed by people I thought loved me and cared about my heart. This willful determination to hurt me, to cause me ruin, has caused my heart to break. I have no feeling for myself. How do I get back to finding worth in myself? You have spoken "rest" to me. What does that look like, Father? Instead of anxiously looking about me, if I will rest in you, perhaps I will have a better perspective on what is happening to me. The enemy of my soul is attempting to rob me of the call I believe you have placed on my life. I will rise up in you! I am worth something, because you say I am. I bless those that have betrayed me. They must be very unhappy people to desire to hurt me like they have. I refuse to allow them to take away my confidence.

Father Speaks

Now, do you understand my direction for you to rest? Give it all to me and leave it with me, child. I am quite able to bring you through this. I who placed a call upon you am able, am faithful, to bring it to fruition. Need you doubt me? The one who called you is able. I am able. I place the call upon your life. I will do it. You will speak nothing but blessings. What you want to see happen. The miracles you are asking for. Speak, child, what is it you want? Speak and ask of me, for I delight in you. I want to see you blessed beyond your imagination. Speak and believe it is yours. Give it all to me, child…all of it. You know!

Scripture

Be strong and courageous. Do not be afraid or terrified because of them, for the LORD your God goes with you; he will never leave you nor forsake you. (Deuteronomy 31:6, NIV)

Let the beloved of the LORD rest secure in him, for he shields him all day long, and the one the LORD loves rests between his shoulders. (Deuteronomy 33:12, NIV)

The one who calls you is faithful, and he will do it. (1 Thessalonians 5:24, NIV)

His delight is not in the strength of the horse, nor his pleasure in the legs of a man, but the LORD takes pleasure in those who fear him, in those who hope in his steadfast love. (Psalm 147:10–11, ESV)

Let's Make It Personal

1. Have you ever been betrayed? Did you think that your friends would think you should have it all together, that incident should not have bothered you? After all, Jesus has it…right?
2. These feeling need to have an outlet. Journal about them. Talk about them with God.
3. For thought: Jesus loved Judas; he cared deeply for him even though he knew he would betray him. Jesus hurt, he wept. Do you think Jesus suffered internal agony over the reality that Judas had sold him out? Can you identify with that pain?
4. Were you angry at your betrayers? Did you want to see them pay for the wrong they did to you? Are you able to step away from that and see that the enemy was behind it all? The people were just pawns in the enemy's assault against you.

Scripture

For if you forgive other people when they sin against you, your heavenly Father will also forgive you. But if you do not forgive others their sins, your Father will not forgive your sins. (Matthew 6:14–15, NIV)

For we do not have a high priest who is unable to empathize with our weaknesses, but we have one who has been tempted in every way, just as we are—yet he did not sin. (Hebrews 4:15, NIV)

Confession

I called out to my Lord with praise because he is so worthy. He is my shepherd; I lack nothing, for he has saved me from my enemies. (Scripture references: 2 Samuel 22:4, NIV; Psalm 23:1, NIV)

Blessed

Holy. Bringing you happiness or something you need.
(*Cambridge English Dictionary*)

Heart's Cry

Is it time, Father? Has my time come to walk into blessing? You have spoken over me that you have blessing in store for me. I have been in a battle. You have been in it with me. If it had not been for you, I don't think I would have made it. You knew that. You never left my side even when I could not find you. During those times, you still blessed me. I found myself looking for your presence in my life, and as I sought you, I found you.

Father Speaks

Good things are on their way to you this very moment. Do you not perceive it, my child? I have released blessing with your name on them. Yes, they are at the door; open it. Receive what your Father has for you. Have you not prayed and asked for blessings? Have you not felt my hand of guidance upon you? Am I a God that does not tell the truth? You know my voice, child; you must trust me.

Scripture

Every good and perfect gift is from above, coming down from the Father of the heavenly lights, who does not change like shifting shadows. (James 1:17, NIV)

And God is able to bless you abundantly, so that in all things at all times, having all that you need, you will abound in every good work. (2 Corinthians 9:8, NIV)

For when God made a promise to Abraham, because He could vow by no one greater, He vowed by Himself, saying, "Surely I will bless you, and surely I will multiply you." (Hebrews 6:13–14, MEV)

God is not a man, so he does not lie. He is not human, so he does not change his mind. Has he ever spoken and failed to act? Has he ever promised and not carried it through? (Numbers 23:19, NLT)

Let's Make It Personal

1. In what ways has God blessed you? Were they unexpected?
2. If you journal about the way he blesses you, it can be an encouraging experience and something you can look back on in the future should you need a reminder of his goodness to you.
3. Do you think that the greatest blessings come after the greatest times of testing?
4. Is it possible that your Father knows what is best? He knows when you will be ready and able to receive the blessings he has for you. Perhaps you were to go through or are currently going through those testing times in order to receive and rightly handle the blessings.

Scripture

But as for me, it is good to be near God. I have made the Sovereign LORD my refuge; I will tell of all your deeds. (Psalm 73:28, NIV)
Taste and see that the Lord is good; blessed is the one who takes refuge in him. (Psalm 34:8, NIV)

Confession

My God! You will meet all my needs according to your riches in Christ Jesus. You grant me the desires of my heart and cause all my plans to succeed. (Scripture references: Philippians 4:19, NIV; Psalm 20:4, NIV)

Breaking Point

The point at which a person gives way under stress.
(*Merriam-Webster Dictionary*)

Heart's Cry

So, Father, I fell down last night. My heart was aching and so torn from the pain my family is going thorough. I fell down; grief and sadness had a jab at me. I allowed that to happen, but not for long because of you, Father. You lifted me up; you reminded me of your promises; you reminded me that it is finished. My prayers are already answered. The desires of my heart are on the way. Thank you, Father, for your grace and mercy in my life. Thank you for strengthening me. I am an overcomer in the name of Jesus Christ.

Father Speaks

Today is a breaking point for you. Do you not perceive the changes on the horizon? Your Father is at work to perfect that which concerns you. I desire to bring out in you the ME that dwells there: power, yes; instinct, yes; discernment, yes; all your heart's desires, yes. I have put those desires in your heart. Am I not able to fulfill that which I called you to be? Gifts from me are without repentance. Come allow me to teach you. Listen well to that still, small voice within you, for it is my voice bidding you come, step out, and walk with me. Uncharted territory, child.

Scripture

For where your treasure is, there your heart will be also. (Matthew 6:21, NIV)

Have I not commanded you? Be strong and courageous. Do not be afraid; do not be discouraged, for the LORD your God will be with you wherever you go. (Joshua 1:9, NIV)

For the gifts and the calling of God are irrevocable. (Romans 11:29, ESV)

The LORD will perfect that which concerns me; your mercy, O LORD, endures forever; do not forsake the works of Your hands. (Psalm 138:8, NKJV)

Let's Make It Personal

1. Have your ever fallen down spiritually speaking? What was that like for you? If you are comfortable writing about the experience, grab your journal.
2. Consider this: wherever your life is right now has come to pass under your Father's watchful eye. He has seen it all, and he was there for you.
3. It may be difficult to believe, but it all fits into his plan for you. He has a good plan for your life.
4. Your Father does not keep a record of wrongs. Rather he will help you learn and grow during the tough times.

Scripture

"For I know the plans I have for you," declares the LORD, "plans to prosper you and not to harm you, plans to give you a hope and a future." (Jeremiah 29:11, NIV)

I cry out to God Most High, to God who fulfills his purpose for me. (Psalm 57:2, NLT)

Let us then with confidence draw near to the throne of grace, that we may receive mercy and find grace to help in time of need. (Hebrews 4:16, ESV)

Confession

There is nothing I cannot do through him who strengthens me. Therefore, I will commit to my Father whatever I do, and he will establish my plans. (Scripture references: Philippians 4:13, ESV; Proverbs 16:3, NIV)

Breakthrough

An important discovery or event that helps to improve a situation or provide an answer to a problem. (*Cambridge Dictionary*)

Heart's Cry

It is time, Father. Breakthrough time. I have been obedient to you. When attacks came my way, I did not return evil for evil. I was silent as you directed. Many times, my heart was wrenched, torn, and left bleeding. But, God! You sustained me. You are the lover of my soul. Your love for me is unending, and your strength is mine. Breakthrough is close; I can sense it when I pray. You are a good and faithful Father. You will not stand for your child to be assaulted more than she is able to withstand; you provide the way through. Breakthrough is here for me! Thank you, Father.

Father Speaks

I desire that you see me as your all-consuming lover. One who walks beside you. One who opens the way before you. One who will keep you from dashing your foot upon a stone. I am your Deliverer. I am your Protector. I see the evil that desires to destroy you. The evil plots against you. The lies spoken about you. I declare this day I am dealing with those things. I will silence those who desire to destroy you. I will not allow this assault to continue. Look to me in the midst of this turmoil, for your will see me move on your behalf like never before. I will break through the bronze walls, the briar and thorn bush the enemy has set in place to stop you. I declare not one hair on your head shall be touched. Not one insult to your emotional well-being. For it is my desire to surround you with my hedge of protection. No one and nothing shall come near you to harm you in anyway. Do you believe this? Let your behavior demonstrate my power in you. Breakthrough is upon you.

Scripture

The LORD appeared to him from far away. I have loved you with an everlasting love; therefore I have continued my faithfulness to you. (Jeremiah 31:3, ESV)

You are my war club, my weapon for battle-with you I shatter nations, with you I destroy kingdoms. (Jeremiah 51:20, NIV)

I will go before you and will level the mountains; I will break down gates of bronze and cut through bars of iron. (Isaiah 45:2, NIV)

The One who breaks open the way will go up before them; they will break through the gate and go out. Their King will pass through before them, the LORD at their head. (Micah 2:13, NIV)

Let's Make It Personal

1. When you pray for breakthrough, be specific in what you need. It can be difficult to know what to pray, how to pray it or what to ask for. The Holy Spirit will guide your prayers.
2. The way to help you with this is to find scriptures that address what you are praying about and pray them out loud back to God. Believing that what you speak is bringing about the results you seek. The enemy hears God's Word; he CANNOT withstand it.
3. You are aligning your hearts desires with His. That will bring spiritual breakthrough.
4. Be sure to listen to his voice, heed his direction; walk in obedience.

Scripture

You always hear me, but I said it out loud for the sake of all these people standing here, so that they will believe you sent me. (John 11:42, NLT)

Keep on asking and you will receive what you ask for. Keep on seeking, and you will find. Keep on knocking and the door will be opened to you. For everyone who seeks receives. Everyone who seeks finds. And to everyone who knocks, the door will be opened. (Matthew 7:7–8, NIV)

For I am about to do something new. See, I have already begun! Do you not see it? I will make a pathway through the wilderness. I will create rivers in the dry wasteland. (Isaiah 43:19, NLT)

Confession

I praise my God, the Father of my Lord Jesus Christ, who has blessed me with every spiritual blessing in the heavenly places because I am united with Christ. Therefore, I know the truth, and the truth sets me free. (Scripture references: Ephesians1:3, NLT; John 8:32, NLT)

Breathe

To inhale and exhale freely. (*Merriam-Webster Dictionary*)

Heart's Cry

Show me the way, Father! Draw me deeper into you, Jesus. I want to get back to you, deeper still. The time is now. I must not let any more time pass by. In you, Jesus, I live and breathe and have my being. You are the air I breathe; I need you for every breath. Come, Holy Spirit, fill me, grow me, use me. The spirit is so willing. The flesh is so weak. Only in you will I find my strength. Strengthen me, my Lord. Make me into a vessel suitable for your work.

Father Speaks

Do you feel it? Do you feel it? I AM is in your midst. I AM is here to meet your needs. I hear your cries; I see your need. Come closer to me. Let me breathe upon you my renewing breath. Receive a fresh and a new infilling of the Holy Spirit. He is here. He is here with you. Can you not feel his presence? Allow him in, my child. It is your Father's desire to meet every need you have. Lean into me. Press in. Take your seat beside me. Come, we have much to do. Many places to go, much to say. For it is my desire to use you. Do you not know this yet? I have opened a door for you that no man can close. You must walk through it. All you need is waiting for you. I have provided the way. I have equipped you, child. I am waiting. Come let us begin.

Scripture

Since God is in her midst, she will not be shaken. God will help her at the break of dawn. (Psalm 46:5, ISV)

The LORD your God is in your midst, a victorious warrior he will exult over you with joy, He will be quiet in His love, He will rejoice over you with shouts of joy. (Zephaniah 3:17, NASB)

Show me the right path, O LORD; point out the road for me to follow. (Psalm 25:4, NLT)

God planned for us to do good things and to live as he has always wanted us to live. This is why he sent Christ to make us what we are. (Ephesians 2:10, CEV)

So, you too, when you see all these things, recognize that he is near, right at the door. (Matthew 24:33, NASB)

Let's Make It Personal

1. Has your heart been longing for more of him? Ask him for more; he will show you the way.
2. Is he everything to you? Can you express your feelings on paper? If so, journal about them.
3. Quiet yourself as you sit at the feet of your Savior, Jesus Christ. Listen for his still, small voice.
4. Do you believe that he wants to use you? That he takes delight in you? Journal your thoughts.

Scripture

Whom have I in heaven but you? I desire
you more than anything else.
(Psalm 73:25, NLT)

He must become greater and greater, and
I must become less and less.
(John 3:30, NLT)

He brought me out into a broad place; he rescued me,
because he delighted in me. (Psalm 18:19, ESV)

After the earthquake came a fire, but the LORD was not in the fire.
And after the fire came a gentle whisper. (1 Kings 19:12, NIV)

Confession

Your Word says that I have asked nothing in your name.
It is your breath within me, Father, that helps me to
understand what I should ask for. You want me to ask
you and you will answer and my joy will be full.
(Scripture references: John 16:24, ESV; Job 32:8, ESV)

Broken Heart

Broken Heart is a metaphor for intense emotional, and sometimes physical stress or pain one feels at experiencing great longing. (*Wikipedia*)

Heart's Cry

Words cannot express what I am feeling. Such deep sadness that has become physical pain. The only thing I can do, the only thing there is to do, is to run to you, Father. You have the words of life. You will reach down and touch me, strengthen me. If I will just keep my eyes on you, and spend time in your Word, I will come through this. It is your grace that sustains me. Your love guides me through to the other side of this pain. Thank you, Father.

Father Speaks

Pieces, pieces of your heart, I hold. I am the glue that will mend your broken heart. I am the one that loves you with a never-ending love. Do you think that I did not see, that I did not hear? Am I a God that is just far away and not close up? There is nothing I cannot put back together, nothing. For what I created I know well how to fix. This heart of yours that is in pieces, I have it, I have every piece. Fear not and cry no more, child. What desired to take you out of my will has served to make you stronger.

Scripture

The righteous cry out, and the LORD hears them; he delivers them from all their troubles. The LORD is close to the brokenhearted and saves those who are crushed in spirit. (Psalm 34:17–18, NIV)

Be strong and take heart, all you who hope in the Lord. (Psalm 31:24, NIV)

God, pick up the pieces. Put me back together again. You are my praise! (Jeremiah 17:14, MSG)

Let's Make It Personal

1. God's grace will help you seek him. It is a gift extended to us that helps us with the desire to seek more of him.
2. We have access to his voice, which is his Word. His Word envelops us and makes it possible for us to continue living our lives with him. Journal what he speaks to you.
3. We have access to his ear through prayer. He hears and answers us. Keep record of answered prayers.
4. We have fellowship with other believers. They can hold you up in prayer and help with anything you may need. They are his hands and feet.

Scripture

But he said to me, "My grace is sufficient for you, for my power is made perfect in weakness." (2 Corinthians 12:9a, NIV)

You have turned for me my mourning into dancing; you have loosed my sackcloth and clothed me with gladness. (Psalm 30:11, ESV)

Confession

O Lord, you are a shield about me, my glory, and the lifter of my head. Therefore, there is nothing I cannot do through you, Lord, for you strengthen me. (Scripture references: Deuteronomy 31:8, ESV; Philippians 4:13, ESV)

Bury

Completely cover; cause to disappear or become inconspicuous. (*Online Dictionary*)

Heart's Cry

Others so want me to disappear. Are the things I stand for too much for them? I desire to serve you and stand for what is right. Is that so wrong, Father? What rejoicing there would be if they could see me no longer. Yet you have a purpose for me. You have created me and put your life in me. I have a purpose. To follow and serve you, not to please man. Is it possible that my getting buried is part of your plan? I have been planted, I must die, then I will come up and out stronger and more fit for your purposes. Father, your will be done in my life.

Father Speaks

Today is going to be like none other. Time to push through. Time to see clearly. The things you have longed for are starting to manifest in your life. Dreams you thought were lost are even now awakening. Time has come, child. Push through. Time has come for you to come up higher. Come walk with me above the chaos, for I have a plan for you. If you keep your eyes upon me, you will see as I see. You will manage your life from a new perspective. What better way to live but by my side? You have desired to see as I see, hear as I hear, touch as I touch, go as I go, and do as I do. Is there anything too hard for me?

Scripture

Arise, shine; for your light has come, and the glory of the LORD has risen upon you. (Isaiah 60:1, NASB)

He put another parable before them, saying, "The kingdom of heaven is like a grain of mustard seed that a man took and sowed in his field. It is the smallest of all seeds, but when it has grown it is larger than all the garden plants and becomes a tree, so that the birds of the air come and make nests in its branches. (Matthew 13:31–32, ESV)

Whatever you do, work at it with all your heart, as working for the Lord, not for human masters, since you know that you will receive an inheritance from the Lord as a reward. It is the Lord Christ you are serving. (Colossians 3:23–24, NIV)

I am the LORD, the God of all mankind. Is anything too hard for me? (Jeremiah 32:27, NIV)

Let's Make it Possible

1. Do you feel as though you have been buried? The pressures of this world are just too much to bear. Pushing up through the "dirt" takes great strength and persistence.
2. There is a choice, however. You can continue to persevere and break through, or you can remain buried and rot away. It is your choice.
3. Father's choice for you is to push through! He is rooting you on! Grab ahold of his hand, and he will help you.
4. You must leave the past in the past. Don't set up camp and dwell there.

Scripture

Forget the former things; do not dwell on the past. (Isaiah 43:18, NIV)

Still other seeds fell on fertile soil, and they produced a crop that was thirty, sixty, and even a hundred times as much as had been planted! Anyone with ears to hear should listen and understand. (Matthew 13: 8–9, NLT)

Confession

Father, don't be far from me; come quickly to help me. You are my strength; therefore I am strong because of your mighty power. (Scripture references: Psalm 22:19, NIV; Ephesians 6:10, NIV)

Called

A strong inner impulse toward a particular course of action especially when accompanied by conviction of divine influence. (*Merriam-Webster Dictionary*)

Heart's Cry

Father, have I heard you call me? I think you have spoken words to me regarding a direction for my life. My calling. What does this mean, and what is it, Father? Help me to understand what it is that you are doing in my life. If you have called me, if you are calling my name, I want to answer you. I am saying to you, Father, "Here I am, send me." Show me your will, and I will do it.

Father Speaks

You are where I called you to be for such a time as this. I have called you. I will do it. You are to be used mightily, powerfully, for I decree it. I have called you forth. Listen, listen closely, child, for I have much to speak to you. Hear your Father's voice, for I am speaking. Ask for more, and you shall have more. Ask for boldness, for it is yours. Ask for miracles, signs, and wonders, for this is my will. I Am have spoken. I Am will do it. Ask, and ye shall receive. Speak, and it shall be done for you. Go where I call you, for I have gone before you. Behold, the doors are open for you. I Am has opened them. Come, my child, believe. For if I decree a thing, it shall come to pass

Scripture

We know that all things work together for good to those who love God, to those who are called according to His purpose. For those whom He foreknew, He predestined to be conformed to the image of His Son, so that He might be the firstborn among many brothers. And those whom He predestined, He also called; and those whom He called, He also justified, and those whom He justified, He also glorified. (Romans 8:28–30, ESV)

Call to me and I will answer you, and will tell you great and hidden things that you have not known. (Jeremiah 33:3, ESV)

I can't do a solitary thing on my own: I listen, then I decide. You can trust my decision because I'm not out to get my own way but only to carry out orders. (John 5:30, MSG)

Let's Make It Personal

1. Do you think you have heard the Father call you? Seek out someone you trust, such as a trusted pastor or close friend, and tell them what you think that calling is. Ask for feedback.
2. Take your journal and seek his face regarding your discussion with that person.
3. Ask him to confirm your calling with scripture. Be sure to write it down.
4. Now take time to meditate and pray about what he has shown you and journal your next steps.

Scripture

All that the Father gives Me will come to Me, and the one who comes to Me, I will certainly not cast out. (John 6:37, NIV)
You did not choose me, but I chose you and appointed you so that you might go and bear fruit—fruit that will last—and so that whatever you ask in my name the Father will give you. (John 15:16, NIV)

Confession

Jesus Christ, I thank you for giving me strength and judging me faithful to be appointed to your service. You have called me, and you are faithful to do what you have spoken.
(Scripture references: 1 Thessalonians 5:24, NIV; 1 Timothy 1:12, ESV)

Capable

Having the ability, fitness, or quality necessary to achieve efficiently whatever one has to do; competent. (*Online Dictionary*)

Heart's Cry

As I write, I find I must believe it is you, Father, speaking through me. I am the vehicle for your words to flow through me. Cause me to be your vessel. Help me to receive you. Oh, Lord, my Rock and my Redeemer. Praise, praise, I praise your name. You are my God, my Lord in whom I trust. Who else is there but you, my Father? You are the giver of all good gifts. You speak and mountains move for your beloved. Draw me close, Lord, my Lord, Father, Friend, Lover, Brother—draw me to you. Cause me to see you. Cause me to hear your voice.

Father Speaks

I am here, child! I am here in your midst. I join in with the praises. Angels, angels attending your every need. Come take what you need. Come take what you want. It is my desire to give you all good and perfect gifts. Blessings upon blessings are in this place. Come, I say again, come take from me that which only I can give to you. Life, abundant life, joy in abundance, healing, health. Needs met. Financial need met, yes, I will meet those needs also. Come take what you desire from me. I am ravished by your gaze. There is nothing I will not do for you. Ask of me, I am able. Believe, believe. Why would I withhold good things from you when I am your good, good Father? Believe, ask of me. Believe, you shall receive what you ask of me if you believe. Is there anything I cannot do?

Scripture

See, I will do a new thing, now it shall spring forth; shall you not be aware of it? I will even make a way in the wilderness, and rivers in the desert. (Isaiah 43:19, MEV)

For we are God's handiwork created in Christ Jesus to do good works, which God prepared in advance for us to do. (Ephesians 2:10, NIV)

And also for me, that words may be given to me in opening my mouth boldly to proclaim the mystery of the gospel. (Ephesians 6:19, ESV)

Delight yourself in the LORD, and he will give you the desires of your heart. (Psalm 37:4, ESV)

For the LORD God is a sun and shield; the LORD bestows favor and honor; no good thing does he withhold from those whose walk is blameless. (Psalm 84:11, NIV)

Let's Make It Personal

1. You must know that God uses you because he loves you. He has planted specific gifts in you. Only you can flow in those gifts. He is no respecter of persons; even though you feel weak, it is his desire is to use you.
2. Praise him for the wisdom and the ability to hear his voice.
3. Because of his grace toward you, he graciously uses you even though you are a weak human being. He knows you are capable to do what he has called you to do.
4. Always remember that your usefulness to him stems from your relationship with him. Worship him in all things all the time.

Scripture

But he said to me, "My grace is sufficient for you, for my power is made perfect in weakness.' Therefore I will boast all the more gladly of my weaknesses, so that the power of Christ may rest upon me. (2 Corinthians 12:9, ESV)

Show me someone who does a good job, and I will show you someone who is better than most and worthy of the company of kings. (Proverbs 22:29, GNT)

In the same way, let your light shine before others, so that they may see your good works and give glory to your Father who is in heaven. (Matthew 5:16, ESV)

Confession

The Lord is my helper, and I can boldly say that I will not fear, for what can man do to me? I will wait on the Lord and be courageous, for he will strengthen my heart. (Scripture references: Hebrews 13:6, ESV; Psalm 27:14 ISV)

Cares

A state of mind in which one is troubled; worry, anxiety, or concern. (*Dictionary.com*)

Heart's Cry

Cares, cares, cares. I refuse to allow them to smother me. My mind has been troubled by them long enough. Father, show me how to cast them at your feet. You can handle them; I cannot. You are my burden-bearer. I choose to allow you to help me. Thank you, Father, for loving me enough to be patient with me as I wrestled with the cares of this life that you have told me are not mine to wrestle with. You can have them.

Father Speaks

Child, why are you so consumed with the cares of this world? Do you not know that your Father in heaven sees it all? That he cares for you? Be encouraged, child, I have a plan that will help you, not harm you. I have a future for you that I planned for you. Listen closely, and you will hear the still, small voice saying, this is the way, walk in it. Then and only then will you be able to step out, walk with me, and touch those around you. You must discard the cares of this world that you carry in order to be used of me. Learn from me, learn from your trials, and you will be able to extend a hand of hope to others going through what you have gone through. Only then will you be confident and powerful in others' lives.

Scripture

For I know the plans I have for you, declares the LORD, plans to prosper you and not to harm you, plans to give you a hope and a future. (Jeremiah 29:11, NIV)

Your own ears will hear him. Right behind you a voice will say, "This is the way you should go," whether to the right or to the left. (Isaiah 30:21, NLT)

Take my yoke upon you. Let me teach you, because I am humble and gentle at heart, and you will find rest for your souls. (Matthew 11:29, NLT)

For God, the Faithful One, is not unfair. How can he forget the work you have done for him? He remembers the love you demonstrate as you continually serve his beloved one for the glory of his name. (Hebrews 6:10, TPT)

Let's Make It Personal

1. Are there cares of this world that are bogging you down? Journal about those. Take them to the Father in prayer. Ask him how he sees them. What does he want to be to you in this?
2. Have you made some mistakes that you think can never be overcome? Please know that with the Father, the mistakes you have made have the power to turn you into something stronger than ever.
3. You will be transformed into the vessel he desires you to be as you come before him with a teachable spirit. Mistakes are learning tools.
4. During the worst times in your life, the greatest lessons can be learned. Father will help you through them. They will strengthen you so you can help someone else.

Scripture

Repent, then, and turn to God, so that your sins may be wiped out, that times of refreshing may come from the Lord. (Acts 3:19, NIV)
For whoever has [a teachable heart], to him more [understanding] will be given; and whoever does not have [a yearning for truth], even what he has will be taken away from him. (Mark 4:25, AMP)
I pray that out of his glorious riches he may strengthen you with power through his Spirit in your inner being. (Ephesians 3:16, NIV)

Confession

The joy of the Lord is my strength, and the name of the Lord is a fortified tower that I run to and am kept safe. (Scripture references: Nehemiah 8:10b, NIV; Proverbs 18:10, NIV)

Celebrate

To do something enjoyable in order to show that an occasion or event is special. (*Macmillan Dictionary*)

Heart's Cry

Father, you told me that today was not a day for regret but celebration. Celebrate what you have done for me. I am to let the past stay there, in the past. I have no right to resurrect something you call dead. It has no power to hurt or have me unless I give it that power. Father, you have been calling me to walk out of that oppressive place and find the freedom you have for me. I need to see my past covered with your blood and myself washed clean from every bit of defilement. It is a new season. I must step into it and leave the past where it belongs. Let me move ahead with you, Father. I am ready for what you have called me to. Let's go, Father.

Father Speaks

Yes, new beginnings. You have closed the door to the torment. The enemy used your family and others to torment you. No more. You have come up higher. You have passed another challenging trial in your life. You have been successful, my child. I am very pleased with you. I do cherish you. You are my chosen jewel. You shine like the noonday sun. I have placed that glow within you. You will shine light into the dark places of those I bring to you. You will deliver them in my power and name. People will be set free from bondages. Come, my precious jewel. Let's begin today! I can hardly wait to be who I am in power and might in you, with you. We shall set the captives free.

Scripture

Blessed is the man who remains steadfast under trial, for when he has stood the test he will receive the crown of life, which God has promised to those who love him. (James 1:12, ESV)

The light shines in the darkness, and the darkness has not overcome it. (John 1:5, NIV)

You will be a crown of splendor in the LORD's hand, a royal diadem in the hand of your God. (Isaiah 62:3, NIV)

He makes my feet like hinds' feet, and sets me upon my high places. (2 Samuel 22:34, NASB)

The Spirit of the Lord God is upon me, because the Lord has anointed me to bring good news to the poor; he has sent me to bind up the brokenhearted, to proclaim liberty to the captives, and the opening of the prison to those who are bound. (Isaiah 61:1, ESV)

Let's Make It Personal

1. When you seek God's direction, be aware that he will help you close doors that are not the best for you. You can then celebrate that your Father has heard your prayers and he has come to your rescue.
2. Are you willing to close the door to the past and follow the Lord?
3. Do you trust that he has everything under control and that your past when left in his hands cannot resurrect itself and torment you? Remember, it is all covered in the blood of Jesus Christ.
4. If you are ready to move out with the Lord, tell him so and be ready for a splendid journey. Be sure to journal.

Scripture

For we are God's handiwork, created in Christ
Jesus to do good works, which God prepared in
advance for us to do. (Ephesians 2:10, NIV)
Arise, shine; for your light has come, and the glory of
the LORD has risen upon you. (Isaiah 60:1, ESV)
Those who know your name trust in you, for you, O LORD,
do not abandon those who search for you. (Psalm 9:10, NLT)

Confession

Thank you that Jesus Christ is the same yesterday,
today, and forever. I am encouraged because every good
and perfect gift comes from the Father and he gives
them to me. I am confident in his leading as he never
changes. (Hebrews 13:8, NIV; James 1:17, NKJV)

Change

To transform or convert. (*Dictionary.com*)

Heart's Cry

I so long for change. My life is so gray, lifeless. My days are spent waiting for something to change in my life, yet I do not know where to begin. You understand this, Father. I know all good things come to those who wait. Help me keep believing that you have a good plan for my life.

Father Speaks

Today this hour change is taking place. Change you have desired. Change you have wrestled for. Time to come up and out, child. Time of waiting is no more. Listen for my voice. You will hear it more often and at times louder than others. Each situation you encounter requires my perfect direction. Fear not, daughter, for it is I.

Scripture

Jesus replied, "But even more blessed are all who hear the word of God and put it into practice." (Luke 11:28, NLT)

Do not be afraid or discouraged, for the LORD will personally go ahead of you. He will be with you; he will neither fail you nor abandon you. (Deuteronomy 31:8, NLT)

I will instruct you and teach you in the way you should go; I will counsel you with my eye upon you. (Psalm 32:8, ESV)

Let's Make It Personal

1. Are you longing for change in your life? Are you trying to make it happen on your own?
2. Have you asked Father what he is doing in your life? What direction does he want you to go?
3. During your time of seeking Father and journaling what he says to you, believe that it is, indeed, him speaking to you.
4. A good way to be sure it is his voice is to ask for scripture to confirm what he has spoken to you.

Scripture

Guide my steps by your word, so I will not be overcome by evil. (Psalm 119:133, NLT)

Call to me and I will answer you, and will tell you great and hidden things that you have not known. (Jeremiah 33:3, ESV)

When he brings out his own sheep, he goes before them. And the sheep follow him, for they know his voice. (John 10:4, MEV)

Confession

Holy Spirit, you give me life when my flesh is no help at all. The words you have spoken to me are spirit and life. I am a child of God and am led by the Holy Spirit. (Scripture references: John 6:63, ESV; Romans 8:14, NLT)

Chaos

Complete disorder and confusion. Behavior so unpredictable as to appear random, owing to great sensitivity to small changes in conditions. (*Online Dictionary*)

Heart's Cry

No one knows what is happening inside of me. No one has a clue. How can they? They do not know my inner most thoughts that drive me. No one knows the deep anguish I have felt; I have endured. The battle to keep my mind. To have the strength to shut out the enemy's barrage of arrows, attacks, insults, insinuations, fears, anxiety…darkness. Father, no one knows! But wait! Are you allowing this for a purpose? This inner tumult, sadness, desperation, fury, confusion…for a purpose? It drives me deeper into you as I fall at your feet and cry out to you.

Father Speaks

Child, as you call upon me all of heaven comes to attention. Angels anticipate my directions. I delight in answering you. I have angels on assignment around you, around your family, just as you have asked of me. Think it not strange, these things happening around you. You will look with your eyes, but the destruction will not come near you. You have plans; I have given them to you. You have direction; I have guided you. You will have victory in the things you set your hand to. I have called you. I have equipped you. I will do it. Run to me. I am the lover and perfecter of your very life. I have called you. I have equipped you; I will continue guiding you. Walk this way, not that, you will hear me say. Speak this word, not that. Touch this one, not that one. Arise and go out in victory. For what I have called you to do, I will bring to completion in your life. You are mine! You were created for my purposes.

Scripture

But truly God has listened; he has attended
to the voice of my prayer.
(Psalm 66:19, ESV)

For he will command his angels concerning you to
guard you in all your ways. (Psalm 91:11, ESV)

And they went and woke him, saying, 'Master, Master, we are perishing!" and he awoke and rebuked the wind and the raging waves, and they ceased, and there was a calm. (Luke 8:24, ESV)

So the LORD must wait for you to come to him so he can show you his love and compassion. For the LORD is a faithful God. Blessed are those who wait for is help. (Isaiah 30 :18, NLT)

Make you full of every good work and ready to do all his desires, working in us whatever is pleasing in his eyes through Jesus Christ; and may the glory be given to him for ever and ever. So be it. (Hebrews 13:21, BBE)

Let's Make It Personal

1. Did a personal storm blow the doors off of your life? Would you say you have been forever changed? Chaos and its companion confusion will cause you to reevaluate many aspects and assumptions about yourself.
2. These storms are not just about survival but of learning to thrive in spite of them. Perhaps a shift in perception is needed. There is something the Holy Spirit can teach you, if you seek his guidance. It may be difficult for you to surrender and allow him to teach and guide you.
3. You will grow not in spite of your circumstances but because of them. Run to the Lord and seek shelter with him. Don't focus on the bad; instead focus on his promises. Keep that in mind as you navigate your way through with him.
4. As you choose to surrender to the Father and learn from your situation, your will grow, mature in your spiritual life, and glean tools to survive chaos in your life. Be sure to journal.

Scripture

Then they cried out to the LORD in their trouble, and he brought them out of their distress. He stilled the storm to a whisper; the waves of the sea were hushed. They were glad when it grew calm, and he guided them to their desired haven. (Psalm 107:28–30, NIV)

The LORD is good, a strong refuge when trouble comes. He is close to those who trust in him. (Nahum 1:7, NLT)

But you are a tower of refuge to the poor, O LORD, a tower of refuge to the needy in distress. You are a refuge from the storm and a shelter from the heat. For the oppressive acts of ruthless people are like a storm beating against a wall. (Isaiah 25:4, NLT)

Confession

Because God is my refuge and my shield, I put my hope in him. He tells me to call out and he will answer and tell me great and unsearchable thing I do not know. I will not plan my own course because my God establishes my steps. (Scripture references: Jeremiah 33:3, NIV; Psalm 119:114, NIV; Proverbs 16:9, NIV)

Chosen

Selected from a number; picked out; taken in preference; elected; predestined; designated to office. (*Webster's American Dictionary of the English Language, 1828*)

Heart's Cry

Have you really chosen me? Who am I? What have I done to be called by the Most High? My past is not something I am proud of. In my heart I felt that it disqualified me. Yet my heart burns inside of me with desire to be used by you. If there is something here you can salvage, Father, here I am. Use me, send me, have your will with me.

Father Speaks

Child, child, child. Do you not yet see what I am trying to do with and through you? You must learn to walk with me. Come up higher. No longer walk the path of my servant Moses. He was caused to linger in the desert by those around him in unbelief. You must shake off the tethers that are restraining you. No one, no human should ever have the right to hold you down from your Father's best. I cry out to you, child, walk this way, not that. I put words in your mouth to speak. You must listen for them. Step out of yourself; remove you from the picture. Count yourself as nothing for my everything. In me is your everything. Anything you could ever ask or desire is found in me. Come, I will teach you how to live above the chaos.

Scripture

Walk with me and work with me—watch how I do it. Learn the unforced rhythms of grace. I won't lay anything heavy or ill-fitting on you. (Matthew 11:29, MSG)

Now go! I will be with you as you speak, and I will instruct you in what to say. (Exodus 4:12, NLT)

Then the LORD reached out his hand and touched my mouth and said to me, "I have put my words in your mouth." (Jeremiah 1:9, NIV)

And the Spirit entered into me when He spoke to me and set me upon my feet, and I heard Him speaking to me. (Ezekiel 2:2, AMP)

Let's Make It Personal

1. Have you heard the Father's call to step out with him? Trusting him for everything that concerns you? If so, what has he spoken to you? Have you journaled about it?
2. Are you still living in and walking out the past? Is this his will for you? Journal your thoughts on this.
3. As he said, "Step out and remove yourself from the picture." This will take an acute focus on him and his Word.
4. Seek his will and determine to follow it. Fear has no place when your Father speaks. Fear must bow its knee and leave you in the name of Jesus Christ. Don't waste any more time on the past or on worry about how this will all work out. He has the plan. He will do it for and with you.

Scripture

Whether you turn to the right or to the left, your
ears will hear a voice behind you saying, "This is
the way; walk in it." (Isaiah 30:21, NIV)
Do nothing from selfish ambition or conceit, but in humility count
others more significant that yourselves. (Philippians 2:3, ESV)
The LORD himself goes before you and will be
with you; he will never leave you nor forsake you.
Do not be afraid; do not be discouraged.
(Deuteronomy 31:8, NIV)

Confession

I will come to you and listen to you; you will teach me the
fear of the LORD. I will praise you! I am blessed because
I fear you. I greatly delight in your commandments.
(Scripture references: Psalm 34:11, NLT; Psalm 112:1, ESV)

Come Away

If something comes away from something else, it becomes separated from it. (*Cambridge English Dictionary*)

Heart's Cry

How I desire to come away with you, my Lord. I want to be tucked away safe under your protection. I know changes are coming, and I feel that I must draw in close ever closer to you. You have the answers that will come up during this change. You have seen it coming; your hand is in it and you have called me forth to walk it out. Show me your paths, and I will walk on them. I will remain under the shadow of your wings, for I am your child. Speak, Father, I am listening.

Father Speaks

Come away with me, child. Change, change is coming. Can you not sense it? Can you not feel it? Change is coming. I am calling you out. Walk with me. Take the high road through this change. Allow me to elevate you. I tell you, without me, you will be unable to withstand the wind of change. Come take my hand, and I will draw you close to me. I will keep you safe under my wings of protection. I will keep you in my secret pavilion. Safe from the assaults of the enemy. I call you my child. I call you my beloved child. I call you MINE!

Scripture

You hide them in the shelter of your presence, safe from those who conspire against them. You shelter them in your presence, far from accusing tongues. (Psalm 31:21, NLT)

For in the time of trouble he shall hide me in his pavilion: in the secret of his tabernacle shall he hide me; he shall set me up upon a rock. (Psalm 27:5, KJV)

Have I not commanded you? Be strong and courageous. Do not be afraid; do not be discouraged, for the LORD your God will be with you wherever you go. (Joshua 1:9, NIV)

And a highway will be there; it will be called the Way of Holiness; it will be for those who walk on that Way. The unclean will not journey on it; wicked fools will not go about on it. (Isaiah 35:8, NIV)

Let's Make It Personal

1. Are you sensing something stirring in the Spirit? Have you asked the Holy Spirit about it?
2. The change he is calling you to is a powerful one. Things will never be the same afterward. This is a good time to get your journal out and start writing what he is showing you.
3. Do you believe he is able to keep you safe? Perfect love, which comes from the Father, casts out fear. He loves you perfectly.
4. You are his child! He calls you his child! Get into the Word and find scriptures that speak to you regarding his love for you and his protection.

Scripture

He will cover you with his feathers. He will shelter you with his wings. His faithful promises are your armor and protection. (Psalm 91:4, NLT)
Humble yourselves before the Lord, and he will lift you up. (James 4:10, NIV)

Confession

I will be strong and courageous; I will not be afraid or terrified. The Lord my God goes with me; he will never leave or forsake me. Even though new things are coming, he will make a way through the wilderness and streams in the wasteland. (Scripture references: Deuteronomy 31:6, NIV; Isaiah 43:19, NIV)

Come

When a specified time is reached or event happens. (*Online Dictionary*)

Heart's Cry

Father, bid me come to you, for I am weak and heavy laden with the cares of this world. Surely, you have all the answer to my cries. I must know your heart, Father. I desire to draw closer, to come up higher with you. Bid me come, and I will follow.

Father Speaks

Today there is a change taking place. Listen, do you not hear the rumbling? My Spirit is hovering over my people. Biding them to come, to seek and to find me. The days are short, my children. Soon you will walk in step with me closer than you ever have. Those who will, I am calling up higher. Come and see what I have to offer you. Come up higher, come up here. Let me show you great and mighty things you know not of. For these are the days my children will hear my voice louder than ever. Many have cried out to me, "Father, I cannot hear you, where are you?" I say to you, I am right next to you, yes, I dwell within you. I walk with you, and I talk to you. You have sensed my presence yet questioned, could this really be you? Your hearts have burned inside of you, yet you have asked, "Is this you, Father?" Ask no more. Believe only. I am the one that calls you by name. I am the one that is calling you out! Come, harken to my voice and none other. I speak, and you will hear. I command, and you will obey. I desire, and you will know what it is. I go, and you will know where. For I am calling you to do not your will but MINE. Hearken not to your voice or the voice of another but to MINE. For those who will, I am calling you. Seek me, hear me, come up higher with me. Let's look at things from my perspective now, not yours. Many are called, my precious children; few are chosen. I am calling; will you follow?

Scripture

Listen! Listen to the roar of his voice, to the rumbling that comes from his mouth. (Job 37:2, NIV)

Search for the LORD and for his strength; continually seek him. (1 Chronicles 16:11, NLT)

After this I looked, and there before me was a door standing open in heaven. And the voice I had first heard speaking to me like a trumpet said, "Come up here, and I will show you what must take place after this." (Revelation 4:1, NIV)

They said to each other, "Didn't our hearts burn within us as he talked with us on the road and explained the Scriptures to us?" (Luke 24:32, NLT)

Let's Make It Personal

1. Have you heard the call? Come up higher? He is calling you.
2. What does he want to do when you come up higher? He wants to reveal himself to you, to reveal secrets of the kingdom to you. Grab your journal.
3. He is calling you into new realms of revelation. Revelation of his protection, miracles. and intimacy.
4. He has new gifts, new treasures, new places in the spirit for you. He says, "Come…"

Scripture

He called you to this through our gospel, that you might share in the glory of our Lord Jesus Christ. (2 Thessalonians 2:14, NIV)
It is He who reveals the profound and hidden thing; He knows what is in the darkness, and the light dwells with Him. (Daniel 2:22, NIV)
He replied, "You are permitted to understand the secrets of the Kingdom of Heaven, but others are not." (Matthew 13:11, NLT)

Confession

When I call out, you answer me. You tell me great and mighty things which I do not yet know. You have manifested to me mysteries that have been hidden from past generations. (Scripture references: Jeremiah 33:3, NASB; Colossians 1:26, NASB)

Commune

To converse or talk together usually with profound intensity, intimacy. (*Dictionary.com*)

Heart's Cry

Father, I wish to commune with you more and more. To come away with you. To be intentional about that intimate place, that secret place where we meet. There I am refreshed and empowered to face the day. To begin my days with you is the most vital thing I can do for myself.

Father Speaks

For these are the days that you must walk ever so closely with me. Listen for my foot fall and set yourself in step with me. I desire that none be left behind. All who will—come follow me. Walk with me. Commune with me. Refresh yourself with me for it is my desire for you to come deeper with me. I am yearning to fill you up. Fill you up, child. My power is your power. What you have seen me do in scripture, I wish for you. Did I not tell you that greater things shall you do than I did when I walked the earth? Is there anything too hard for me to fulfill in you? Now you understand the necessity of communing with me. Strengthen, child. Prepare, child. Soon.

Scripture

Since we live by the Spirit, let us keep in step with the Spirit. (Galatians 5:25, NIV)

He said to them "Come away with me by yourselves to a quiet place and get some rest." (Mark 6:31b, NIV)

I will refresh the weary and satisfy the faint. (Jeremiah 31:25, NIV)

Very truly I tell you, whoever believes in me will do the works I have been doing, and they will do even greater things than these, because I am going to the Father. (John 14:12, NIV)

Let's Make It Personal

1. What are your thoughts on doing even greater things than Jesus did while he was on this earth? Scripture is true: you are to be doing great things in Jesus's name.
2. How important is intimacy with God? Is that something that is imperative to you?
3. Examine yourself. Are there things that have kept you from connecting with the Father? Write your thoughts out in your journal.
4. If there are things that get in the way of your quiet time with God, purpose to resolve those issues. Ask him how he sees them and what he wants you to do with them.

Scripture

He restores my soul. He leads me in the paths of righteousness for his name's sake. (Psalm 23:3, ESV)
For I will satisfy the weary soul, and every languishing soul I will replenish. (Jeremiah 31:25, ESV)

Confession

I am blessed because I take refuge in God and I worship him in spirit and truth he has allowed me to taste and to see how good he is. (Scripture references: Psalm 34:8, ESV; John 4:24, ESV)

Comparison

The act of comparing two or more people or things. (*Cambridge English Dictionary*)

Heart's Cry

Please forgive me for comparing myself to others. That is not what you want for me. You have a plan for my life unlike the others. None of us carry the same calling. I must keep seeking your identity for me. My identity in you! I am ready. Lead and guide me. I do not want to miss one thing.

Father Speaks

Come away with me, my child. We have such a great adventure ahead of us. Are you ready? Just tell me, and we will begin. I have so much to tell you. So much to teach you. Your heart is open to me. Much can be done. Listen for my voice, my direction. This is the beginning of a grand adventure. Come take my hand and let us begin. Your walk with me is like none other. I waited until you were ready for it. No one else can walk this out for you. You have been called to it, prepared for it. Let others do what they do. Keep yourself rooted in me.

Scripture

My beloved speaks and says to me: "Arise, my love, my beautiful one, and come away." (Song of Solomon 2:10, ESV)

Preach the word; be prepared in season and out of season; correct, rebuke and encourage—with great patience and careful instruction. (2 Timothy 4:2, NIV)

Now then go, and I, even I, will be with your mouth, and teach you what you are to say. (Exodus 4:12, NASB)

Stay on the path that the LORD your God has commanded you to follow. Then you will live long and prosperous lives in the land you are about to enter and occupy. (Deuteronomy 5:33, NLT)

Let's Make It Personal

1. Have you fallen into the comparison trap? If so, what is it about the others that causes you to compare yourself to them? Perhaps they are comparing themselves to you.
2. If that is the case, you must show by your actions how you stay in your own lane.
3. Your Father has placed a specific call on your life that only you can walk out.
4. You may be strong in the gift of prophecy and someone else in mercy. Each is just as important as the other. While your gift is bold and outspoken, another's could be quiet and gentle. You will complement each other, not compare with each other.

Scripture

Not that we dare to classify or compare ourselves with some of those who are commending themselves. But when they measure themselves by one another, and compare themselves with one another, they are without understanding. (2 Corinthians 10:12, ESV)

We have different gifts, according to the grace given to each of us. If your gift is prophesying, then prophesy in accordance with your faith. (Romans 12:6, NIV)

Confession

I thank you, Lord, that there are different kinds of gifts. But the same spirit distributes them. If I pay careful attention to my own work, I will get the satisfaction of a job well done, and I won't need to compare myself to anyone else. (Scripture references: 1 Corinthians 12:4, NIV; Galatians 6:4, NLT)

Compassion

Sympathetic consciousness of others' distress
together with a desire to alleviate it.
(*Merriam-Webster Dictionary*)

Heart's Cry

Father, this day I need you to show up. I know it is I who have moved away from you. Forgive me. I must find my way back. Spending time with you. Loving you. Loving our meeting together. You alone hold the keys to my very existence. You alone I love and adore with everything within me. Have you allowed this situation I am going through? Others do not understand me. You do! Speak to me; let me see you today, Father. For without you I will surely perish. You are filled with compassion for me. Walk with me. I invite you to come alongside me. Thank you.

Father Speaks

Child, these days have been challenging to you. You have done well running back to me to quiet your soul. I have allowed this situation for a purpose. That purpose is to fine-tune you even more. Each step is an act of obedience to me, to what I know is the right thing to do. Ask me, and I will show you how to handle these things that present themselves to you. There is never "no way out." As you have felt trapped by circumstances and situations, I have been ready with the way out. I have shown you; do you not perceive it? I will continue to show you, to guide you. The peace you desire is here for you. Seek it out, and it will be found by you. I am the peace-giver. In me you will find everything your soul desires. Seek me with an open and ready heart, and I will be found by you greater than you expect. We have much to accomplish. Must you waste time on things that are not productive for you?

Scripture

Ask me and I will tell you remarkable secrets you do not know about things to come. (Jeremiah 33:3, NLT)

The name of the LORD is a strong fortress; the godly run to him and are safe. (Proverbs 18:10, NLT)

Therefore I tell you, do not worry about your life, what you will eat or drink; or about your body, what you will wear. Is not life more than food, and the body more than clothes? Can any one of you by worrying add a single hour to your life? (Matthew 6: 25, 27, NIV)

Peace I leave with you; my peace I give you. I do not give to you as the world gives. Do not let your hearts be troubled and do not be afraid. (John 14:27, NIV)

I love those who love me, and those who seek me diligently find me. (Proverbs 8:17, ESV)

Let's Make It Personal

1. Can you journal about a time that you felt far from the Lord? Do you think it was because you moved away or because he did?
2. Is it possible that sometimes the Lord is quiet? Perhaps during those times, he wants us to seek him. Look for him in the scriptures and through prayer.
3. He has promised us that he will be found by us if we seek him.
4. Write down obstacles you encounter when you want to read the Word and seek him. Pray about those things and ask Father for a strategy to avoid such interruptions.

Scripture

Seek the LORD and his strength; seek his presence continually! (1 Chronicles 16:11, ESV)

God did this so that they would seek him and perhaps reach out for him and find him, though he is not far from any one of us. (Acts 17:27, NIV)

Confession

Because I have not departed from the commands of your lips, and I have treasured the words of your mouth more than my daily bread, I can ask you and you will tell me remarkable secrets that I do not know, about things to come. (Scripture references: Job 23:12, NIV; Jeremiah 33:3, NLT)

Concern

To cause worry to someone: to be important to someone or to involve someone directly. (*Cambridge English Dictionary*)

Heart's Cry

How do I thank you for counting me worthy to grandparent your children? Father, I have deep concerns for them. Their lives have not been peaceful. They are so young and have seen much too much sadness and anger. Revenge and hate. Only you can protect them. Guide me as I spend time with them. May my mouth speak over them your words of affirmation.

Father Speaks

These children you are so concerned about have been called by me. They reside in the palm of my hand. My name is written in their hearts. They are engraved in my palm; my hands hold them, child. They have a purpose and destiny to fulfill for me, child. If I have placed my hand upon these children; I will not remove it. No fear! They are called by my name. I will fill them; I am filling them. I will never let go of them! They are MINE. They are safe under the protective wings of my spirit. I have put the enemy on alert. See, Satan! They are MINE! You shall not harm one hair on their heads. They are MINE! Nothing shall harm them. I have encapsulated them in my blood. You shall not touch them. They are MINE! They were mine before time began. I knew them. They were planned and expected by me. Woe be to the one that touches my called children. They are sheltered, covered, protected by my hand. Worry not, child. I have heard your cries. Authority has been sent forth from my throne room to protect and keep. I take such delight in these children. They are MINE!

Scripture

See, I have engraved you on the palms of my hands. (Isaiah 49:10a, NIV)

Before I formed you in the womb I knew you, before you were born I set you apart. (Jeremiah 1:5a, NIV)

I sought the LORD, and he answered me; he delivered me from all my fears. (Psalm 34:4, NIV)

Do not fear, for I have redeemed you; I have summoned you by name; you are mine. (Isaiah 43:1b, NIV)

We know that anyone born of God does not continue to sin; the One who was born of God keeps them safe, and the evil one cannot harm them. (1 John 5:18, NIV)

For he will conceal me there when troubles come; he will hide me in his sanctuary. He will place me out of reach on as high rock. (Psalm 27:5, NLT)

Let's Make It Personal

1. Do you have loved ones that you are concerned about? Journal about your concerns. Take them to the Lord in prayer. Listen for the Holy Spirit while you read the scriptures. Take the scriptures you are given and make them personal. You can speak them over yourself and the children you are concerned about.
2. Trust that your Father loves the ones you are concerned about much more than you are capable of.
3. Write out your heart's desire for your loved ones. Submit it to God and trust that he has heard you.
4. Reread "Father Speaks." Believe what he said. Trust that your loved ones are truly kept under the shadow and protection of your Father in heaven.

Scripture

May he give you the desire of your heart and make all your plans succeed. (Psalm 20:4, NIV)
But let all who take refuge in you be glad; let them ever sing for joy. Spread your protection over them, that those who love your name may rejoice in you. (Psalm 5:11, NIV)

Confession

I thank you, God, that you are my refuge and strength, an ever-present help in trouble. You go with me and fight for me against my enemy; you give me victory!
(Scripture references: Psalm 46:1, NLT; Deuteronomy 20:4, NLT)

Confident

A feeling or belief that you can do something well or succeed at something. (*Merriam-Webster Dictionary*)

Heart's Cry

Yes! I am stronger because of you, Father! I have my confidence back. Knowing that my life has been plotted out and directed by you gives me such relief. I knew that, yet I tried to live life my way. That did not work out so well. Now that I have purposed to keep my eyes fixed on you and my ears trained to hear your voice, there is nothing I cannot do. No longer do I get concerned about speaking to others with the Word you have given me for them. Or reaching out to touch someone that you want healed. I can finally leave my concerns about that with you. If you have a Word for someone, and they receive it, it becomes a blessing. If they don't receive it, I can now leave it in your hands, having confidence I did what your Spirit directed and the outcome is in your hands. What freedom you have granted me! You taught me how to rely on you and not on myself! It is NOT about me anyway.

Father Speaks

Move forward, no looking back. For I have a plan for you, my child. Plans that will prosper you, take you deeper into me, to use you, to prove you, to make you my own, my own tool. I desire to reach the downtrodden the outcast the sad the happy with my words. Words I will speak through you for such a time as this. I take you by the hand to guide you to direct your path so that you will not stumble. Hear the Word of your Father; I am calling you out this day. Out of bondage, out of lack, out of sadness—into glorious joy and happiness such as you have never experienced. This day you will begin your new journey with me. Come, let us begin. I am excited for you, my child. We have much to do. Trust me, walk with me. I will open doors, and I say to you, no man will close them. I am taking you higher, deeper than you have ever gone. This new journey is for a time such as this. Come my beloved child, take hold of my hand. Let us begin.

Scripture

And he said, "Behold, I am making a covenant. Before all your people I will do marvels, such as have not been created in all the earth or in any nation. And all the people among whom you are shall see the work of the LORD, for it is an awesome thing that I will do with you." (Exodus 34:10, ESV)

Those who love Your instructions have
great peace, and do not stumble.
(Psalm 119:165, NLT)

For I know the plans I have for, declares the LORD, plans to prosper you and not to harm you, plans to give you a hope and a future. (Jeremiah 29:11, NIV)

I know your works. Behold, I have set before you an open door, which no one is able to shut. I know that you have but little power, and yet you have kept my word and have not denied my name. (Revelation 3:8, ESV)

Let's Make It Personal

1. Have you ever lost confidence in yourself? Did you know that your confidence is not to be found only in human strength? What role do you believe faith in the Lord plays?
2. If you seek to find confidence only in your own abilities, you will be sorely disappointed.
3. Focus on the ultimate reliable goal of confidence in Almighty God.
4. Grab your journal and begin to examine your heart. Whom do you trust in? Where does your confidence rest?

Scripture

This is the confidence we have in approaching God: that if we ask anything according to his will, he hears us. And if we know that he hears us—whatever we ask—we know that we have what we asked of him. (1 John 5:14–15, NIV)

For surely, LORD, you bless the righteous; you surround them with your favor as with a shield. (Psalm 5:12, NIV)

Let us fix our eyes on Jesus, the author and perfecter of our faith. (Hebrews 12:2a, BSB)

Confession

My God has not given me a spirit of fear and shyness, but of power, love, and self-discipline. I hope in the Lord, and I am strong and fortified. (Scripture references: 2 Timothy 1:7, NLT; Psalm 31:24, NIV)

Conflict

Fight, battle, war. (*Merriam-Webster Dictionary*)

Heart's Cry

My humanness gets in the way of my heart's desires. I want to be used by you! My soul rises up and begins questioning, "What if, did he really say that, look at your life, can you really hear from God?" I use your Word and your promises to silence the chatter in my head. I know that my soul challenges me; the enemy of my soul is very active in setting up roadblocks to keep me from having the determination to do as you have called me to do. Forgive me, Father. I will not allow my flesh or the enemy to hold me back any longer. I am willing, and I believe I am ready to do as you direct.

Father Speaks

I am quieting your soul right now. You need to listen well tonight, hear me, listen. I hear the pondering of your thoughts. What are you doing? Who do you love, my child? Who is the lover of your soul? Do you believe? Have you heard? Am I more to you than you are in you? Are you ready to live breathe and have your being in me? Are you now able to move out, do, touch, speak as if I were doing it? I will be the one doing it. All power is yours. Do you believe that which I said before I left this world, that greater things shall you do than I did when I walked this earth? Yes, your thoughts are what my desire and will is for you.

Scripture

When doubts filled my mind, your comfort gave me renewed hope and cheer. (Psalm 94:19, NLT)

But I have calmed and quieted myself, I am like a weaned child with its mother; like a weaned child I am content. (Psalm 131:2, NIV)

For it is not you who will be speaking—it will be the Spirit of your Father speaking through you. (Matthew 10:20, NLT)

Very truly I tell you, whoever believes in me will do the works I have been doing, and they will do even great things than these, because I am going to the Father. (John 14:12, NIV)

Let's Make It Personal

1. Are you aware of the head chatter that goes on when you want to step out and do something for the Lord? Do you think it is all you? Or do you see the enemy's attempt at keeping you from God's best? Journal about that.
2. Does your heart burn inside you when you think about stepping out to serve the Lord?
3. What holds you back? Examine yourself. Journal about your fears and insecurities. When you get those out on paper, they are not as powerful. You can now deal with them. Father will help you with a strategy straight out of his Word.
4. Begin to thank the Holy Spirit for showing up. Thank him for his comfort, counseling, and his guidance as you plot out your plan to serve the Father in a greater way than ever before.

Scripture

You make known to me the path of life; you will fill me with joy in your presence, with eternal pleasures at your right hand. (Psalm 16:11, NIV)
And I will do whatever you ask in my name, so that the Father may be glorified in the Son. You may ask me for anything in my name, and I will do it. (John 14:13–14, NIV)

Confession

As I cast all my anxieties on you because you care for me. You are my strength and my song; you have given me victory. I will praise and exalt you! (Scripture references: 1 Peter 5:7, ESV; Exodus 15:2, NLT)

Confused

Unable to think clearly or to understand something; not clear and therefore difficult to understand. (*Cambridge English Dictionary*)

Heart's Cry

I know I have all power in you. I must believe and rely on that. You have given me a measure of faith. I get so confused about things in my life. I struggle with what I am to do with my life, what is my vision? You speak a thing to me, and my heart jumps for joy. As soon as I hear your Word, the enemy comes along to steal it. I find myself unsure, at times very confused, about which way I am to go, what voice am I hearing. Especially in the morning hours, Father. Feelings of worthlessness cloud my thinking. I know those thoughts are not from you, yet I give ear to them. Your Word tells me that I am victorious over these things. Therefore I am. I will meditate on and speak your Word over my situation. I am victorious.

Father Speaks

My child, my child, calm, calm. I will never let you down. I am taking you places, doing things, you do not know of yet. Those things have been kept hidden away with me, awaiting the right time to be revealed to you. The enemy has no rights to you, my child. In the morning hours, call out my name, and the demons of hell must flee from you. It is my will for you to think clearly, to hear with precision and to move in the direction I call you. Your life belongs to me. Did I not die for you? For I say you are mine; you will hear my voice and none other. Peace be unto you. The peace I give no other can give. Stop running to and fro looking for your purpose in this life, your place in this world. I have the place; I will put you there.

Scripture

We continually ask God to fill you with the knowledge of his will through all the wisdom and understanding that the Spirit gives. (Colossians 1:9b, NIV)

Oh, that we might know the LORD! Let us press on to know him. He will respond to us as surely as the arrival of dawn or the coming of rains in early spring. (Hosea 6:3, NLT)

The night is nearly over; the day is almost here. So let us put aside the deeds of darkness and put on the armor of light. (Romans 13:12, NIV)

The thief comes only to steal and kill and destroy; I have come that they may have life, and have it to the full. (John 10:10, NIV)

Let's Make It Personal

1. In what way have you experienced confusion? Is it possible to be into confusion for a while before you realize it? Has someone spoken something to you that caused confusion? Can you journal about that?
2. What a relief it is to know that confusion is not from your Father. He is the author and finisher of your faith, not confusion.
3. Confusion is not a matter of right or wrong. It is all about your Father taking you through something that you temporarily do not understand.
4. It will only be by going through the confusion that you will be able to understand what your Father wants for you. When you get through this, you will be prepared the next time confusion shows its ugly head. You will be better prepared to discern rightly. Be sure to journal.

Scripture

May the God of hope fill you with all joy and peace as you trust in him, so that you may overflow with hope by the power of the Holy Spirit. (Romans 15:13, NIV)

For God is not a God of confusion but of peace. (1 Corinthians 14:33a, ESV)

Dear friends, do not believe every spirit, but test the spirits to see whether they are from God, because many false prophets have gone out into the world. (1 John 4:1, NIV)

Confession

How thankful I am that your Word is a lamp to guide my feet and a light for my path. As I call out, you answer me and tell me great and unsearchable things that I do not yet know. (Scripture references: Psalm 119:105, NLT; Jeremiah 33:3, NIV)

Conqueror

A person who conquers a place or people; a vanquisher.
(*Oxford Dictionary*)

Heart's Cry

My life has been so wrecked by the enemy and his tactics against me. Father, I do not know how I will overcome, but your Word tells me that I will. That I am an overcomer, a conqueror. If I keep my eyes on you, the author and finisher of my faith, I will learn how to live above the chaos. There from that place I will be able to hear your direction regarding the battles that come against me. I will put on the entire armor of God! I am not defeated! I am the conqueror with you at my side! Thank you, Father!

Father Speaks

Daughter, you must put the enemy under your feet and keep him there. Spirits of confusion, doubt, and fear present themselves as concerns to you. In your life there is no fear or concern. I have declared you are free from that demonic stronghold in your life. If you stay close to me and listen to me and no other voice, you will shed the shackles of fear and concern in your life. Come up higher, sit with me. Let's look with our eyes and observe the destruction of the enemy in your life. Let me take you higher. Above the chaos, where I sit enthroned over the flood waters that seek to overtake you. You are mine! I made you. I handpicked you for such a time as this. Can you not perceive how close, so very close you are to not only coming up higher but remaining here seated with me? Together we are conquerors over your very existence. The closer you draw to me, the more you become like me.

Scripture

The God of peace will soon crush Satan under your feet. The grace of our Lord Jesus Christ be with you. (Romans 16:20, NLT)

The LORD sits enthroned over the flood; the LORD is enthroned as King forever. (Psalm 29:10, NIV)

Don't copy the behavior and customs of this world, but let God transform you into a new person by changing the way you think. Then you will learn to know God's will for you, which is good and pleasing and perfect. (Romans 12:2, NLT)

And in Your lovingkindness, cut off my enemies and destroy all those who afflict my soul, for I am Your servant. (Psalm 143:12, NASB)

And God raised us up with Christ and seated us with him in the heavenly realms in Christ Jesus. (Ephesians 2:6, NIV)

Let's Make It Personal

1. Are you getting weary of the enemy's assaults against you? Your health, finances, family issues? Would you enjoy crushing Satan under your feet? Scripture has something to say about that.
2. How would it feel to take your foot up as high as you can and slam it down upon Satan and crush and pound him into bits under your feet?
3. In Romans 16:20 (NLT), you are told that Jesus crushes Satan under your feet. However, this takes partnership. You and Jesus. Don't try to crush Satan with your own strength. He would be too much for you. With Jesus as your partner, Satan has no chance.
4. Keep walking forward. If Satan gets in your way, crush him under your feet with the Word of God.

Scripture

Submit yourselves, then, to God. Resist the devil,
and he will flee from you. (James 4:7, NIV)
Be alert and of sober mind. Your enemy the devil
prowls around like a roaring lion looking for someone
to devour. Resist him, standing firm in the faith.
(1 Peter 5:8–9a, NIV)

Confession

I thank you, God, that you have given me victory over sin
and death. I belong to you, and your Spirit that lives in
me is greater than the spirit that lives in the world.
(Scripture references:1 Corinthians 15:57, NLT; 1 John 4:4, NLT)

Consequence

The direct, result or outcome of something
occurring earlier. (*Dictionary.com*)

Heart's Cry

Yes, I did make a mistake. I messed up. I sinned against you, Father. Funny how I was foolish enough to think that after I asked for and received your forgiveness, that there would be no consequences. Father, now with very a repentant heart, I am asking you to help me handle these outcomes. I know that you did not cause this; I did. However, I know you love me enough to never leave me as I am.

Father Speaks

Arise and shine, for my favor is upon you child. Is there anything too hard for me? Why is it that you take troubled thought for other things, the things you have given me? I love you, child. I have a wonderful plan for your life and for those you love so dearly. Would I take part of me and wound it? No, I tell you, I would heal it. It will be better for that which you concern yourself with after you call upon me for help. I can do what no man can do. I can deliver, heal, sooth, comfort, and bring joy and peace in the midst of turmoil. Trust me, child.

Scripture

For the LORD God is a sun and shield; the LORD bestows favor and honor. No good thing does he withhold from those who walk uprightly. (Psalm 84:11, ESV)

See what kind of love the Father has given to us, that we should be called children of God; and so we are. (1 John 3:1a, ESV)

I am the LORD, the God of all mankind. Is anything too hard for me? (Jeremiah 32:27, NIV)

But there's also this, it's not too late. God's personal message! "come back to me and really mean it! Come fasting and weeping sorry for your sins!" Change your life, not just your clothes. Come back to God, your God. And here's why: God is kind and merciful. He takes a deep breath, puts up with a lot, this most patient God, extravagant in love, always ready to cancel catastrophe. Who knows? Maybe he'll do it now, maybe he'll turn around and show pity. Maybe, when all's said and done, there'll be blessings full and robust for your God! (Joel 2:12–14, MSG)

Let's Make It Personal

1. Have you ever had consequences for the choices you made? We call making choices against what scripture says, sin. If the Bible says something is wrong, it is wrong.
2. There are no "little or big" sins in God's eyes. James 4:17 (ESV) addresses this, "So whoever knows the right things to do and fails to do it, for him it is sin." He is a forgiving Father and does not hold our sins against us.
3. He loves you too much to leave you as you are. He uses problems to direct you. There are times he may need to get your attention and steer you in the direction he has for you. Consequences are used for that purpose. Painful situations can facilitate change.
4. Have you ever heard the saying "If you want to know what is inside a person, drop them in hot water"? If you are dealing with consequences, know this: he loves you and forgives you; there is nothing that he will not use for your good and to his glory.

Scripture

My little children, these things write I unto you, that ye sin not. And if any man sin, we have an advocate with the Father, Jesus Christ the righteous.
(1 John 2:1, KJV)

He has told you, O man, what is good; and what does the LORD require of you but to do justice, and to love kindness, and to walk humbly with your God?
(Micah 6:8, ESV)

Dear brothers and sisters, when troubles come your way, consider it an opportunity for great joy. (James 1:2–3, NLT)

My suffering was good for me, for it taught me to pay attention to your decrees. Your instructions are more valuable to me than millions in gold and silver.
(Psalm 119:71–72, LB)

Confession

God blesses me because my heart is pure, and
he surrounds me with his shield of love.
(Scripture references: Matthew 5:8, NLT; Psalm 5:12)

Consolation

Comfort received by a person after a loss or disappointment. (*Oxford Dictionaries*)

Heart's Cry

You are the most important thing in my life, Father! You are my eternal salvation, my eternal love. I must see the goodness of God among the living. Speak, and I will listen. I don't have much confidence right now; I am disappointed in myself. I need your infusion of determination and set will. You I do not want to disappoint with my life choices. Keep the enemy of my soul far from me. Allow me some breathing room. I will reset and come back stronger than ever. You are my God; there is no one and nothing else. I will keep my eyes upon you. For in you I live, breathe, and have my being. Speak, and I will hear; the Holy Spirit will enable me to hear your voice.

Father Speaks

Child, child, why do you worry so? Why is your heart so burdened with the cares of this world? Have you not heard, I have overcome the world? I have overcome the turmoil and worry in you. I am the overcomer in and for you. Is there too much power in this world for you to handle? Which power are you contending with? My power? Or that of the enemy of your soul? Have you not heard? Has no one told you that the one who loves you with an everlasting love is the same one that delights in delivering you and in answering your prayers. Nothing, NO THING, takes me by surprise. I was there before time began. I saw you then; I loved you then; I had a plan for your deliverance then. There is nothing too hard for me. Can you believe this? You can say to me, "I believe, Father! Help my unbelief," and at that moment, the moment you speak, I have answered. I have encouragement for you. Reach out to me, child. Look for me. I will be found by you. I am waiting to open the windows of heaven to pour out blessings upon you. Believe.

Scripture

I have told you these things, so that in me you may have peace. In this world you will have trouble. But take heart! I have overcome the world. (John 16:33, NIV)

I am the LORD, the God of all mankind. Is anything too hard for me? (Jeremiah 32:27, NIV)

The Lord is my strength and my shield; in him my heart trusts, and I am helped; my heart exults, and with my song I give thanks to him. (Psalm 28:7, ESV)

I do believe; help me overcome my unbelief. (Mark 9:24b NIV)

If you look for me wholeheartedly, you will find me. (Jeremiah 29:13, NLT)

Let's Make It Personal

1. Are you aware of the Holy Spirit's role in bringing comfort to you? Jesus sent him to you to be a consolation to you. In prayer ask him to speak to you. He will guide your quite time in the Word. You will find comfort there.
2. Consolation from the Father will restore you and refresh your vision. You acquire energy from the Father through scripture reading.
3. You will see where God is active in your life and where he is leading you. Journal.
4. With the scriptural information he gives, you are armed with the correct words of your mouth to speak out loud over your life. Your words are not powerless in your life. They have creative power. God created the heavens and the earth with the words of his mouth. You have that same power residing within you.

Scripture

Since we are living by the Spirit, let us follow the Spirit's leading in every part of our lives. (Galatians 5:25, NLT)

But when he, the Spirit of truth, comes, he will guide you into all the truth. He will not speak on his own; he will speak only what he hears, and he will tell you what is yet to come. (John 16:13, NIV)

The heart of the godly thinks carefully before speaking. (Proverbs 15:28, NLT)

When she speaks, her words are wise, and she gives instructions with kindness. (Proverbs 31:26, NLT)

Confession

If I talk too much, I can get into sin. Therefore, I will be sensible and keep my mouth shut. I know that wise words bring many benefits. So I ask that you set a guard over my mouth Lord and keep watch over the door of my lips. (Scripture references: Proverbs 10:19, 12:14, NLT; Psalm 141:3, NIV)

Control

The power to influence or direct people's behavior or the course of events. (*Online Dictionary*)

Heart's Cry

Oh, how I want to fix the things that are coming at me. I am the one that wants to bring some type of justice to the situations that I am faced with. Yet, Father, you have taught me about control. When I wanted to lash out at those who have wounded me, when I wanted to seek some type of revenge on those who hurt my family, you always calmed the storm raging inside of me, and you comforted me.

Father Speaks

Child, child, why do you wrestle so with the things you cannot control? Am I not capable of handling your issues? Has anything happening to you taken me by surprise? No, I have gone the paths before you. I have seen the obstacles. I have disarmed them for you. Yet you run ahead with a preconceived idea of what I am doing. Child, let go! Let me guide you through troubled waters, briar paths, and the fire. I go before you. I have it all under control. Allow me to handle things. I will navigate you through to the other side.

Scripture

For since the beginning of the world men have not heard, nor perceived by ear, neither has the eye seen a God beside You, who acts for the one who waits for Him. (Isaiah 64:4, MEV)

Have I not commanded you? Be strong and courageous. Do not be afraid; do not be discouraged, for the LORD your God will be with you wherever you go. (Joshua 1:9, NIV)

For My eyes are on all their ways; they are not hidden from My face, nor is their iniquity concealed from My eyes. (Jeremiah 16:17, NIV)

Let's Make It Personal

1. Have you been wrestling with things you cannot control? How has that made you feel? How has that worked out for you? Journal about it.
2. God will release his blessing upon you; however, oftentimes it is after a period of wrestling with him. Are you capable of holding on until the breakthrough happens?
3. How badly do you want your breakthrough, your blessing? Journal your thoughts.
4. If you are wrestling with God over control of something, it is time you release it to him. When he calls you to wrestle, there is always more going on than what you first understood. Our Father in heaven, filled with mercy and grace, will always use this time to transform you for his good. You must believe this. He is a good, good God!

Scripture

And without faith it is impossible to please God, because anyone who comes to him must believe that he exists and that he rewards those who earnestly seek him. (Hebrews 11:6, NIV)
Do not be anxious about anything, but in every situation, by prayer and petition, with thanksgiving, present your requests to God. And the peace of God, which transcends all understanding will guard your hearts and your minds in Christ Jesus. (Philippians 4:6–7, NIV)

Confession

I will set my mind on things above, not on earthly things. As I remain steadfast, I will be kept in perfect peace because of my trust in you. (Scripture references: Isaiah 26:3, NLT; Colossians 3:2, NIV)

Declare

If you declare that something is true, you say that it is true in a firm, deliberate way. (*Collins English Dictionary*)

Heart's Cry

I declare, Father, my heart is yours and yours alone. Guide me and open my mouth; fill it with your words. Let the meditations of my heart and the words of my mouth be pleasing to you my rock and my redeemer. Anoint my very breath, my lips, my heart, my mind, my soul, with you and only you. You hear the words of my mouth, and you will answer. I will be used by you in new and powerful ways, as you will.

Father Speaks

I will bring those to you that need a bit of your anointing placed upon them. They are hungry for more of me, and they are searching. You, my child, have come from a place of deep pain that reached into your soul. Only I heard your soul cries; only I knew the level of pain you walked in. Now, child, I say to you, rise up! My other children need you to speak into their lives. Bring hope to them; encourage them. I will tell you one by one what they need. Listen closely to me.

Scripture

Blessed are those who hunger and thirst for righteousness, for they will be filled. (Matthew 5:6, NIV)

O God, you are my God; I earnestly search for you. My soul thirsts for you; my whole body longs for you in this parched and weary land where there is no water. (Psalm 63:1, NLT)

The righteous cry out, and the LORD hears them; he delivers them from all their troubles. (Psalm 34:17, NIV)

As for that in the good soil, they are those who, hearing the word, hold it fast in an honest and good heart, and bear fruit with patience. (Luke 8:15, ESV)

Then the way you live will always honor and please the Lord, and your lives will produce every kind of good fruit. All the while, you will grow as you learn to know God better and better. (Colossians 1:10, NLT)

Let's Make It Personal

1. Do you think you have completely given your heart to the Lord?
2. What type of life do you think someone would lead if Jesus was their Lord, all the time? Can you journal about that?
3. Have you ever known someone, or are you the one that calls Jesus Lord without doing his will? Do you go your own way? He sees your heart. He forgives, and he desires to use you.
4. Do you want to be used by him? Would you like to walk in his will? Tell him so, and purpose to draw close to him in Bible reading and quiet time with him. You will grow in him, and soon you will be hearing his voice clearer. He will be able to direct your path.

Scripture

May the words of my mouth and the meditation of my heart be pleasing to you, O LORD, my rock and my redeemer. (Psalm 19:14, NLT)

Why do you call me, Lord, Lord, and do not do what I say? (Luke 6:46, NIV)

Jesus replied, "I am the bread of life. Whoever comes to me will never be hungry again. Whoever believes in me will never be thirsty." (John 6:35, NLT)

But in my distress I cried out to the LORD; yes, I prayed to my God for help. He heard me from his sanctuary; my cry to him reached his ears. (Psalm 18:6, NLT)

Confession

My Lord, I lift my hands to you. My soul thirsts for you as parched land thirst for rain. As I take delight in you, I receive my heart's desires. I will not be ruled by a spirit of timidity, but of power and love and self-control. (Scripture references: Psalm 143:6, 37:4, NLT; 1 Timothy 1:7, ESV)

Deeper

Penetrating or entering deeply into subjects of thought
or knowledge; having deep insight or understanding:
a profound thinker. Origination in or penetrating
to the depths of one's being.
(*Dictionary.com*)

Heart's Cry

I have longed for and yearned to understand you better. Your Word tells me that deep calls to deep. If I understand that correctly, I can come to you, commune with you, and learn from you. By doing that I am going from deep to deeper in my walk and love for you, Father. Guide me along this walk from deep to deeper.

Father Speaks

Deeper, come deeper, daughter. I am calling you into the deep waters. Fear not, I am here. I have your hand. You will walk with me onto, into, and above the deep waters. Much to show you. So much to reveal to you. Do you desire to know me? Do you desire to know me, daughter? My desire to reveal myself to you is greater than your desire to know me. Nothing can you do on your own. I have designed it that way. For I love you so intensely I cannot bear not having you. Come, child, come! You ravish my heart. For one look from your eyes and there is nothing I will not do for you. Understand, daughter! There is nothing I will not do for you, NO THING! Keep your gaze upon me. I need you, child. I desire you. Nothing will be able to remove my hand from you. Nothing will ever take you out of my grip. My grip is a loving grip. Child, I love you. Come sit with me. Sit at my right hand. Come, my precious child, my bride. I love you intensely and forever.

Scripture

Deep waters call out to what is deeper still; at the roar of your waterfalls all your breakers and your waves swirled over me. (Psalm 42:7, ISV)

I will give them hearts that recognize me as the LORD. They will be my people, and I will be their God, for they will return to me wholeheartedly. (Jeremiah 24:7, NLT)

I give them eternal life, and they shall never perish; no one will snatch them out of my hand. (John 10:28, NIV)

For you reach into my heart. With one flash of your eyes I am undone by your love, my beloved, my equal, my bride. You leave me breathless-I am overcome by merely a glance from your worshiping eyes, for you have stolen my heart. I am held hostage by your love and by the graces of righteousness shining upon you. (Song of Songs 4:9, TPT)

Let's Make It Personal

1. When was the first time you realized what the word *deeper* meant regarding your relationship with the Father?
2. Was it difficult to believe that he loves you too much to leave you as you are?
3. Sit quiet in his presence with your journal. Allow him to guide and direct your deeper walk with him.
4. Realize that there is nothing you can do to stop his great love for you and his great desire to commune with you. He is extending his hand to you, saying, "Come to me and I will show you great and mighty things that you know not of."

Scripture

Call to me, and I will answer you; I will tell you wonderful and marvelous things that you know nothing about. (Jeremiah 33:3, GNT)
The LORD is near to all who call on him, to all who call on him in truth. (Psalm 145:18, NIV)

Confession

Thank you, Father, for the assurance that when I call out to you, you answer me. Your Word is a lamp unto my feet and a light unto my path. There is no God greater than you. I know when I call upon you and pray, you listen to me. You are always ready to hear my petitions and bring a swift answer. (Scripture references: Psalm 119:105, NIV; 1 John 5:15, ESV)

Defeat

Win a victory over in a battle or other contest; overcome or beat. (*Online Dictionary*)

Heart's Cry

Father, give me a second chance to confront and deal with those things that defeated me in the last season. Show me what I need to do.

Father Speaks

Child, child, the enemy has taken another shot at you. He slipped in when you were not prepared or aware. He caused you sadness and some confusion for a short period of time. You have come through that by the words of your mouth and my power within you. You are victorious once again. Be more on the lookout for the whiles of the enemy. Don't forget your armor! It is available for you to put on every morning! Keep your eyes on me and my power. Never allow an opening or occasion for the enemy of your soul to slide in. Ask me and I will give you your own alarm system. My spirit shall be your keeper, and my spirit will sound the alarm when danger is approaching; hear him, child, and arm yourself for offensive battle. You be the aggressor; always move forward wielding the sword of the spirit, of my Spirit. Gird yourself child with the shield of faith and praise; rejoice in me. Take no thought for the day; take no concerns. For I hold your day and your future in the palm of my hand. I decree and declare to you, my precious child; if you abide in me, I will abide in you and no harm shall befall you.

Scripture

The heart of the godly thinks carefully before speaking. (Proverbs 15:28, NLT)

Finally, be strong in the Lord and in his mighty power. Put on the full armor of God, so that you can take your stand against the devil's schemes. (Ephesians 6:10–11, NIV)

From eternity to eternity I am God. No one can snatch anyone out of my hand. No one can undo what I have done. (Isaiah 43:13, NLT)

God means what he says. What he says goes. His powerful Word is sharp as a surgeon's scalpel, cutting through everything, whether doubt or defense, laying us open to listen and obey. Nothing and no one is impervious to God's Word. We can't get away from it, no matter what. (Hebrews 4:12–13, MGS)

We know that anyone born of God does not continue to sin; the One who was born of God keeps them safe, and the evil one cannot harm them. (1 John 5:18, NIV)

Let's Make It Personal

1. If you want to take your life back, then you must control the words of your mouth.
2. Of course, you will miss it now and then; do not be discouraged. Repent, receive forgiveness, and get right back on track. Do not give the devil a foothold to come in and harass you.
3. As long as your words line up with the Word of God, Satan cannot touch you.
4. The Word of God is powerful, the most commanding tool you will ever have. Use it, and you will have what you say.

Scripture

If we confess our sins, he is faithful and just to forgive us our sins and to cleanse us from all unrighteousness. (1 John 1:9, ESV)
And do not give the devil a foothold. (Ephesians 4:27, NIV)
And so blessing and cursing come pouring out of the same mouth. Surely, my brothers and sisters, this is not right! (James 3:10, NLT)

Confession

When I speak, my words are wise, and I give instructions with kindness. I want to enjoy my life and see many happy days, so I keep my tongue from speaking evil, and I do not tell lies. (Scripture references: Proverbs 31:26, NLT; 1 Peter 3:10, NLT)

Defender

To ward off attack from; guard against
assault or injury. (*Dictionary.com*)

Heart's Cry

How did I get to this place? The place where ones I trusted treat me with such disregard. My heart has been bruised. Who gave them the right to speak to me in such a way? My heart is hurt. Where is there for me to go? You are my only safe place. You see me as someone that is worthy of love and acceptance. You are my great Defender. In you I put my trust; what can man do to me? Thank you, Father, for loving me so much.

Father Speaks

Child, child, you take thought for much. Yet you seek me and my hand; this pleases me, for when you seek me, I am found by you. When you cry out, all of heaven hears and I command an answer. Before your heart cries out, I have heard and prepared an answer that will bring you much joy. My hand is forced to bring justice upon those who have slandered my chosen. I have been patient with the ones who have hurt you, my child. I am a loving and kind father, and when injustice comes upon my daughter, I must act. Be prepared, for the coming days will bring turmoil, and I will settle the water. Out of that will come mighty blessings beyond that which you have requested of me. I will embarrass your enemy in front of you. You will put to death all words spoken against you, and this will be done as you sit in my presence quiet, holding your peace the peace I give to you. Destruction of your enemies. I am a righteous God, and I demand justice. I will set you free, child. You will go forth soon, oh, so very soon, leaping laughing and praising my name. Prepare, daughter. Even now, pray for your enemies. Your Father has spoken.

Scripture

In my distress I called to the LORD; I cried to my God for help. From his temple he heard my voice; my cry came before him, into his ears. (Psalm 18:6, NIV)

And will not God bring about justice for his chosen ones, who cry out to him day and night? Will he keep putting them off? (Luke 18:7, NIV)

May all my enemies be disgraced and terrified. May they suddenly turn back in shame. (Psalm 6:10, NLT)

Vengeance is Mine, and retribution, in due time their foot will slip; for the day of their calamity is near, and the impending things are hastening upon them. (Deuteronomy 32:35, NASB)

Then you will experience God's peace, which exceeds anything we can understand. His peace will guard your hearts and minds as you live in Christ Jesus. (Philippians 4:7, NLT)

God is not man, that he should lie, or a son of man, that he should change his mind. Has he said, and will he not do it? Or has he spoken, and will he not fulfill it? (Numbers 23:19, ESV)

Let's Make It Personal

1. As you strengthen yourself in God's Word, you may run into some giants that want to keep you from overcoming. Once you get God's perspective on the situation, those giants will turn into nothing more than grasshoppers.
2. Think about this: your enemies can be defined as anyone who doesn't want you to succeed. However, it is not the enemy that can stop your progress; it is your response that determines your outcome.
3. The Holy Spirit is ready to show you the way out of hurt and frustration into peace and victory. He does this through the Word.
4. When Father tells you he is bringing justice to your situation do you know what he means? Journal about that. Are you prepared? Can you pray for others?

Scripture

You have heard that it was said, you shall love your neighbor and hate your enemy. But I say to you, love your enemies and pray for those who persecute you. (Matthew 5:43–44, ESV)

Because he holds fast to me in love, I will deliver him; I will protect him, because he knows my name. When he calls to me, I will answer him; I will be with him in trouble; I will rescue him and honor him. (Psalm 91:14–15, ESV)

The Lord will rescue me from every evil deed and bring me safely into this heavenly kingdom. To him be the glory forever and ever. Amen. (2 Timothy 4:18, ESV)

So we can confidently say, "The Lord is my helper; I will not fear; what can man do to me?" (Hebrews 13:6, ESV)

Confession

The angel of the Lord encamps around me because I fear him and he rescues me. He is my hiding place and keeps me from trouble. He surrounds me with shouts of deliverance. (Scripture references: Psalm 34:7, NASB; Psalm 32:7, ESV)

Defenseless

Someone completely vulnerable that has no form of protection or no means of protection. (*YourDictionary*)

Heart's Cry

Oh, Father, how I am wounded by the lash of tongues. People speaking lies about me. I am completely defenseless. No one understands. No one cares what this is doing to me. Yet I must continue to face another day. I looked at my picture of you, and I thought you looked angry. I asked if you were angry at me. You told me, "No, child, I have righteous anger."

Father Speaks

I am a God of justice. The time has come. For I have wooed the sinner to me. I have shown them the right way. Yet they have scorned me. Said to themselves, "He does not know, he will not care, he understands." Therein is the lie. I do understand those that wish to practice deception. I do understand those that claim that pain and suffering make them behave the way they behave. I say to you that enough is enough. You shall hurt my beloved no longer. I have called her to me to do my bidding, and others have distracted her, caused her great pain and distress, gotten her off the path I cleared before her. Yet she held on to me. I sustained her through the vicious attacks of the enemy. She clung to me, her rock, her Deliverer. I say to you, this day is the day of deliverance. The tide has changed. The waves will no longer cover her, assault her, or attempt to take her under. I am her life raft. I am her Savior. I am the one to reach down into the troubled waters and free her. She will run to me and allow me to wrap my arms of love and assurance around her. I have come to set the captive free. I have come to set her free. Now is the time.

Scripture

Perhaps they will bring their petition before the LORD and will each turn from their wicked ways, for the anger and wrath pronounced against this people by the LORD are great. (Jeremiah 36:7, NIV)

The LORD lives! Praise be to my Rock! Exalted be my God, the Rock, my Savior. (2 Samuel 22:47, NIV)

When they call on me, I will answer; I will be with them in trouble. I will rescue and honor them. (Psalm 91:15, NLT)

He reached down from heaven and rescued me; he drew me out of deep waters. (Psalm 18:16, NLT)

Let's Make It Personal

1. Have you been lied about? Others thought they could rob you of the calling Father has placed on you.
2. Take your journal and sit quietly before the Lord. He desires to speak with you about your pain. He has a way through it for you.
3. He fights the fight for you; you need not engage. You are to forgive those who persecute you and say all sorts of derogatory things about you.
4. As difficult as it may be, forgive them, for this is the Father's will for you. Release them into his hands.

Scripture

The righteous hate what is false, but the wicked make themselves a stench and bring shame on themselves. (Proverbs 13:5, NIV)

For if you forgive others their trespasses, your heavenly Father will also forgive you, but if you do not forgive others their trespasses, neither will your Father forgive your trespasses. (Matthew 6:14–15, ESV)

Confession

You send me a sign of your favor. Those who hate me will be put to shame because you, O LORD, help and comfort me. I will proclaim who is my God besides the LORD? And who is my Rock except my God? (Scripture references: Psalm 18:31, NIV; Psalm 86:17, NLT)

Delight

A strong feeling of happiness. Something that makes you very happy: something that gives you great pleasure or satisfaction. (*Merriam-Webster Dictionary*)

Heart's Cry

I have spent time in your Word and have had wonderful time in prayer with you. Today I sense you are very close to me, Father. I am filled with joy knowing that you are my best friend. I pray that you find delight in spending time with me. It is my greatest desire to bring you joy.

Father Speaks

This is a day of change, transformation, crossing over. Yet you know it not. Such is how I choose to move with you at this time. I delight to surprise you, child. I have many surprises arranged for you. Divine surprises, arranged by me for you! Because you are my beloved daughter, upon whom I place my love. I delight in you, and you know it not. I delight in you. I am pleased in the way you cling to me. You run to me; you must have me. Therefore, I am yours. You are my beloved, and I am yours. I have called you into a rest. Rest in ME. For soon, child, oh, so soon, you will be called to move out in me and with me. I can hardly constrain myself from starting you.

Scripture

But the LORD your God, he's the one who will cross over before you! (Deuteronomy 31:3, CEBa)
And a voice from heaven said. "This is my dearly loved Son, who brings me great joy." (Matthew 3:17, NLT)
Surprise us with love at daybreak; then we'll skip and dance all the day long. (Psalm 90:14, MSG)
For the LORD you God is living among you. He is a mighty savior. He will take delight in you with gladness. With his love, he will calm all your fears. He will rejoice over you will joyful songs. (Zephaniah 3:17, NLT)
Come to me, all you who are weary and burdened, and I will give you rest. (Matthew 11:28, NIV)

Let's Make It Personal

1. Have you ever felt your Father's delight in you? He is living with you; he is a mighty Savior; he takes delight in you; with his love he will calm your fears and rejoice over you with singing. Journal about that.
2. Did you have to perform for him to be happy with you? He offers his love through Jesus Christ as a free, undeserved gift to you.
3. His love and adoration come in spite of us. We are not deserving, yet he loves us unconditionally.
4. Take time to enter into his presence. Allow him to love you, to speak to you.

Scripture

The LORD your God is in your midst, a mighty one who will save; he will rejoice over you with gladness; he will quiet you by his love; he will exult over you with loud singing. (Zephaniah 3:17, ESV)

We know how much God loves us, and we have put our trust in his love. God is love, and all who live in love live in God, and God lives in them. (1 John 4:16, NLT)

The LORD delights in those who fear him, who put their hope in his unfailing love. (Psalm 147:11, NIV)

Confession

You tell me that you walk with me and you are my God. Therefore, I desire to live in harmony with others. Your Word tells me that I must put on love, which binds everything together. (Scripture references: Colossians 3:14, ESV; Leviticus 26:13, NJV)

Deliverance

Deliverance is rescue from imprisonment, danger, or evil.
(*Collins English Dictionary*)

Heart's Cry

Father, only you know the thoughts the enemy has brought to my mind. I know they are all lies. You are my God, my Provider, my Healer, my Deliverer. All I need. I will focus on the goodness of the Lord during this dry and barren time. When all seems wrong, when words spoken by others would slice me into pieces, you raise up a standard of mighty protection for me. You decree and declare no harm will come to your child. You pluck me up from the rubble and dust me off. You place me on high ground where the accusations of the enemy cannot reach me. There you pour oil over my wounds. You touch my fragmented heart; you heal my mind. You put a right spirit in me. You call me forth after a period of rest. I am strengthened. I am dressed in fresh, powerful armor. I am ready to get back into the battle. For my Father goes before me and he levels the path before me. I will keep my eyes on him. He is my deliverer. In his name I will rejoice.

Father Speaks

Woe be to those who have hurt and continue to hurt, my child. When I say vengeance is mine, you need to begin praying for mercy for those who have hurt you. For there are those that call my name, yet have no relationship with me. They live by their own rule and religion. This angers me. They know the right and perfect way. They have allowed the enemy to pollute their minds with greed and vengeance. Woe be unto them that desire to hurt my child.

Scripture

It is mine to avenge; I will repay. In due time their foot will slip; their day of disaster is near and their doom rushes upon them. (Deuteronomy 32:35, NIV)

Woe to you, destroyer, you who have not been destroyed! Woe to you, betrayer, you who have not been betrayed! When you stop destroying, you will be destroyed; when you stop betraying, you will be betrayed. (Isaiah 33:1, NIV)

Righteousness and justice are the foundation of Your throne; loving devotion and faithfulness go before You. (Psalm 89:14, ESV)

The Lord passed before him and proclaimed, "The Lord, the Lord, a God merciful and gracious, slow to anger, and abounding in steadfast love and faithfulness, keeping steadfast love for thousands, forgiving iniquity and transgression and sin, but who will by no means clear the guilty, visiting the iniquity of the fathers on the children and the children's children, to the third and the fourth generation." (Exodus 34:6–7, ESV)

Let's Make It Personal

1. Can you pray that God has mercy for someone that has hurt you or someone you love? Jesus is your greatest example of this.
2. Deliverance can be God walking through the trials by your side, comforting and encouraging you. His desire is to help you mature in your faith.
3. You have your spiritual armor found in Ephesians 6:12–17. You can defend yourself with the power tools found in that scripture. The Word of God is an offensive weapon we are to use continually.
4. Your Father is going to defend you and see to it that justice is done. You can lay your anger, resentment, bitterness down and allow him to do what is necessary. It is not for you to seek these things, you dare not. Heed the words of Jesus in Matthew when he says that an unforgiving heart will destroy you.

Scripture

But if you do not forgive others their trespasses, neither will your Father forgive your trespasses. (Matthew 6:15, ESV)
Having a good conscience, so that, when you are slandered, those who revile your good behavior in Christ may be put to shame. (1 Peter 3:16, ESV)
Beloved, never avenge yourselves, but leave it to the wrath of God, for it is written, "Vengeance is mine, I will repay, says the Lord." (Romans 12:19, ESV)

Confession

You will be merciful to me as I show mercy to others. You will fight for me, and all I have to do is be silent. I will be found blameless in your sight.
(Scripture references: 2 Samuel 22:26, ESV; Exodus 14:14, ESV)

Dependence

The state of relying on or being controlled by someone or something else. (*Online Dictionary*)

Heart's Cry

There is nothing I would rather read than your Word, Father. In it is found rivers of living water. It refreshes me and qualifies me to live this life I have to live. My desire is to represent you well. To live in forgiveness and love. Without you and your Word, I can do nothing. I am nothing without you. I am completely dependent on you. With you I can scale a wall and tear down strongholds. With you I will live a victorious life.

Father Speaks

Are you ready, daughter? For the time is quickly approaching. You must remain close to me. It is good, your dependence on me. I will put my words into your mouth. Speak them with power and conviction. Fear not! I have your back. The doors are opening even now as I speak this to you. You have my Dunamis power within you. Ask me what you will and I will do it. You have been walking alone for some time. This was necessary for me to fine tune your spiritual ears to hear me, know my direction. I have spoken to you about our journey together; the time has come. No, you do not feel equipped; you will never feel equipped. I am your equipping. Open your mouth, and I will fill it. You shall move forth in great power, mercy, grace, and glory. My glory is all over you! You know not how others being in your presence causes them to feel me, my presence. Yes, there is great power in your hands because I am your hands. Everything you have requested of me is yours. I care not about money; your heart is what I want, and as I look upon you and your devotion to me, I delight in giving you anything you want: money and all it can buy for you. That means nothing to me; to see you happy means everything to me. Because she loves me, because she calls upon my name, because she is lost without me, because she would die without me. That is what moves me. Daughter, you have no idea, no concept of the love I have for you. Come! As we journey together, I will see to it that you begin to see just how high and how deep how wide my love is for you. Come! Let us begin! I can hardly wait!

Scripture

Trust in the LORD with all your heart, and do not depend on your own understanding. (Proverbs 3:5, ISV)

For though we walk in the flesh, we are not waging war according to the flesh. For the weapons of our warfare are not of the flesh but have diving power to destroy strongholds. We destroy arguments and every lofty opinion raised against the knowledge of God, and take every thought captive to obey Christ. (2 Corinthians 10:3–5, ESV)

Open your mouth wide, and I will fill it with good things. (Psalm 81:10b, NLT)

He brought me out into a broad place; he rescued me, because he delighted in me. (Psalm 18:19, ESV)

Let's Make It Personal

1. What does total dependence on God look like to you? Journal about that. Ask the Holy Spirit to show you areas that need improvement.
2. I think a good example of dependence on God is Shadrach, Meshach, and Abednego. They had to depend on him to keep them safe in the fiery furnace. Or Daniel in the lion's den. Noah and the flood. There are many examples of others being totally dependent on God.
3. Praying is a great way to encourage yourself by acknowledging his provision, power, and promises in your life.
4. Become a living sacrifice to God, purified from sin and dedicated to him in all things.

Scripture

My soul, wait in silence for God only, for my hope is from Him. (Psalm 62:5, NASB)

So let us keep on coming boldly to the throne of grace, so that we may obtain mercy and find grace to help us in our time of need. (Hebrews 4:16, NIV)

Confession

For I know that nothing can separate me from my Father's love. Neither death nor life, angels nor demons, nothing I have done in my past or anything I can do in the future. No matter how high or how deep, or anything else in all creation, has the power to separate me from the love of God that is in Christ Jesus. Therefore, I will trust in him with all my heart, and I will not lean on my own understanding; he will make my paths straight because in everything I do, I submit to him. (Scripture references: Romans 8:38–39, NIV; Proverbs 3:5–6, NIV)

Desire

A strong feeling of wanting to have something or wishing for something to happen. (*Oxford Dictionaries*)

Heart's Cry

My one deepest desire is to know YOU. My heart searches for you in the night as I lay on my bed. Out of my heart my mouth praises you, Father. I long for you as a deer longs for water. As I wait upon you, I know you will reveal yourself to me. I will find you in your Word and in the quiet place. You, the lover of my soul, will never let me down.

Father Speaks

Yes! Yes! I have heard your prayer, child. I have heard and am answering. Keep your eyes set on me. Know that I love you tenderly and everlasting. It is my delight to grant to you the desires of your heart. Ask me, and I shall answer. Trust me, child. Can you feel it? Yes, my power is here. My desire is here. Ask and I will show you deep yet deeper things. Come to the feet of your Savior, child. I am beckoning you come. More, I have more for you. We have just begun. My precious child. Come to me, I am calling, drawing you. Come, for I have something new for you. New, now come and take it.

Scripture

Because he bends down to listen, I will pray as long as I have breath! (Psalm 116:2, NLT)

No one comes to me unless the Father who sent me draws them, and I will raise them up at the last day. (John 6:44, NIV)

The Spirit and the Bride say, "Come." And let the one who hears say, "Come." And let the one who is thirsty come; let the one who desires take the water of life without price. (Revelation 22:17, ESV)

Take delight in the LORD, and he will give you the desire of your heart. (Psalm 37:4, NIV)

The one who calls you is faithful, and he will do it. (1 Thessalonians 5:24, NIV)

Let's Make It Personal

1. What is your deepest heart's desire? Have you spoken to Father about that?
2. As you search for him do you have assurance he can be found by you? Why or why not?
3. Journal about this. What is that assurance?
4. Spend some time just praising him. Pour your heart out to him for he is listening,

Scripture

As the deer longs for streams of water, so I long for you, O God.
(Psalm 42:1, NLT)
You will seek Me and find Me when you search for
Me with all your heart. (Jeremiah 29:13, NAS)

Confession

Thank you, Father, for hearing my cry. You know my
deepest longings. My tears are liquid words, and you
have read them all. I will praise you with my mouth
for you have saved me out of all my troubles.
(Scripture references: Psalm 34:6, NIV; Psalm 38:9, TPT)

Desolation

A state of complete emptiness or destruction, great unhappiness or loneliness. (*English Oxford Dictionary*)

Heart's Cry

Is there a limit that one reaches that has the effect of the straw that broke the camel's back? Inside there is such emptiness like a crystal glass that has been drained of its contents. Still clear, crystal clear, and yet streaked by its previous contents. As I watch the wind blow the dead leaves around in the air, I think of how my fragmented emotions are blown around by circumstances beyond my control, and like the leaves, dry, brittle, and fragile is my life. I will say to myself, surely God lives and he cares for me! He is coming to my rescue.

Father Speaks

These difficult days for you are coming to an end. If it were not for your faithfulness and holding on to me, times could have been worse. Yet I heard your pleas for help, for deliverance, and I have answered. Though you do not see the answer yet, do not become discouraged, for it is my good pleasure to answer your cries for help. Child, hear me. I am as close as the air that you breathe. Again, is there anything to hard for me? In the gray days, you will find me if you seek me with your whole heart. I will be found by you. I am closer to you than a brother. I am your lover, lover of your soul, your very being. How can the maker disown his own? I molded you, I made you. I formed you in your mother's womb. I knew you before time began. I rejoiced in you before the heavens were created. I loved you; I was anticipating your arrival on planet Earth. Yet even so, I waited for you to find me, to recognize me, the one who loves you perfectly, without judgement, purely. My love for you is perfect, without flaw. I watched as you searched for love, finding only disappointment and pain. I watched and

I waited. I yearned for you to turn to me. Oh, child, just one glance from your eyes! One word from your mouth, one call of my name, and I would have rushed to your side. There is nothing I would withhold from you. You are my child, my beloved child. Still I wait, I yearn, I desire your presence with me. Come, child, let us reason together, for I have many things to tell you. I have prepared a way through the desert for you. You will not journey alone. Come, take my hand, let us begin our glorious joyful life together. I love you with an everlasting and deep love.

Scripture

I call on the LORD in my distress, and he answers me. (Psalm 120:1, NIV)

You will seek me and find me when you seek me with all your heart. (Jeremiah 29:13, NIV)

For you formed my inward parts; you knitted me together in my mother's womb. I praise you, for I am fearfully and wonderfully made. Wonderful are your works; my soul knows it very well. (Psalm 139:13–14, ESV)

For the LORD God is a sun and shield; the LORD bestows favor and honor; no good thing does he withhold from those whose walk is blameless. (Psalm 84:11, NIV)

Let's Make It Personal

1. Journaling helps get the feeling of sadness out on paper. There you can better evaluate them in the light of God's Word.
2. Something to ponder: In Matthew 14:13–19 (ESV), Jesus disciples called the place where the five thousand were fed, desolate, and wanted to send them away to find provisions. Jesus fed them all with a few loaves and some fish. They were all satisfied. He met all their needs.
3. Is it possible that Jesus wants to encounter you in your desolate place and meet all your needs?
4. He loves you with an everlasting love. He is calling you to come sit with him and allow him to satisfy your every need.

Scripture

The LORD appeared to us in the past, saying: "I have loved you with an everlasting love; I have drawn you with unfailing kindness." (Jeremiah 31:3, NIV)

The LORD your God in your midst, the Mighty One, will save; He will rejoice over you with gladness, he will quiet you with his love, he will rejoice over you with singing. (Zephaniah 3:17, NKJV)

Confession

I will open my mouth and taste and open my eyes and see how good God is. Your unfailing love is wonderful. I run to you, and I am blessed, for your mercy is so abundant. (Scripture references: Psalm 43:8 MSG; Psalm 69:16, NLT)

Destiny

Something that is to happen or has happened to a particular person or thing; usually inevitable course of events. The power that determines the course of events. (*Dictionary.com*)

Heart's Cry

Father, I believe you have a destiny for each of your kids. I know you have one for me. Help me to recognize what mine is. It is my heart's desire to walk in obedience to you; my heart is yours. I desire to hear your voice. I am getting so much better at hearing and understanding your voice. As I grow in you, I see others that seem to be sitting on the sidelines, expecting you to do something for them, yet unwilling to count the cost of serving you. It is as though they are unaware of who you really are and that you not only choose us, you need us to answer your call. I am willing to count the cost; I hear you calling.

Father Speaks

Tonight will be a time of great awakening for my people. Many have fallen asleep. No longer. Time is too short for those who choose lethargy over my fire. Those who choose to walk in victory must also choose to step out into my plan for them. For I say, arise, sleeper, come out from the slumber that has kept you blinded to my works. Come out, sleeper, harken to my voice. My sheep hear my voice and none other. My sheep obey me. Many are called; few are chosen. Are you one of the called? Examine yourself. Who has your heart? I did not come to bring peace but a sword. It is written that anyone who loves others more than me is not worthy of me. I am calling those that will, come get out of the boat, walk with me. Come leave all behind for my sake. I say to you, truly you will lose nothing by serving me. You will gain much. I delight in giving you the kingdom.

Scripture

For anything that becomes visible is light. Therefore it says, "Awake, O sleeper, and arise from the dead, and Christ will shine on you." (Ephesians 5:14, ESV)

For everyone born of God overcomes the world. This is the victory that has overcome the world, even our faith. (1 John 5:4, NIV)

For many are called, but few are chosen. (Matthew 22:14, KJV)

Anyone who loves their father or mother more than me is not worthy of me; anyone who loves their son or daughter more than me is not worthy of me. (Matthew 10:37, NIV)

Let's Make It Personal

1. Do you serve God wholeheartedly? What does that look like to you? Journal about this.
2. Have you been one of those sleepers? If so, what woke you up? Your Father wants to take you from where you are to where he wants you to be.
3. He has perfect timing. The best thing you can do is to be patient. Don't rush ahead of him.
4. He has a divine connection for you where your gifts, skills, passions, and your personality merge together. At that time, he will use you to reach others as only you can. Hence his plan for you.

Scripture

My sheep hear my voice, and I know them, and they follow me. (John 10:27, ESV)

Anyone who wants to serve me must follow me, because my servants must be where I am. And the Father will honor anyone who serves me. (John 12:26, NLT)

I seek you with all my heart; do not let me stray from your commands. (Psalm 119:10, NIV)

Confession

I will worship my Lord with gladness and come before him with joyful songs. He loves me and all things will work together for my good because I am called according to his purpose. (Scripture references: Psalm 100:2, NIV; Romans 8:28, ESV)

Devastation

Causing great damage or harm. (*Merriam-Webster Dictionary*)

Heart's Cry

Father! Father! I am being buried alive by the assaults against me. Words that cut like a surgeon's scalpel. I cannot speak one Word without the caustic response from another. I must be saying things that bring conviction or guilt upon others. I have no intent to do that. When I try to explain, there is no listening to reason. I am wrong in everything I speak. Am I so awful, Father? Are my words so worthless? Help me to watch the words of my mouth and the meditation of my heart that I may please you.

Father Speaks

Child, child, come sit at my feet for a while. Let me refresh you. You have been in battle for a time without much reprieve. Now I speak that you are to come. Come, child, settle yourself before me. Not just a quick visit, but come for a prolonged stay. Refresh, refresh, for the battle does rage on. You have already been deemed victor. Now, my precious child, it is time to know that. Really know in your spirit, deep within, that the battle has been won. You are the victor. Nothing can hamper my plans for you. You can slow them down, child, but nothing can take them from you. I gave them to you before the beginning of time. You must see with your spiritual eyes, not with worldly eyes. Step up into the realm of the supernatural and remain there. Let nothing rob you, child. You must allow what man has to say to you and about you to roll off as water on a duck's back. You see, they do not speak for me.

Scripture

I have told you all this so that you may have peace in me. Here on earth you will have many trials and sorrows. But take heart, because I have overcome the world. (John 16:33, NLT)
I will give you the keys to the kingdom of heaven; whatever you bind on earth will be bound in heaven, and whatever you loose on earth will be loosed in heaven. (Matthew 16:19, NIV)
No one will be able to stand against you. The LORD your GOD, as he promised you, will put the terror and fear of you on the whole land wherever you go. (Deuteronomy 11:25, NIV)
And in your steadfast love you will cut off my enemies,
and you will destroy all the adversaries of my soul,
for I am you servant. (Psalm 143:12, ESV)
May the words of my mouth and the meditation
of my heart be pleasing to you, O LORD, my rock
and my redeemer. (Psalm 19:14, NLT)

Let's Make It Personal

1. Are you dealing with family members, perhaps good friends, that have a spirit of anger or rebellion?
2. Have you bound the spirit/sprits that are causing the problems? What was the outcome? Journal about what worked, and perhaps what did not work.
3. You love your family and your friends, and perfect love casts out fear. No need to be in fear of them. The enemy wants you to shy away from loving them. Jesus wants you to be able to stand your ground in love.

Scripture

For our struggle is not against flesh and blood, but against the rulers, against the authorities, against the powers of this dark world and against the spiritual forces of evil in the heavenly realms. (Ephesians 6:12, NIV)

At once the Spirit sent him out into the wilderness, and he was in the wilderness forty days, being tempted by Satan. He was with the wild animals, and angels attended him. (Mark 1:12–13, NIV)

No man can enter into a strong man's house, and spoil his goods, except he will first bind the strong man; and then he will spoil his house. (Mark 3:27, KJV)

The "strong man" is Satan; his House or Palace is this Lower world; the Stronger than the Strong is Christ, who first bound the Evil One, when He triumphed over his temptations. (Cambridge Bible for Schools and Colleges Commentary on Mark 3:27 [strong man's house])

Confession

My God is faithful, and he will strengthen me and guard me from the evil one. I may face troubles, but my God comes to rescue me. He will be with me as I speak and instruct me in what to say. (Scripture references: 2 Thessalonians 3:3, NLT; Psalm 34:19, NLT; Exodus 4:12, NLT)

Difficult Path

Not easily or readily done. A way for walking. (*Online Dictionary*)

Heart's Cry

I cannot breathe! Help me, Father, for this path is too difficult for me. I cannot navigate through this alone. The pressure is too much for me. Wave after wave of assault and conflict threaten to take away my mental stability.

Father Speaks

For the path has been a difficult one. You almost fainted because of the pressure upon you.
Child, I did not bring the sorrow. I saw it coming, yea I knew it before the beginning of time. This was no surprise to me, your Father. I was there beside you to hold you up under the intense pressure of the trial. The enemy thought he had you. But he underestimated your hold on me, your rock. I sustained you. I rebuked the enemy. I took hold of your hand and offered my peace to withstand. Even though you felt as though you were bouncing off the bottom of a great ocean tide, you still were able to come up for air. During that time, I refreshed you. Each time you came up to breathe, I was with you, sustaining you, strengthening you. While the enemy of your soul was bound away from you, your mind and thoughts continued to pummel you. I was there ready to help you get your thoughts under control, yet in your humanness you missed me. I saw your struggle to hold on to me, my Word. I held on to you. I am still holding on to you. Strengthen, my child, strengthen, for I have poured myself upon you; within you. Your strength has come from me, your Father. Seek me, child, and I will be found—greater and more magnificent than you ever imagined. For it is the Father's will to bless you.

Scripture

He reached down from on high and took hold of me; he drew me out of deep waters. He rescued me from my powerful enemy, from my foes, who were too strong for me. They confronted me in the day of my disaster, but the Lord was my support. He brought me out into a spacious place; he rescued me because he delighted in me. (2 Samuel 22: 17–20, NIV)

For in the day of trouble he will keep me safe in his dwelling; he will hide me in the shelter of his sacred tent and set me high upon a rock. (Psalm 27:5, NIV)

May the LORD show you his favor and give you his peace. (Numbers 6:26, NLT)

I lie down and sleep; I wake again, because the LORD sustains me. (Psalm 3:5, NIV)

For I am the LORD your God who takes hold of your right hand and says to you, do not fear, I will help you. (Isaiah 41:13, NIV)

Let's Make It Personal

1. When you are in crisis, you desperately want your normal back, whatever that looks like to you.
2. Often God takes you through the desert and feeds you with his manna. What is this manna? The Word of God. You need a steady stream of words from God's mouth.
3. If you look for it, for him, you will find what you need and your soul will be comforted. Your needs will be met by your Father. You will rest under the shadow of his wings as he teaches you though the crisis.
4. You need to figure out how to serve him in the midst of your misfortune. You will learn how to accept his grace in the middle of your trial.

Scripture

Jesus answered, "It is written: 'Man shall not live on bread alone, but on every word that comes out from the mouth of God.'" (Matthew 4:4, NIV)

But if from there you seek the LORD your God, you will find him if you seek him with all your heart and with all your soul. (Deuteronomy 4:29, NIV)

Each time he said, "My grace is all you need. My power works best in weakness." So now I am glad to boast about my weaknesses, so that the power of Christ can work through me. (2 Corinthians 12:9, NLT)

Confession

My eyes are toward you, my Lord; in you I seek refuge. You will not leave me defenseless. Grace and peace is mine in abundance through the knowledge of God and of Jesus my Lord. (Scripture references: Psalm 141:8, ESV; 2 Peter 1:2, NIV)

Discernment

(In Christian contexts) Perception in the absence of judgment with a view to obtaining spiritual guidance and understanding. (*Online Dictionary*)

Heart's Cry

Many times, Father, I have had to check myself to be sure what I was sensing was, indeed, you and not me. Sometimes the things I felt were harsh. I am so grateful I sought your thoughts before opening my mouth. Father, I want to grow in hearing and discerning your voice. Teach me.

Father Speaks

You must have discernment in a solid place in your spirit to walk where I have called you to walk. Discernment and a cloak of humility are upon you, daughter. I am preparing you. I am pleased with your restraint to speak when I direct not to, when your emotions dictate.

Scripture

My sheep hear my voice, and I know them, and they follow me. (John 10:27, KJV)

As God's chosen ones, holy and beloved, clothe yourselves with compassion, kindness, humility, meekness, and patience. (Colossians 3:12, NRS)

Do not be quick to speak with your mouth, nor let your heart be hasty to utter a word before God. For God is in heaven, and you are on the earth; therefore may your words be few. (Ecclesiastes 5:2, MEV)

Let's Make It Personal

1. Journal about a time that you heard from God but used wisdom to not speak it out.
2. Many times, Father will show us things that are for us to know so we can pray about them. Intercede for others.
3. Now journal about a time that you heard something from God and you spoke it out. Was it edifying to the person? Was it for their good?
4. Take some time to ponder and pray about the difference between speaking out and not speaking out. Journal what the Father shows you.

Scripture

Blessed is the one who finds wisdom, and the one who gets understanding, for the gain from her is better than gain from silver and her profit better than gold. She is more precious than jewels, and nothing you desire can compare with her. Long life is in her right hand; in her left hand are riches and honor. Her ways are ways of pleasantness, and all her paths are peace. (Proverbs 3:13–18, ESV)

My dear brothers and sisters, take note of this: Everyone should be quick to listen, slow to speak and slow to become angry. (James 1:19, NIV)

Confession

I believe in your commands and delight in obeying you. Teach me good judgment and knowledge so that I will not judge by appearance or make decisions based on what I hear. (Scripture references: Isaiah 11:3, NLT; Psalm 119:66, NLT)

Distractions

A thing that prevents someone from concentrating on something else, extreme agitation of the mind. (*English Oxford Dictionary*)

Heart's Cry

How am I to focus on anything! One thing after another happens. Father, when will there be a break in my life? I must learn to sort out all the things coming at me.

Father Speaks

Refuse to get involved in distractions the enemy is sending your way. Relax and let me handle them. It will be an easy transition for you if you allow me to handle them. Get away with me. Sequester yourself away with me. This must be a deliberate act of your will. I can tell you what to do; I will not force you. You must realize that without me, you will NOT win the war you are in. Come, child, spend time with me. I will strengthen you, and you shall walk through the roadblocks Satan has in your way. I say you will not be hindered! Come.

Scripture

If then you have been raised with Christ, seek the things that are above, where Christ is seated at the right hand of God. Set your minds on things that are above, not on things that are on earth. (Colossians 3:1–2, ESV)

Look straight ahead, and fix your eyes on what lies before you. (Proverbs 4:25, NLT)

Stay alert! Watch out for your great enemy, the devil. He prowls around like a roaring lion, looking for someone to devour. (1 Peter 5:8, NLT)

Let's Make It Personal

1. I am sure you are aware that distraction from God is extremely dangerous.
2. He is the director of your path, the captain of your ship. When you begin to lose sight of him, you begin to take back control of your life. Fear and worry creep in. You can start feeling all alone.
3. Have you lost sight of him? Are you missing opportunities, blessings?
4. Spend time with your Father. As you draw near to him, he promises to draw near to you. He will make the way much clearer for you.

Scripture

Don't copy the behavior and customs of this world, bet let God transform you into a new person by changing the way you think. Then you will learn to know God's will for you, which is good and pleasing and perfect. (Romans 12:2, NLT)
Do not love this world nor the things it offers you, for when you love the world, you do not have the love of the Father in you. (1 John 2:15, NLT)

Confession

As I come close to God, he will come close to me. I will seek his will in everything I do, and he will show me which path to take. (Scripture references: Proverbs 3:6, NLT; James 4:8a, NIV)

Door

A moveable, usually solid, barrier for opening and closing an entranceway. (*Dictionary.com*)

Heart's Cry

You love me, Father. You delight in me. I am favored by you. You choose me for such a time as this. Your purpose for me will be fulfilled. I will walk out the call you have placed on my life. From before time began, you saw me, and you chose me to carry your glory, your mercy, your love to others. You have anointed me to walk in the path you have prepared for me. I will walk and not stumble. Your Word tells me you go before me to level the way. As I keep my eyes on you, I shall not stumble.

Father Speaks

Many will hear the words I have for you to speak. For many are waiting for the message you will bring to them. Hope and encouragement. This is my will for you, daughter. From the dark places of your soul, I have drawn you out. I have made a way for you. As you walk this way and not that, I will provide the doors for you to walk through. The doors that I have prepared for you to walk through. Have no fear, for it is I who open the doors and I will close doors. I will guide and direct you. Listen, listen, quiet yourself, and listen for that still, small voice within you that says, this is the way, walk in it. I will be found at each door. I will walk with you through each one. We will walk in victory together, for I have much for you to tell my people. Much for you to teach. No fear, child. Open your mouth, and I will fill it.

Scripture

The LORD himself goes before you and will be with you; he will never leave you nor forsake you. Do not be afraid; do not be discouraged. (Deuteronomy 31:8, NIV)

I know all the things you do, and I have opened a door for you that no one can close. You have little strength, yet you obeyed my word and did not deny me. (Revelation 3:8, NLT)

The Light shines in the darkness, and the darkness did not comprehend it. (John 1:5, NASB)

But you are a chosen people, a royal priesthood, a Holy nation, God's special possession, that you may declare the praises of him who called you out of darkness into his wonderful light. (1 Peter 2:9, NIV)

Let's Make It Personal

1. Each of us has a specific calling on our lives. Can you identify yours? If so, journal about it.
2. Have you met opposition along the way? Be encouraged, for there would not be any struggle if the call was not from the Father.
3. Ask the Holy Spirit to help you identify the things keeping you from moving out in your calling. Journal about those.
4. Go before the Lord and receive your battle plan to defeat the enemy. You will be empowered to take the territory Father has called you to.

Scripture

For everything that is hidden will eventually be brought into the open, and every secret will be brought to light. (Mark 4:22, NLT)
Submit yourselves therefore to God. Resist the devil, and he will flee from you. (James 4:7, ESV)

Confession

My enemy the devil who prowls around like a roaring lion cannot harm me, for I am alert and of sober mind. Because my ways please you, Father, you make even my enemies to be at peace with me. (Scripture references: 1 Peter 5:8, NIV; Proverbs 16:7, ESV)

Doubt

To be uncertain about something. To believe that something may not be true or is unlikely: to have no confidence in. (*Merriam-Webster Dictionary*)

Heart's Cry

How can I speak life to others when I do not see any of my prayers answered? I do not understand. I am to tell others what a good God you are. How much you love them and how you will hear and answer their prayers. I am not the right person, Father. I am not strong enough. You placed a call upon my life that I am not able to fulfill. You are the God of the universe. You love me with an everlasting love. You know what is best. I know that because I don't see my prayers answered, yet you are working on my behalf to bring about a perfect result. Forgive me, Father, for my weakness. I want more of you, to go deeper in the things of my God. In this struggle you are molding and making me into a usable vessel. I believe, help me in my unbelief.

Father Speaks

Child, stress has had a negative impact on you physically and emotionally. You desire to walk deeper with me. I desire that also. You ask for understanding of me. No one will ever fully understand the God of the universe. I knit you together in your mother's womb. I brought you into this life as you know it. From before time began, I knew you. I know the call I have placed upon your life. It is without repentance. I desire to use you. Much more than that, I desire to see you filled up with me. So full that what you have from me will leak out to others. Then, oh, child, then you will move and breathe and touch and see me as you desire to see me. I have a good plan for your life, and no, it is not too late. My calling is without regret. I know you. I knew you, and I will continue to move in and through you. What is it that you desire, my child? Seek and you shall find, knock and know that the doors will be opened for you. Shall we begin?

Scripture

For you created my inmost being; you knit me together in my mother's womb. I praise you because I am fearfully and wonderfully made; your works are wonderful, I know that full well. (Psalm 139:13–14, NIV)

For he satisfies the thirsty and fills the hungry with good things. (Psalm 107:9, NLT)

The Spirit of God has made me; the breath of the Almighty gives me life. (Job 33:4, NIV)

Open your mouth and taste, open your eyes and see-how good God is. Blessed are you who run to him. (Psalm 34:8, MSG)

Keep on asking, and you will receive what you ask for. Keep on seeking, and you will find. Keep on knocking, and the door will be opened to you. (Matthew 7:7, NLT)

Let's Make It Personal

1. Does your soul ache for more of him? Be encouraged; he has the perfect plan to fill satisfy your soul.
2. Are you thirsty for more? He is the river you can drink from and be refreshed.
3. Do you feel weak? If you ignore the weakness in you and deny it, you will never realize or experience God's strength in you. He wants you strong so you can minister to others.
4. Can you believe that God loves you with an everlasting love? That his grace is sufficient for you? Do you understand grace? It is enabling power and spiritual healing offered through Jesus Christ. You have that; you have grace working in your life.

Scripture

But he said to me, "My grace is sufficient for you, for my power is made perfect in weakness." Therefore I will boast all the more gladly about my weaknesses, so that Christ's power may rest on me. (2 Corinthians 12:9, NIV)

For he satisfies the longing soul, and the hungry soul he fills with good things. (Psalm 107:9, ESV)

Let not the wise boast of their wisdom or the strong boast of their strength or the rich boast of their riches, but let the one who boasts boast about this: that they have the understanding to know me, that I am the LORD, who exercises kindness, justice and righteousness on earth, for in these I delight," declares the LORD. (Jeremiah 9:23–24, NIV)

Confession

The call upon my life can never be withdrawn. He fills my life with good things; my youth is renewed like an eagle's. (Scripture references: Romans 11:29, NLT; Psalm 103:4, NLT)

Dross

Things that are a total loss—really worthless or damaging. (*Vocabulary.com*)

Heart's Cry

Father, I not only ask you, I must have more of you. I have asked you purge me, get the dross out. You have been doing that. You helped me when I was quick to judge a situation or person. You know how it grieves me when my thoughts go in that direction. Who am I to judge anyone? Thank you, Holy Spirit, for being quick to convict me. Show me how to walk this day Father, for I do not know how; I know you are with me. I need to focus on you, to draw near to you. Then everything else fades completely away. Praise your Holy name, my Savior, my friend. Speak to me this day; I will hear you.

Father Speaks

The days you have walked through were there to draw you close to me, to purge dross from your soul. You have stayed close to me. I am very pleased with you, child. Hardness of heart knocks on the hearts door when one struggles against what the Holy Spirit is doing. No struggles, no more. Open your heart to all I have prepared for you. Look at each situation and each person with my eyes. See them as I see them. For I have equipped you to do just that. You are my ambassador in this world. You have been called and set apart for such a time as this. You will bring my heart to the people. Healing shall follow.

Scripture

Blessed is the one who fears the Lord always, but whoever hardens his heart will fall into calamity. (Proverbs 28:14, ESV)

I will give you a new heart and put a new spirit in you. And I will remove the heart of stone from your flesh and give you a heart of flesh. (Ezekiel 36:26, ESV)

Wherever your treasure is, there the desires of your heart will also be. (Matthew 6:21, NLT)

Guard your heart above all else, for it determines the course of your life. (Proverbs 4:23, NLT)

We are therefore Christ's ambassadors, as though God were making his appeal through us. We implore you on Christ's behalf: Be reconciled to God. (2 Corinthians 5:20, NIV)

Let's Make It Personal

1. Praising God helps to soften your heart. Praise and worship him for who he is! The more you understand how much you are loved by God, the more you can expect good things to happen to you. You are the object of God's love.
2. Your heart represents the response to your life around you, the demands and trials you go through. During that time, you need to hear just how pleased your Father is with you. He is right there with you to help you understand the meditations of your heart.
3. If you feel that your heart has hardened, ask the Father to reveal when and why that started. Be sure to journal.
4. Be encouraged that the hardness of your heart can be repaired by God's grace. He will restore you by taking away your heart of stone and giving you a heart of flesh.

Scripture

I will give them an undivided heart and put a new spirit in them; I will remove from them their heart of stone and give them a heart of flesh. (Ezekiel 11:19, ESV)

Restore to me the joy of your salvation, and make me willing to obey you. (Psalm 51:12, NLT)

Don't copy the behavior and customs of this world, but let God transform you into a new person by changing the way you think. Then you will learn to know God's will for you, which is good and pleasing and perfect. (Romans 12:2, NLT)

Confession

Father, I am asking you to create in me a clean heart and give me a right spirit. I am under no condemnation because of Jesus Christ in my life. (Psalm 51:10, NIV; Romans 8:1, NLT)

Dwelling Place

A place where one dwells. (*YourDictionary*)

Heart's Cry

How I long for a safe dwelling place Father. Where I can go and be myself, without the judging eyes of others. I should take no concern about what others think of me. I know you approve of me and accept me. You will take up my defense, and I will walk blameless before you. Call me into your dwelling place, and there I will find comfort. When you speak I will answer.

Father Speaks

Child, I always desire to speak with you. You must bring yourself to the place every day where we commune together. Never allow one day to pass without time with me. I have much to show you. There are many things you know not of. Mysteries out of my Word. Mysteries of me. Things you desire to understand. Things you have asked me for. More of me. You cannot get more of someone unless you spend time with them. I am not someone—I AM. I am all you need. I am everything you have ever desired or dreamed about. I am what you have looked for, searched for, longed for. Why, child, do you find yourself longing for comfort and peace when that is what I am. Spend time with me every day. Trust me with the little things in your life, and oh, so soon you will be trusting me with the big things in your life. Nothing will be impossible for you in me. No mountain shall stand when you tell it to move. Nature will come to attention when you speak with the authority I have placed within you. All of heaven is cheering you on to victory in me. You are not alone, have never been alone. Never will be alone. Search yourself, for therein you shall find me. Yes, I reside within you, child. More power than imagined resides within you. Grab ahold of me! I desire to take you places. I need you to go to places and people who are hard-hearted. The words placed in your mouth by me will melt hearts, silence confusion, and deafen the ears to the enemy. Victory for those I am preparing you to speak to is coming soon. You will be a tool in my hand for battle, for comfort, for releasing the captive. Come! Let's set the captives free!

Scripture

Then, because so many people were coming and going that they did not ever have a chance to eat, he said to them, "Come with me by yourselves to a quiet place and get some rest." (Mark 6:31–33, NIV)

My beloved spoke and said to me, "Arise, my darling, my beautiful one, come with me." (Song of Solomon 2:10, NIV)

Behold, I have given you authority to tread on serpents and scorpions, and over all the power of the enemy, and nothing shall hurt you. (Luke 10:19, ESV)

Jesus looked at them intently and said, "Humanly speaking, it is impossible. But with God everything is possible." (Matthew 19:26, NLT)

Let's Make It Personal

1. How many times have you heard the Holy Spirit say to you, "Come away with me?" Did you find time to do just that? What was the result of spending time with him? I hope you found it to be a great blessing to have intimacy with him.
2. In the Gospels you will find many examples of Jesus withdrawing from others to spend time with his Father. That prayer time was strengthening and empowering Jesus to walk out his earthly call.
3. Your life may be filled with unfortunate experiences, yet if you speak the words from Psalm 23:1 (ESV), "The LORD is my shepherd I shall not want," the urgency to engage will fade away.
4. You will be much more aware of the Father taking up your defense as you draw closer to him. He will reveal himself as the powerful God that will never leave you. He is equipping you for his purposes.

Scripture

And God is able to make all grace abound to you,
so that having all sufficiency in all things at all
times, you may abound in every good work.
(2 Corinthians 9:8, ESV)
No one will be able to stand against you as long as you
live. For I will be with you as I was with Moses. I will
not fail you or abandon you. (Joshua 1:5, NLT)
The eternal God is your dwelling place, and
underneath are the everlasting arms. And he thrust
out the enemy before you and said, "Destroy."
(Deuteronomy 33:27, ESV)

Confession

I thank you, Father, that nothing is impossible for me because of you. You are the Lord, and you do not change. If you say it, it will happen without delay. (Scripture references: Luke 1:37, NLT; Malachi 3:6, NLT; Ezekiel 12:25a, NLT)

Empower

Give (someone) the authority or power to do something. Make (someone) stronger and more confident in controlling their life and claiming their rights. (*Online Dictionary*)

Heart's Cry

I love you, Lord. You are my rock, my strong tower. In you I trust. I flee to you, Father, and you hide me under the shadow of your wings. In you I trust, I find safety. I cry out to you; I know you hear me. What am I to do but wait on my Father? He will show me the way I should go. He is God, and there is none other. He is my wonderful Counselor, Peace-Giver, Protector. To him I run. You are a glorious, awesome God. Who dare question your ways? You promote man and bring man down. My very breath is in your hands. You see the future, and you go before me to straighten the path in which I should walk. You speak to me, "This is the way, walk ye in it." Who am I Father to question your ways? I am just a simple breath, a light breeze, here today, gone tomorrow. What can I do for you, Lord? Where do you want me? Here I am, my Father, show me the path to take.

Father Speaks

Many have resisted my call. You, child, have not. You have relied on me in your darkest hour. It is for you I have come. I have come to strengthen and empower you. I will lift you up. Even now I am elevating you to a place I have prepared for you. It is your next step. Will you take my hand and come higher? Come, my child, it is time for empowering. Rest in me.

Scripture

Then your light will shine like the dawning sun, and you will quickly be healed. Your honesty will protect you as you advance, and the glory of the Lord will defend you from behind. (Isaiah 58:8, CEV)

For I know the plans I have for you, declares the Lord, plans to prosper you and not to harm you, plans to give you a hope and a future. Them you will call on me and come and pray to me, and I will listen to you. You will seek me and find me when you seek me with all your heart. (Jeremiah 29:11–13, NIV)

Let's Make It Personal

1. Have you resisted his call? If so, can you identify the things causing you to hesitate? Journal about that.
2. At times the call can be in the form of something big, and sometimes it is a simple task. However, know that God is always asking you to do something for him. Be encouraged that if you allow his truth to shape your heart so that you desire what is right, you will find great joy in obeying him.
3. A good way to test what you hear is to evaluate if it is good, loving, kind. Will it be a blessing?
4. You do not get a free pass to avoid what he is calling you to do. You should never use your free will to make decisions that are out of line with Father's best for you.

Scripture

You did not choose me, but I chose you and appointed you so that you might go and bear fruit-fruit that will last-and so that whatever you ask in my name the Father will give it to you. (John 15:16, NIV)

The one who calls you is faithful, and he will do it. (1 Thessalonians 5:24, NIV)

I press on toward the goal to win the prize for which God has called me heavenward in Christ Jesus. (Philippians 3:14, NIV)

Confession

I take joy in doing your will, my God, for your instructions are written on my heart. I know that the God of hope will fill me with all joy and peace as I trust in him, and I will be filled to overflowing with hope by the power of the Holy Spirit. (Scripture references: Psalm 40:8, NLT; Romans 15:13, NIV)

Empty

Having no purpose or result: marked by the absence of human life, activity, or comfort and empty silence. (*Merriam-Webster Dictionary*)

Heart's Cry

Empty, dry, hollow am I. I want to run somewhere, but where? To where can I run but to you, my Father? Alone, lonely, desolate, I just want to sleep away the heartache and pain. The disbanding of unanswered prayers. To step out of this life for a while. Come back when things are over, better, or completed. Do you still hear my pleas? I have to believe that you hear me even when I am not speaking; you hear my heart's cry. I choose to believe. Refresh me, Father, come breathe life back into these dry bones.

Father Speaks

Today what a change has taken place. It is here, I am here, I am as close to you as your very breath. Breathe, my child, breathe. I am here, breathe me in, and I will come out of you with every word you speak, every prayer you pray. Every direction you turn, my breath will be upon you. I am here. Feel me, hear me, accept what I want to do with you, in you. Allow me access to your heart, child. I am gentle and kind. I would never hurt you. I will never hurt you. I am here. Healing in my wings. Feel the wind of my Spirit. Allow me access to your heart. I will come and sup with you. I will come in and meet every need you have, every need you will ever have. Come, child, allow me to hold you. Allow me to heal you, allow me to mold you, allow me to make you into what your heart desires to be for me. I put that desire in your heart. I will never allow my child to fail. Reach out for me, child. Let me be everything I can be in and through you. Come, breathe, breathe of me, breathe in deep. Allow me to move you. I am calling you out to dance with me. Let's dance a dance of victory. Let us celebrate what I am doing in you!

Scripture

In him we were chosen, having been predestined according to the plan of him who works out everything in conformity with the purpose of his will. (Ephesians 1:11, NIV)

I remain confident of this: I will see the goodness of the LORD in the land of the living. (Psalm 27:13, NIV)

As a face is reflected in water, so the heart reflects the real person. (Proverbs 27:19, NLT)

The Spirit of God has made me, and the breath of the Almighty gives me life. (Job 33:4, NASB)

Answer me, O LORD, for Your lovingkindness is good; according to the greatness of Your compassion, turn to me. (Psalm 69:16, NASB)

Search for the LORD and for his strength; continually seek him. (1 Chronicles 16:11, NLT)

You turned my wailing into dancing; you removed my sackcloth and clothed me with joy. (Psalm 30:11, NIV)

Let's Make It Personal

1. Have you ever or are you currently feeling empty? It is okay to acknowledge your feelings. Journal about them.
2. Do you think you have no value? Let me expose that lie. You are a child of the King of Kings. Jesus bought you with his blood. You are of immeasurable worth. The Father has lavished his love upon you; you are called a child of God! Don't buy into the lie of the enemy.
3. You must look inward, to him, for your sense of purpose; don't look outward. Your tendency may be to compare yourself. Stop now; you are uniquely made. There is no room for comparison. He made you, you are the work of his hands. You were made for a specific purpose. Ask him to reveal it to you.
4. The Holy Spirit desires to speak with you. Take your Bible and your journal and allow the spirit to show you how the Father sees you. Believe what is spoken to you.

Scripture

See what great love the Father has lavished on us, that we should be called children of God! And that we are! The reason the world does not know us is that it did not know him. (1 John 3:1, NIV)

Above all else, guard your heart, for everything you do flows from it. (Proverbs 4:23, NIV)

Joyful are those who obey his laws and search for him with all their hearts. (Psalm 119:2, NLT)

May these words of my mouth and this meditation of my heart be pleasing in your sight, LORD, my Rock and my Redeemer. (Psalm 19:14, NIV)

Then he said to me, "Prophesy over these bones, and say to them, O dry bones, hear the word of the LORD." (Ezekiel 37:4, ESV)

Confession

Father, don't be far from me; come quickly to help me. You are my strength; therefore I am strong because of your mighty power. (Scripture references: Psalm 22:19, NIV; Ephesians 6:10, NIV)

Enemy

A person who feels hatred for, fosters harmful designs against, or engages in antagonistic activities against another; and adversary or opponent. (*Dictionary.com*)

Heart's Cry

There are those around me that have great dislike for me, and they want to see harm come to me and my family. Father, I must remember what you have told me, what your Word says. I am to return kindness for hatred. I am to speak blessings not curses. Oh, Father, sometimes that is hard to do when my heart is being torn in half by others. Yet as an act of my will, I must purpose to obey you. For I believe there is great recompense of reward for obedience. Father, how do you see this?

Father Speaks

The enemy of your soul is fighting to take you out. If he can get you to respond, he has taken your peace and opened the door for more demonic activity around you. You must silence the enemy. Command him to be silent. He must be bound and gagged. Rendered impotent. Ask me, and I will show you the way to freedom from your enemy. I have overcome the world, and I will show you how to move in the power I have provided for you. Seek me, ask me, and I shall do it.

Scripture

You prepare a table before me in the presence of my enemies. You anoint my head with oil; my cup overflows. Surely your goodness and love will follow me all the days of my life, and I will dwell in the house of the LORD forever. (Psalm 23: 5–6, NIV)

For though we walk in the flesh, we do not war after the flesh: For the weapons of our warfare are not carnal, but mighty through God to the pulling down of strong holds; casting down imaginations, and every high thing that exalteth itself against the knowledge of God, and bringing into captivity every thought to the obedience of Christ. (2 Corinthians 10:3–5, KJV)

I have told you these things, so that in me you may have peace. In this world you will have trouble. But take heart! I have overcome the world. (John 16:33, NIV)

Let's Make It Personal

1. How many times have you felt as though your enemy was winning the battle that rages around you, even inside you?
2. Do you think that your Father in heaven does not see? Does not care? Journal about those feelings. Be honest with Father. He already knows. He wants to help you.
3. Perhaps the first thing that is needed for your victory is for you to identify who the enemy is. Scripture tells us that Satan is our enemy.
4. Ask Father to clearly reveal to you who you are fighting against. Once you see who your battle is with, you can take up your sword, the Word of God, and fight the good fight.

Scripture

When the Spirit of truth comes, he will guide you into all truth. He will not speak on his own but will tell you what he has heard. He will tell you about the future. (John 16:13, ESV)

I will instruct you and teach you in the way you should go; I will counsel you with my loving eye on you. (Psalm 32:8, NIV)

Confession

I am secure in the Lord. He watches over everything I do now and forever. Therefore I will be strong and courageous and never terrified because of my enemy. My Father, my God, goes with me and will never leave or forsake me. (Scripture references: Psalm 121:8, NLT; Deuteronomy 31:6, NIV)

Enlighten

To give intellectual or spiritual light to; instruct; impart knowledge to. (*Dictionary.com*)

Heart's Cry

Father, I want to comprehend the riches of your goodness toward me. I must have the eyes of my heart enlightened. I must be able to see the riches of the glory of God. Help me recall how good you are. I want to see displays of your goodness. I want to see them pass before my eyes, demonstrations of your goodness to flood my soul and my mind. Then I will be able to move out in you with reassurance that I do, indeed, hear your voice and can speak what I hear to others.

Father Speaks

I wish to speak with you. This thing I have called you to, I have equipped you for. You do not realize it now; my Word will go forth from your mouth. Many will hear of the goodness of the Lord through you. You will open your mouth, and I will fill it. You shall trust me and me alone to guide and advise you. You have done well. You have heard me speak to you. Now you must prepare for our journey together. Write what I have for you to write. Touch those who I have for you to touch. Speak to those I have for you to speak to. Set free by my Word those I have for you set free. Many will hear of the works I do in you. Many will desire to hear you speak, see you move in me, to experience me through you. Write now, now is the time. You have much to get done with me and for me. Much to be fulfilled. It is just beginning. We shall have the time of your life. You and ME, child, yes! We shall have a grand time together. Many are waiting for you to bring me to them. Hear me, child. It is time to move.

Scripture

May he equip you with all you need for doing his will. May he produce in you, through the power of Jesus Christ, every good thing that is pleasing to him. All glory to him forever and ever! Amen. (Hebrews 13:21, NLT)

I pray that the eyes of your heart may be enlightened, so that you will know what is the hope of His calling, what are the riches of the glory of His inheritance in the saints, and what is the surpassing greatness of His power toward us who believe. These are in accordance with the working of the strength of His might. (Ephesians 1:18–19, NASB)

Then the LORD put out his hand and touched my mouth. And the LORD said to me, "Behold, I have put my words in your mouth." (Jeremiah 1:9, ESV)

Let's Make It Personal

1. Have you ever spoken a Word from the Lord to someone?
2. Did you sense his presence prompting you to speak? What does that feel like? Journal about the times he has had you deliver a Word from him to someone.
3. Does your heart long to be filled with his presence? If you desire him more than anything, he will fulfill that desire.
4. Father is looking for those who are sold out to him, those who want nothing more than to sit at his feet and learn of him.

Scripture

Teach me to do your will, for you are my God; may your good Spirit lead me on level ground. (Psalm 143:10, NIV)

A good man brings good things out of the good stored up in his heart, and an evil man bring evil things out of the evil stored up in his heart. For the mouth speaks what the heart is full of. (Luke 6:45, NIV)

Confession

I can open my mouth and speak with assurance because it will not be me speaking but the Spirit of you speaking through me. I am so thankful that there is nowhere I can go from your Spirit. Your presence is always with me. (Scripture references: Matthew 10:20, NIV; Psalm 139:7, ESV)

Equip

To furnish or provide with whatever is needed for use or for any undertaking. (*Dictionary.com*)

Heart's Cry

There is nothing I need, for you have provided all that is necessary for my life and my well-being. How I praise you and thank you, Father. You are a powerful God. I trust you.

Father Speaks

There are those who still remain on the sidelines, content to watch the spirit move, content to observe only. I say to you, you must pray to be moved by my spirit, that you will be compelled to jump into the move of my spirit! I not only desire you; I need you now! I will equip you, empower you, and move you, but you MUST desire me, want my presence not only around you, but in you. There is no place for fear of failure. Whom my Father calls, HE will also equip. There is no room for fear of man, for I am. I AM will hedge you in and protect you with my mighty spirit. No tongue that rises up against you shall prevail. Keep your eyes upon ME and ME only. I promise as you, look to me; the things of this earth will grow strangely dim because of MY GLORY and GRACE. Learn of me. As you grow closer to me, I will grow closer to you. Can you feel it even now, my child? My wooing you, calling you to come deeper with me, the lover of your soul?

Scripture

And I will put my Spirit in you and move you to follow my decrees and be careful to keep my laws. (Ezekiel 36:27, NIV)

Now may the God of peace, who through the blood of the eternal covenant brought back from the dead our Lord Jesus, that great Shepherd of the sheep, equip you with everything good for doing his will, and may he work in us what is pleasing to him, through Jesus Christ, to who be glory for ever and ever. Amen. (Hebrews 13:20–21, NIV)

Fear of man will prove to be a snare, but whoever trust in the Lord is kept safe. (Proverbs 29:25, NIV)

No weapon forged against you will prevail, and you will refute every tongue that accuses you. (Isaiah 54:17a, NIV)

Let's Make It Personal

1. What has the Father called you to do? There may be a desire in your heart that you are not sure is from him. Ask him and listen for his answer.
2. Write down what Father is speaking to you. If he has called you, he will equip you. Spend some time with your journal writing what you feel he has called you to.
3. Keep your mind and heart set on him. Many times, a calling can seem out of reach, too big. If the call seems to big, it is probably your Father calling. He wants you to rely on him not on yourself.
4. If this is where you are, ask Father to clarify what he is saying and confirm it with his Word. Can you trust the Father to provide you with everything you need to follow him?

Scripture

For to us God revealed them through the Spirit, for the Spirit reaches all things, even the depths of God. (1 Corinthians 2:10, NASB)

However, as it is written: "What no eye has seen, what no ear has heard, and what no human mind has conceived"—the things God has prepared for those who love him. (1 Corinthians 2:9, NIV)

But grow in the grace and knowledge of our Lord and Savior Jesus Christ. To him be glory both now and forever! Amen. (2 Peter 3:18, NIV)

Confession

My Father reveals to me deep and mysterious things; he knows what lies hidden in darkness. He is surrounded by light, and he will show me his glorious presence. (Scripture references: Daniel 2:22, NLT; Exodus 33:18b, NLT)

Experience

The fact or state of having been affected by or gained knowledge through direct observation or participation. (*Merriam-Webster Dictionary*)

Heart's Cry

Father, people try to tell me how I should behave or react to things based on their understanding of my trauma and pain, on their experiences. They mean well. They love me. Help me respond to them with grace and love. Speak to me, Father. I so want to hear your voice, your heart. I want to be tool in your hand to use for your glory. Your Word tells me that you will give me the desire of my heart; right now, all I desire is you. Fill me with your presence and I will rest.

Father Speaks

Child, in the coming days, you will experience me in a greater way. Powerful plans I have for you. You want to know me better; you want to move in my power. You must draw closer to me. Don't question when I have you move. Don't question when I have you speak. Don't question when I have you touch. For your desire has been and will continue to be, that in me you live, move, breathe, and have your being. Tough times are ahead for those called to walk with me. Tough times in battle. I am your victor. I am your conqueror. I will lead and direct your every step. Nothing shall stand in your way. For look! This is the way, not that! Walk this way, not that! Speak this word, not that word! Seek me. I am right here. I am the wind at your back. I am the light in front of you. Oh yes! It is me your feel beside you. Come away with me. I will strengthen you, encourage you, equip you for what is to come. We are victorious, you and I. We will move forward; we will not retreat. I am your God. I am calling you forth. Now is the time.

Scripture

"For I know the plans I have for you," declares the LORD, "plans to prosper you and not to harm you, plans to give you a hope and a future." (Jeremiah 29:11, NIV)

All that belongs to the Father is mine; that is why I said, "The spirit will tell you whatever he receives from me." (John 16:15, NLT)

Now then go, and I, even I, will be with your mouth, and teach you what you are to say. (Exodus 4:12 NASB)

The LORD says, "I will guide you along the best pathway for your life. I will advise you and watch over you." (Psalm 32:8, NLT)

He let loose the east wind from the heavens and by his power made the south wind blow. (Psalm 78:26, NIV)

For he says, "In the time of my favor I heard you, and in the day of salvation I helped you." I tell you, now is the time of God's favor, now is the day of salvation. (2 Corinthians 6:2, NIV)

Let's Make It Personal

1. Journal about a time that well-meaning friends or family attempted to tell you how you should handle your life situations.
2. How did you grow from that experience? If you are still in that place, ask the Holy Spirit to give you understanding of it. Ask him to help you see others the way the Father sees them. Be sure to write down what you are told.
3. God must have your attention in order to use you as he desires. He wants to speak, touch, and move through you. Consider what you have gone through as light affliction in order to gain the upward call of Christ Jesus.
4. Prepare yourself to walk this way and not that way, according to what Father has spoken. Become acutely aware of his voice. That happens by spending time with the Holy Spirit. He will guide you into all truths and prepare you to be used by the Father.

Scripture

Lord, I will offer myself freely, and everything I am I give to you. I will worship and praise your name, O Lord, for it is precious to me. (Psalm 54:6, TPT)

I press on toward the goal to win the prize for which God has called me heavenward in Christ Jesus. (Philippians 3:14, NIV)

Surely God is my help; the Lord is the one who sustains me. (Psalm 54:4, NIV)

The Lord looks down in love, bending over heaven's balcony. God looks over all of Adam's sons and daughters, looking to see if there are any who are wise with insight—any who search for him, wanting to please him. (Psalm 53:2, TPT)

Confession

The light of my Father shines in the darkness, and the darkness cannot overcome it. So that in him I can live and move and have my being. (Scripture references: John 1:5, NIV; Acts 17:28a, NIV)

Faith

Belief and trust in and loyalty to God. (*Merriam-Webster Dictionary*)

Heart's Cry

I believe in you, Father! I know that you are the God of the universe! You are the God of everything there is. You hold all things together. Without you nothing would exist. Thank you for loving me. I must have faith to believe, really believe, the things you have spoken to me are really for me. You have spoken to me, and I have a choice to believe, to have the faith of a mustard seed, to see what you have spoken come to pass. Help me, Father. I believe; help me with my unbelief. I choose faith over doubt. I choose to believe you, and with your help, I will have faith to move mountains; your Word has said so. I know that when I ask you for something, you hear and will answer me.

Father Speaks

Why do you wonder at the Word I have spoken to you? Am I not able to bring it to pass? Who do you think I am? Just a God who sits in the heavenlies and watches his children toil and suffer? Is that who you think I am? One who cannot or will not meet your needs? Why are you angry at me, child? What is it that I have done that has not been in the best interest for you? Does my Word say I come to hurt my people? No, I say it says I come to help save and deliver my children. Who am I to you? When you discover who I really am, then nothing will be impossible for you. Find you, you ask me? I tell you, yes, you seek, and I will be found by you. I am not a God who hides in the shadows. Stop looking for me there. Look for me, find me in my Word. Look for me, and I will be found in your praises. Look and see, I am in your midst. Come, all who will, I will cause the blinders to break off your eyes, then you will see clearly who I am. Seek me, and I promise I will be found by you.

Scripture

Jesus answered him, “I am the way, the truth, and the life; no one goes to the Father except by me.” (John 14:6, GNT)
Jesus drew near and said to them, “I have been given all authority in heaven and on earth.” (Matthew 28:18a, GNT)
But seek first the kingdom of God and his righteousness, and all these things will be added to you. (Matthew 6:33, ESV)
I have been crucified with Christ and I no longer live, but Christ lives in me. The life I now live in the body, I live by faith in the Son of God, who loved me and gave himself for me. (Galatians 2:20, NIV)
My Christian friends, who also have been called by God! Think of Jesus, whom God sent to be the High Priest of the faith we profess. (Hebrews 3:1, GNT)
I have been given the mind of Christ. (1 Corinthians 2:16)

Let's Make It Personal

1. Do you find it hard to have faith without having to add your own works to the mix? Remember, it is by grace alone and not works. Can you journal about this?
2. It is possible that pride interferes with your faith? Keep in mind that it takes humility to ask God for help.
3. The Holy Spirit will teach willingly; however, he does this when he is asked to.
4. Do you feel that belief is the same as faith? See scriptures below. Ponder what James has to say. Look these scriptures up for yourself and pray about them. Let the Holy Spirit speak to your spirit, journal.

Scripture

You believe that there is one God. Good! Even the demons believe that-and shudder. (James 2:19, NIV)
So it is with faith: if it is alone and includes no actions, then it is dead.
(James 2:17, GNT)
But he gives us more grace. That is why Scripture says: "God opposes the proud but shows favor to the humble." (James 4:6, NIV)
I am blameless and free from accusation. (Colossians 1:22)
I was chosen in Christ before the foundation of the world to be holy and without blame before Him. (Ephesians 1:4)
And God is able to make all grace abound to you, so that having all sufficiency in all things at all times you may abound in every good work.
(2 Corinthians 9:8, ESV)

Confession

I am firmly rooted and built up in Christ, strengthened in faith and overflowing with thankfulness. I have received God's spirit, not the worlds. I recognize the wonderful things God has freely given me. (Scripture references: Colossians 2:7, NIV; 1 Corinthians 2:12, NLT)

Faithless

Faithless applies to any failure to keep a promise or pledge or any breach of allegiance or loyalty. (*Merriam-Webster Dictionary*)

Heart's Cry

Forgive me, Father. I have not remained faithful to what you have told me to do. Your Word should be the light upon my path, and I have sought out my own way. With my own will and my way, I have seen in the dark dimly and have stumbled into many deceptive things. It is my heart's desire to follow you. I choose to walk in your ways, on the path you have called me to walk. Take my hand, Father, and lead me where you will. I am yours.

Father Speaks

My daughter, why do you call yourself faithless? Has it not taken great faith to hang on to me in the fires you have walked through? Do you see me as your friend as well as your Father? Look, see me, child. I am your friend, your confidant, your brother, your Savior. It is not me that has moved, daughter, you have moved. Return to me, the stronghold of your life. Return to me, and I will hide you under the shadow of my wings where no harm can touch you, where you will be strengthened. I do not regret the call I have placed upon your life. That call is stronger now than in the past for you are growing closer to the open door I have prepared for you. Come, take my hand. I will walk with you.

Scripture

If we are faithless, He remains faithful; He cannot deny Himself. (2 Timothy 2:13, ESV)

Now you are my friends since I have told you everything the Father told me. (John 15:15b, NLT)

Return to your stronghold, O prisoners of hope; today I declare that I will restore to you double. (Zechariah 9:12, ESV)

He will cover you with his feathers. He will shelter you with his wings, His faithful promises are your armor and protection. (Psalm 91:4, NLT)

For I hold you by your right hand—I, the LORD your God. And I say to you, don't be afraid. I am here to help you. (Isaiah 41:13, NLT)

Let's Make It Personal

1. Do you feel faithless? Remember that when you are faithless, he remains faithful.
2. Is it possible that you see yourself as faithless when the Father sees you as a child in need of his guidance? Journal about this.
3. When you are walking in darkness and find yourself stumbling, all you need to do is call out his name. He is as close as the mention of his name.
4. You must take your thoughts captive to the Word of God. Make no room for the counterfeit from Satan.

Scripture

For though we walk in the flesh, we are not waging war according to the flesh. For the weapons of our warfare are not of the flesh but have divine power to destroy strongholds. We destroy arguments and every lofty opinion raised against the knowledge of God, and take every thought captive to obey Christ. (2 Corinthians 10:3–5, ESV)

As the body without the spirit is dead, so faith without deeds is dead. (James 2:26, NIV)

The LORD is near to all who call on him, to all who call on him in truth. (Psalm 145:18, NIV)

As obedient children, do not be conformed to the passions of our former ignorance, but as he who called you is holy, you also be holy in all your conduct, since it is written, "You shall be holy, for I am holy." (1 Peter 1:14–16, ESV)

Confession

The Word of my Lord is truth, and I trust everything he does. His love for me reaches to the heavens. Great is his faithfulness; his mercies begin fresh each morning. (Scripture references: Psalm 33:4, NLT; Psalm 36:5, NIV; Lamentations 3:23, NIV)

Fear

A distressing emotion aroused by impending danger, evil, pain, etc., whether the threat is real or imagined. (*Oxford Dictionary*)

Heart's Cry

When does this stop, Father? Every day there is some type of fear coming at me, threatening to rob me of what joy is left inside me. Will this ever stop? I choose to hold on to you, yet there are days I feel my grip slipping. You will hold on to me. You will never leave me. You are my Defender and my Protector. Thank you, Father.

Father Speaks

I made you did I not? If the master says to the clay, I will make you into this or that, does the clay have any say in that? If I called you to go here and there am I not able to qualify you to go? I do not call the qualified, I call the willing. I will qualify you. You shall go where I send you. Speak what I put in your mouth to speak. Touch those I bring to you and with my power cast out demons, see the dead rise and heal all those who come to you because of me. Our time is close child. Do not fear for He who calls you is able. Watch as I put everything in perfect order for you, your household, your children, your grandchildren, your time, my time, my time daughter. We will spend time together just you and I.

Scripture

Now my daughter, do not fear. I will do for you whatever you ask, for all my people in the city know that you are a woman of excellence. (Ruth 3:11, NASB)

Surely he will save you from the fowler's snare and from the deadly pestilence. (Psalm 91:3, NIV)

The LORD is my protector; he is my strong fortress. My God is my protection, and with him I am safe. He protects me like a shield; he defends me and keeps me safe. (Psalm 18:2, GNT)

Until I humble your enemies, making them a footstool under your feet. (Luke 20:43, NLT)

The LORD your God is in your midst, a mighty one who will save; he will rejoice over you with gladness; he will quiet you by his love; he will exult over you with loud singing. (Zephaniah 3:17, NLT)

When you walk through the fire, you will not be burned; the flames will not set you ablaze. (Isaiah 43:2b, NIV)

Let's Make It Personal

1. Can you identify obstacles or fears that you need Father's help in overcoming?
2. Ask him to give you the resources you need to overcome as you seek him in prayer.
3. If you ask, he will reveal the fears or obstacles that stand in your way. He will give you his strategy to overcome. Journal what he tells you.
4. Ask him to align your will with his. Seek him in the Word.

Scripture

For the Spirit God gave us does not make us timid, but gives us power, love and self-discipline. (2 Timothy 1:7, NIV)
For I, the LORD your God, hold your right hand; it is I who say to you, "Fear not, I am the one who helps you." (Isaiah 41:13, ESV)
Such love has no fear, because perfect love expels all fear. If we are afraid, it is for fear of punishment and this shows that we have not fully experienced his perfect love. (1 John 4:18, NLT)
Say to those with fearful hearts, "Be strong, and do not fear, for your God is coming to destroy your enemies. He is coming to save you." (Isaiah 35:4, NLT)

Confession

Thank you, Father, that I am kept from all harm because you watch over my life. You have assigned your angel as my guard. He surrounds and defends me. (Scripture references: Psalm 121:7, NLT; Psalm 34:7, NLT)

Focus

The state or quality of having or producing clear visual definition. (*Online Dictionary*)

Heart's Cry

Days upon days pass me by. I struggle to remain focused upon necessary daily duties. Father, I want to hear your voice and follow you. I choose to be used by you, and I have no idea what that looks like. Will you please open my eyes to see where you want me, what you want me to be doing? All else holds little interest for me. I must seek you and hear from you. Thank you for hearing me and guiding me.

Father Speaks

We meet again, my child. I have been waiting for you. I have much to share with you. Much to give you. As I have told you, we have much to do. You must get your eyes off yourself and on to me, your Father and your guide. The days ahead shall be filled with me, with my presence. For I desire to walk more closely with you. Come sit with me, talk with me, receive from me all that you desire. Your heart is growing in me. I am becoming more and more the desire of your heart. One day soon I will be the only true desire of your heart. As deep calls to deep, so my heart calls to yours. Are you ready? Are you fully prepared? For to feel as I feel, to have my heart is an awesome thing. What I am asking of you will not always be easy. Are you ready? Gird yourself, my child. Come prepare with me. Let us get you ready for your new journey with me.

Scripture

Don't get sidetracked; keep your feet from following evil. (Proverbs 4:27, NLT)

You will do everything you have promised; LORD, your love is eternal. Complete the work that you have begun. (Psalm 138:8, GNT)

I am overwhelmed with joy in the LORD my God! For he has dressed me with the clothing of salvation and draped me in a robe of righteousness. (Isaiah 61:10a, NLT)

Deep calls to deep in the roar of your waterfalls; all your waves and breakers have swept over me. (Psalm 42:7, NIV)

The bow of the mighty is now broken and those who stumbled are now strong. (1 Samuel 2:4, NLT)

Let's Make It Personal

1. Can you recall a time that you have not been focused on the things of God? Sometimes it is the distractions within the home; other times it is the distractions in your mind.
2. It helps to realize what you can control and what you cannot control. Perhaps the home distractions can be overcome by getting up before anyone else in the morning.
3. The mental distractions are a bit peskier. What consumes your mind controls your life. Try reading your Bible out loud to yourself. Pray out loud as well. Ask the Holy Spirit to calm your thoughts as you pray about the things you will be facing that day.
4. Set a specific time each day to spend with God. You will begin to look forward to that time as does the Holy Spirit. Always journal about your time spent with the Holy Spirit.

Scripture

I will give them a heart to know me, that I am the LORD. They will be my people, and I will be their God, for they will return to me with all their heart. (Jeremiah 24:7, NIV)
You will keep the mind that is dependent on you in perfect peace, for it is trusting in You. (Isaiah 26:3, CSB)
I press on toward the goal to win the prize for which God has called me heavenward in Christ Jesus. (Philippians 3:14, NIV)
My son, pay attention to my wisdom; listen carefully to my wise counsel. (Proverbs 5:1, NLT)

Confession

If I look for God wholeheartedly, I will find him. And I pray that the words of my mouth and the meditation of my heart is pleasing to him, for he is my rock and my redeemer. (Scripture references: Jeremiah 29:13, NIV; Psalm 19:14, NLT)

Foiled

To prevent (something considered wrong or undesirable) from succeeding. (*Online Dictionary*)

Heart's Cry

Things have tugged so hard on me, Father, that I now feel lost. Which way do I turn? You have assured me that you have this all under control. That you have foiled the plans of the enemy. I wish to see the defeat of the enemy. You will show me because you love me so deeply. I will hear the defeat with my ears, I will feel the defeat in my spirit, and I will SEE the defeat with my eyes. Thank you, Father.

Father Speaks

No more feeling lost, left out or left behind by me. I have called you out. I have equipped you. The journey has been a rough one. You have kept your eyes on me. I am moved by your gaze. I am ravished by your love. There is nothing I will not do for you. Ask and you shall receive, for I am waiting.

Scripture

You have stolen my heart, my sister, my bride; you have stolen my heart with one glance of your eyes… (Song of Solomon 4:9, NIV)

May he equip you with all you need for doing his will. May he produce in you, through the power of Jesus Christ, every good thing that is pleasing to him. All glory to him forever and ever! Amen. (Hebrews 13:21, NLT)

Let's Make It Personal

1. During your time with Father, sit in silence and have your journal available.
2. Have you ever been aware of the Lord thwarting an enemy attack against you?
3. Ask the Holy Spirit to reveal to you, through the Word of God, how that took place. What scripture were you prompted to use? Journal about that. In the future you will be able to utilize that strategy.
4. Take time to thank the Holy Spirit for being with you always. Thank Jesus for interceding on your behalf, and thank the Father for answered prayers.

Scripture

God will defeat your enemies who attack you.
They'll come at you on one road and run away on
seven roads. (Deuteronomy 28:7, MSG)
Then he opened their minds so they could
understand the Scriptures.
(Luke 24:45, NIV)
For the LORD Almighty has purposed, and who
can thwart him? His hand is stretched out, and
who can turn it back? (Isaiah 14:27, NIV)
Trust in the LORD with all your heart and lean not on your
own understanding; in all your ways submit to him, and he
will make your paths straight. (Proverbs 3:5–6, NIV)

Confession

I thank you, Father, that your Word is a lamp for my feet and
a light for my path. If I lack wisdom, I will ask God, and he
will give it to me generously. He will not find fault in me.
(Scripture references: Psalm 119:105, NIV; James 1:5, NIV)

Forgive

Stop feeling angry or resentful toward someone for an offense, flaw or mistake. (*Online Dictionary*)

Heart's Cry

Father, I know your Word tells me to forgive. So many times, I have been lashed out at. I have never returned evil for evil. There is never a time that one has done such a horrible thing that there is no forgiveness available. I have obeyed you and declared that I would forgive. You are a good, good God, a forgiving God. You are the only one that can bring healing to a wounded soul, cover over mistakes, and forgive sins. I want to give it all to you. I refuse to be tainted by my past. The same forgiveness you have given to me I will walk in. All is well under your sheltering wings.

Father Speaks

All things you desire, child, are within your reach. When will you understand that asking with wrong motives is giving Satan a stronghold in your life? Your request, your motives must line up with me and my Word. There is Word within you; be sure it is my Word, not counterfeit, no making my Word fit you. You line up with my Word. I delight in giving you the kingdom, kingdom spiritually and kingdom worldly. You must take my kingdom with you into the world. Don't bring the world into my kingdom. You must walk the path I have planned for you. It is time. No more delay. People are waiting for you. All heaven is waiting and watching to see what you will do with the gifting I have given you. Move out, move on, move upward. Now is the time. No more delay, child.

Scripture

Search me, O God, and know my heart; try me, and know my anxieties; and see if there is any wicked way in me, and lead me in the way everlasting. (Psalm 139:23–24, KNJV)

Blessed are the peacemakers, for they will be called children of God. (Matthew 5:9, NIV)

So don't be afraid, little flock. For it gives your Father great happiness to give you the Kingdom. (Luke 12:32, NLT)

So in everything, do to others what you would have them do to you, for this sums up the Law and the Prophets. (Matthew 7:12, NIV)

Therefore say to them, "This is what the Sovereign LORD says: None of my words will be delayed any longer; whatever I say will be fulfilled, declares the Sovereign LORD." (Ezekiel 12:28, NIV)

Make allowance for each other's faults, and forgive anyone who offends you. Remember, the Lord forgave you, so you must forgive others. (Colossians 3:13, NLT)

Let's Make It Personal

1. Forgiveness is for you. You are not condoning the wrong done against you; you are letting it go. Be quick to forgive rather than allowing the wrong done to cause anger to rise up inside of you. Walking in forgiveness clears the path for the Father to answer your prayers. Journal about this.
2. When you forgive others, you will receive forgiveness from God for your own sins.
3. Walking in forgiveness can contribute to your happiness and improve your health.
4. No one is exempt from wrongdoing; each has sinned. Do you feel free once you have confessed your sin and received forgiveness? Extend that empathy, that forgiveness to others.

Scripture

For if you forgive other people when they sin against you, your heavenly Father will also forgive you. But if you do not forgive others their sins, your Father will not forgive your sins. (Matthew 6:14–15, NIV)
We all stumble in many ways. Anyone who is never at fault in what they say is perfect, able to keep their whole body in check. (James 3:2, NIV)
In your anger do not sin: Do not let the sun go down while you are still angry, and do not give the devil a foothold. (Ephesians 4:26–27, NIV)

Confession

Jealousy is like a cancer; therefore I purpose to have peace of mind, and it makes my body healthy. And when I stand praying, I will forgive others so that my Father in heaven will forgive me. (Scripture references: Proverbs 14:30, GNT; Mark 11:25, NIV)

Gift

A thing given willingly to someone without payment. (*Oxford Dictionary*)

Heart's Cry

You, Father, gave me the gift of your Son, Jesus Christ. In him is everything I could ever ask for or want. This gift is one that compels me to keep on living. He is the one that sustains me and gives me life. This gift, Jesus, is my reason for being. Through him I can overcome any obstacle that stands in my way. Through him I can silence the thoughts in my head. Through and with him, I can survive. There is nothing I cannot do through Jesus Christ, my Savior. How I cherish the time I spend with you. I cannot live without you; I must have you. Thank you for giving me more; it is my heart's cry. Burn out the dross in me; clean me out; burn out all that is not pleasing to you. Fill me up with more of you.

Father Speaks

Daughter, oh, how I love you! How I rejoice in you, your love for me. Cling to me, child, draw from me for I delight in filling you up with me. You ask for more, more you shall have. It has begun; have you not sensed it? My hand is upon you, daughter, my hand of love, protection, development. I want to develop you. I want you for myself; my tool. My gift to you is me. Abide in me; I shall abide in you. We have many adventures ahead of us child. Oh, how I delight in you. You are mine, and I am yours. Tell me, daughter, what is it I can do for you? So be it.

Scripture

If you abide in me, and my words abide in you, ask whatever you wish, and it will be done for you. (John 15:7, ESV)

For My hand made all these things, thus all these things came into being. But to this one I will look, to him who is humble and contrite of spirit, and who trembles at My word. (Isaiah 66:2, NASB)

"Do I bring to the moment of birth and not give delivery?" Says the LORD. "Do I close up the womb when I bring to delivery?" says your God. (Isaiah 66:9, NIV)

The LORD appeared to us in the past, saying: "I have loved you with an everlasting love; I have drawn you with unfailing kindness." (Jeremiah 31:3, NIV)

Let the glory of the LORD endure forever: let the LORD be glad in his works. (Psalm 104:31, NASB)

Let's Make It Personal

1. Abiding in Christ is like a branch that is attached to the vine; it is abiding, living. Are you abiding in Christ, receiving all he has for you?
2. Can you be used by the Father as he chooses to use you if you are not abiding in him, in his Word? See John 15:7. Journal your thoughts.
3. Yes, he did choose you; he does have a plan for you, and he wants to use you. Only you can do the things he has placed within you.
4. Are you ready to answer his call? "The one who calls you is faithful, and he will do it" (1 Thessalonians 5:24, NIV).

Scripture

To whom will you compare me? says the Lord. Is there anyone else like me? (Isaiah 46:5, GNT)

He fills my life with good things. My youth is renewed like the eagle's. (Psalm 103:5, NLT)

If you keep My commandments, you will abide in My love; just as I have kept My Father's commandments and abide in His love. (John 15:10, NASB)

And we know that in all things God works for the good of those who love him, who have been called according to his purpose. (Romans 8:28, NIV)

Confession

Faith, hope, and love will always remain. The greatest of them all is love. I am to love others as he loves me. Love always protects, always trusts, always hopes, always preserves. Because I choose love, you open your hand and satisfy the desire of my heart. (Scripture references: 1 Corinthians 13:7,13, NIV; Psalm 145:16, ESV)

Grace

An accurate, common definition describes grace as the unmerited favor of God toward man. (*Bible Study Tools Dictionary*)

Heart's Cry

Where would I be without your grace? You have been so good to me, Father. You have reached down into the pit and drawn me out. Blessings have come my way. Nothing I asked for or deserved. I walk in favor that is so unexpected. I am so thankful for the grace you have bestowed on me.

Father Speaks

Do you hear, my grace is coming in a more powerful way? My grace I give to you, child. Not as the world gives to you. The world does not know grace. I do. Grace shall infiltrate your life. You will walk forward in my grace. You shall lead many to me. You will do everything; all for me. You have seen nothing yet. Wait! It is here, yes, at the doorstep of your life. All you need to do is to open that door. Just say yes. Yes, and I will fill you to overflowing with my power. My grace, my healing, my deliverance. All you can ever ask for or hope that I will do for with and through you is yours, child.

Scripture

For by grace you have been saved through faith. And this is not your own doing; it is the gift of God, not a result of works, so that no one may boast. (Ephesians 2:8–9, ESV)

Do not be conformed to this world, but be transformed by the renewal of your mind, that by testing you may discern what is the will of God, what is good and acceptable and perfect. (Romans 12:2, ESV)

Ask and it will be given to you; seek and you will find; knock and the door will be opened to you. (Matthew 7:7, NIV)

I pray that God, the source of hope, will fill you completely with joy and peace because you trust in him. Then you will overflow with confident hope through the power of the Holy Spirit. (Romans 15:13, NLT)
Now to him who is able to do immeasurably more than all we ask or imagine, according to his power that is at work within us. (Ephesians 3:20, NIV)
Each time he said, "My grace is all you need. My power works best in weakness." So not I am glad to boast about my weaknesses, so that the power of Christ can work through me. (2 Corinthians 12:9, NLT)

Let's Make It Personal

1. The grace of God is necessary for everyday living. Each morning you need his Spirit to fill you up again, to prepare you for the day ahead.
2. The Holy Spirit speaks to your heart in a fresh new way each morning. The Word he speaks to you will keep your focus on the most important thing, Jesus Christ and your walk with him.
3. Attempting to run the race of life without Jesus can cause defeat in your life and drain you of any joy. You may be spinning your wheels, hoping for change, when you have forgotten the very thing that means the most to your life of victory. That is your foundation in God and his grace in your life. Journal about his grace in your life.
4. His grace is there for you; always at work for and within you. His patience never runs out. Begin to look for the miraculous all around you each day.

Scripture

So we have not stopped praying for you since we first heard about you. We ask God to give you complete knowledge of his will and to give you spiritual wisdom and understanding. (Colossians 1:9, NLT)

Your own ears will hear him. Right behind you a voice will say, "This is the way you should go," whether to the right or to the left. (Isaiah 30:21, NLT)

May God give you more and more grace and peace as you grow in your knowledge of God and Jesus our Lord. (2 Peter 1:2, NLT)

Confession

The grace of my Lord Jesus is with me. Out of the fullness of his grace, he blesses me with one blessing after another. (Scripture references: Revelation 22:21, ESV; John 1:16, NIV)

Healing

To restore to health or soundness; cure. To ease or relieve emotional distress. (*The Free Dictionary*)

Heart's Cry

My body hurts. My mind hurts. My feelings hurt. My heart hurts. My finances hurt. My family hurts. Father, my world hurts. Come to me, Father, and bring healing for my emotional and physical wounds. How do I escape something like this? I have been praying. As I call out to you and seek you with all my heart, you will draw near to me. I do not understand why I don't see healing in myself or the people I pray for. Come with healing, touch my woundedness, and I will be healed. Father, help me.

Father Speaks

Healing is what you want to see, to experience. Healing is what you shall have. Not just for yourself but for those you pray for. Healing is my will for you. Not just to experience for yourself but for those you pray for. Healing shall burst forth from you, for I have ordained it. It is my will that you walk in healing, to be complete body, soul, and spirit. It is my desire that as you touch others for me, they shall receive their healing. Soon, child, so very soon you will see an explosion of healing. Ask and you shall receive. Trust me in this. Soon.

Scripture

Keep on asking, and you will receive what you ask for. Keep on seeking, and you will find. Keep on knocking, and the door will be opened to you. (Matthew 7:7, NLT)

For I will restore health to you, and your wounds I will heal, declares the LORD. (Jeremiah 30:17, ESVa)

Nevertheless, I will bring health and healing to it; I will heal my people and will let them enjoy abundant peace and security. (Jeremiah 33:6)

Behold, it was for my welfare that I had great bitterness; but in love you have delivered my life from the pit of destruction, for you have cast all my sins behind your back. (Isaiah 38:17, ESV)

He heals the brokenhearted and binds up their wounds. (Psalm 147:3, NIV)

Let's Make It Personal

1. Are you burdened with health problems, relationship issues, bad news? God promises good things are in store; his supernatural help. Do not give up. Ask Father to help you to keep your focus on him when pain and hurt is overwhelming.
2. Go to the Word and find scriptures on encouragement, healing, and hope. Journal them. Then speak them out loud; pray them back to God.
3. Praying this way helps you stay focused on his promises and provision for your needs. He will strengthen your mind, your heart, and your body.
4. You can find his promises and pray them out for others; you will see his hand move on their behalf.

Scripture

O LORD, if you heal me, I will be truly healed;
if you save me, I will be truly saved. My praises
are for you alone! (Jeremiah 17:14, NLT)
LORD, be gracious to us; we long for you. Be our strength every morning, our salvation in time of distress. (Isaiah 33:2, NIV)

Confession

My God will meet all my needs according to the riches of his glory in Christ Jesus. He gives me strength and increases my power in my weakness. (Scripture references: Philippians 4:19, NIV; Isaiah 40:29, NIV)

Hearing

Opportunity to be heard, to present one's side of a case, or to be generally known or appreciated. (*Merriam-Webster Dictionary*)

Heart's Cry

I have become so weary, Father. I know you have heard my case, that I have been able to stand in the courtroom of heaven before you and because of Jesus found not guilty. Not only am I not guilty, but you have assured me that whatever my heart so desires, if I believe, I can have it. I have asked for more of you, asked for wisdom. I have asked that you find me a fit vessel for your use. For me to be used by you, I must be able to hear your voice. Right now, I am questioning my ability to hear you clearly. Speak to me, Holy Spirit.

Father Speaks

So you think are not hearing me? Is this what you are thinking, daughter? For I have seen your heart, the meditation that are there. When will you relax in me, my child, and know you hear my voice? I will not allow you to hear the voice of another. You have my name inscribed in your heart. Your ear is turned toward me. I have your attention. What more do I need from you? Your belief in the calling that has been placed upon your life. I have so filled you, daughter, with myself, with my words, with my heart. You have desired me; I have given me to you. You have desired to walk ever so close with me. That you are doing, walking closely with me, and you will walk closer and closer to me until what I feel you feel, what I speak you speak, where I go you go, whom I touch you touch. For you and I are melded together. You and I are one as you so desire, child. We are one. Trust me in this. Powerful, powerful you are. I will help you with that. I will help you understand it. I will help you walk in that power, for it is yours. More so much more is yours. I am empowering you. I am healing you. I am meeting all your

needs. Soon, oh, so soon, you will move much more freely in me. Step by step, moment by moment, I am yours and you are mine.

Scripture

Let the words of my mouth, and the meditation of my heart, be acceptable in thy sight, O Lord, my strength, and my redeemer. (Psalm 19:14, KJV)

Listen for God's voice in everything you do, everywhere you go; he's the one who will keep you on track. (Proverbs 3:6, MSG)

Your words were found, and I ate them, and your words became to me a joy and the delight of my heart, for I am called by your name, O LORD, God of hosts. (Jeremiah 15:16, ESV)

Whoever claims to live in him must live as Jesus did. (1 John 2:6, NIV)

Let's Make It Personal

1. To hear the Holy Spirit speak, you must not be conformed to the world. You must have your mind transformed by renewing it. You have to be able to discern what the will of God is.
2. You renew your mind by reading scripture and prayer. Soak your mind, saturate your mind, with God's Word. You mind will be shaped by his Word.
3. Your renewed mind will want to glorify God above anything else. You will want others to see him.
4. During the process of renewing your mind, the call he has placed upon you will begin to rise up. If you already know the call, it will become sharper and more achievable. If you don't know the call on your life, you will feel the stirring of the Holy Spirit as he reveals it to you.

Scripture

Do you be conformed to this world, but be transformed by the renewal of your mind, that by testing you may discern what is the will of God, what is good and acceptable and perfect. (Romans 12:2, ESV)
Each of you should use whatever gift you have received to serve others, as faithful stewards of God's grace in its various forms. (1 Peter 4:10, NIV)

Confession

There are great and hidden things that I have not known about, and as I call out to my Father, he will answer me and tell me about them. Then I will walk in wisdom and not trust my own insight. (Scripture references: Jeremiah 33:3, ESV; Proverbs 28:26, NLT)

Heart

Heart is the organ that controls the flow of blood in the body, or the center of human emotion. (*YourDictionary*)

Heart's Cry

You made me. This heart that beats inside my chest, you made it. The emotions that can bring great joy or deep sadness, you made them. Now, Father, teach me how to deal with the matters of my heart. My heart loves and desires you, Father. How can I love you more? I have been searching for you, for your direction in my life. You have heard my petitions, and you have an answer. Reveal it to me.

Father Speaks

Yes, I know your heart. I knew your heart on the day of your rebirth into my kingdom. I gave you your heart that seeks me, loves me, cries out to me. I know you right well, my child. I know the plans I have for you. Today I begin to reveal them. Do you not perceive it? I am moving in your life for you this day. Love, Jesus.

Scripture

As water reflects the face, so one's life reflects the heart. (Proverbs 27:19, NIV)

For you have been born again, not of perishable seed, but of imperishable, through the living and enduring word of God. (1 Peter 1:23, NIV)

Wherever your treasure is, there the desires of your heart will also be. (Matthew 6:21, NLT)

My flesh and my heart may fail, but God is the strength of my heart and my portion forever. (Psalm 73:26, NIV)

And the peace of God, which transcends all understanding, will guard your hearts and your minds in Christ Jesus. (Philippians 4:7, NIV)

Let's Make It Personal

1. Are you comfortable calling the Lord Jesus Christ your light and life? Has he become your closest friend? Does he walk with you and talk with you? Have you journaled about some of the discussions you have had with him?
2. You must know that you are not in charge of the heart transformation you are seeking. That is God's business. You are to be totally dependent on him to accomplish the work of transforming your heart.
3. Your heart is to become the dwelling place for the Holy Spirit. In order for him to dwell with you, there may be some cleaning up to do. A prayer could be, "Search me and know me and see if there is any wicked thing in me." Be sure to have your journal close.
4. God has invited you to participate in the deep work of transforming your heart. He will not come to you uninvited. If during your prayer time things were revealed to you that need surrendering to him, gladly give him permission to do the work necessary in order to make your heart the dwelling place of the Holy Spirit. He is a jealous God and longs to dwell with you.

Scripture

And I will ask the Father, and he will give you another advocate to help you and be with you for ever—the Spirit of truth. The world cannot accept him, because it neither sees him nor knows him. But you know him, for he lives with you and will be in you. I will not leave you as orphans; I will come to you. (John 14:16–18, NIV)

Put to death therefore, whatever belongs to your earthly nature: sexual immorality, impurity, lust, evil desires and greed, which is idolatry. (Colossians 3:5, NIV)

May the Lord direct your hearts into God's
love and Christ's perseverance.
(2 Thessalonians 3:5, NIV)

Confession

I will trust in my Lord with all my heart, and I will not lean on my own understanding. Everything I do flows from my heart, so I must guard it. Then as I delight in the Lord, he will give me the desires of my heart.
(Scripture references: Proverbs 3:5, 4:23, NIV; Psalm 37:4, NIV)

Heartache

Emotional pain; the horrible feeling of a black hole sitting in your chest where your heart should be. (*Urban Dictionary*)

Heart's Cry

I know you hear my prayers. How long can this heart carry the heartache and pain? It is too much some days, Father. I don't know how much more I can endure. My heart is in pieces. Sharp, broken. I am wondering why you don't seem to take notice of the deep pain and chaos here in my life. Yet I know you hear me; I know you are a good God. You will not allow this turmoil to continue beyond what I can handle. There is a way out, and you will show me. You will answer. I will yet see the goodness of my Father in the land of the living.

Father Speaks

Child, child, it has been a while since we have talked. Once again you have been consumed with the cares of this world. So consumed you forgot who holds your future. It is in my hands. I am capable of taking care of you, my precious child. Don't look to the right or left. Do not look behind you. Child, do you not yet know that it is I that goes before you. I clear the path; I surround you. I bring up your rear guard. Daughter, I bring up your rear guard. Nothing in your past can hurt you any longer for I have sent out a decree for the things in your past to be dispensed with. Those who continually rise up to accuse you, to shoot arrows of destruction at you, shall be no more, for I do not abide deceit nor do I condone retribution. Just as I crushed Satan's head will I crush the head of your enemy and stop the assault against you.

Scripture

I remain confident of this: I will see the goodness of the LORD in the land of the living. (Psalm 27:13, NIV)

But God did listen! He paid attention to my prayer. (Psalm 66:19, NLT)

In your unfailing love, silence my enemies; destroy all my foes, for I am your servant. (Psalm 143:12, NIV)

Then your light will break forth like the dawn, and your healing will quickly appear; then your righteousness will go before you, and the glory of the LORD will be your rear guard. (Isaiah 58:8, NIV)

He will call on me, and I will answer him; I will be with him in trouble, I will deliver him and honor him. (Psalm 91:15, NIV)

Let's Make It Personal

1. Have you ever wondered if the Father has heard your prayers? If so, why have they not been answered?
2. David in scripture did not get his prayer answered for the life of his and Bathsheba's child. Paul had a "thorn" in the flesh that he asked the Father to remove, and the answer to him was, "My grace is sufficient."
3. We don't understand why prayers are not answered, at least not the way we want them to be. Every prayer is answered. Prayer is a mystery. It cannot be explained. It must be embraced by faith.
4. There is nothing wrong with being honest about your frustration and pain. He hears your prayers even when times are the darkest. He may seem to be removed, silent. However, have the assurance that he will never leave or forsake you.

Scripture

LORD, I wait for you; you will answer, Lord my God. (Psalm 38:15, NIV)

For everyone who asks receives; the one who seeks finds; and to the one who knocks, the door will be opened. (Matthew 7:8, NIV)

In those days when you pray, I will listen. (Jeremiah 29:12, NLT)

Confession

I will set my mind on things above, not on earthly things. When I ask, I receive; when I seek, I find; and when I knock, the door will be opened for me. This is the confidence I have in him, that if I ask anything according to his will, he hears me. (Scripture references: Colossians 3:2, ESV; Matthew 7:7, ESV; 1 John 5:14, NIV)

Heartbroken

A feeling you can never understand until you experience it. It is a constant pain and discomfort that you struggle with all day. It is a sickness in your stomach and a knot in your throat. (*Urban Dictionary*)

Heart's Cry

Father, Father! This pain in my chest is unbearable. I cannot breathe. I cannot eat. How can this broken heart be mended?

Father Speaks

Child, run to me. My arms are open wide. Is there anything I cannot mend? Nothing has taken me by surprise. I saw the pain coming and prepared a place of comfort for you. Come away with me, the lover of your soul. I have a place of comfort and healing for you. Allow me to pour out upon you my grace for such a time as this. Come sit upon my lap, and I will surround you with my wings of comfort. Wisdom will pour into you. Life I give to you. All is well when you are in my presence. I bid you come, child, allow me to fill you up with me. It will be well with your soul.

Scripture

He will cover you with his feathers. He will shelter you with his wings. His faithful promises are your armor and protection. (Psalm 91:4, NLT)

Then Jesus said, "come to me, all of you who are weary and carry heavy burdens, and I will give you rest." (Matthew 11:28, NLT)

The Spirit of God has made me; the breath of the Almighty gives me life. (Job 33:4, NIV)

He heals the brokenhearted and binds up their wounds. (Psalm 147:3, NIV)

Let's Make It Personal

1. Are you wondering if you will ever recover from a broken heart? You must allow yourself to believe that your Father sees you and loves you.
2. He wants to be close by your side during your recovery. No specific amount of time can heal the wounds only he can see.
3. The deep ache of a broken heart can be as isolating as a locked room. Your enemy wants to keep you in that locked room, isolated from others. Journal your thoughts about that.
4. Your Father wants the opposite. He wants you to be with those who can come alongside you offering friendship and comfort. Don't forsake yourself from gathering with others.

Scripture

The LORD is near to the brokenhearted
and saves the crushed in spirit.
(Psalm 34:18, ESV)

I remain confident of this: I will see the goodness of the LORD in the land of the living. Wait on the LORD; be strong, and take heart and wait for the LORD. (Psalm 27:13–14, NIV)

Confession

My Father is close to me in my brokenness, and he saves me because I am crushed in spirit. He heals my broken heart and binds up my wounds. (Scripture references: Psalm 34:18, 147:3, NIV)

Help

To give or provide what is necessary to accomplish a task or satisfy a need; contribute strength. (*Dictionary.com*)

Heart's Cry

Your Word tells me you are as close as the mention of your name. I understand that Word. My desire is to experience it now in my time of need. You are a God of truth, I trust you. Let me see your deliverance of me in this time of need. There is nowhere else to turn. Where would I go? You are my strong tower; I run to you. I abide with you. Helper, Comforter, my best friend, that is who you are to me. I will wait upon you, Father, for I know my help is on the way.

Father Speaks

Though you do not see the answer yet, do not become discouraged, for it is my good pleasure to answer your cries for help. Child, hear me. I am as close as the air that you breathe. Is there anything too hard for me? In the gray days you will find me if you seek me with your whole heart. I will be found by you. I am closer to you than a brother. I am your lover, lover of your soul, your very being. How can the Maker disown his own? I molded you in your mother's womb. I knew you before time began. I rejoiced in you before the heavens were created. I loved you. I was anticipating your arrival on planet Earth. Even so, I waited for you to find me, to recognize me, the one who loves you perfectly without judgement. Purely. My love for you is perfect, without flaw. I watched as you searched for love, finding only disappointment and pain. I watch and I waited. I yearned for you to turn to me. Oh, child, just one glance from your eyes! One word from your mouth, one call of my name, and I would have rushed to your side. There is nothing I would withhold from you. You are my child, my beloved child. Still I wait. I yearn, I desire your presence with me. Come, child, let us reason together, for I have many things to tell you. I have prepared a way through the desert for you. You will not journey alone. Come, take my hand. Let us begin our glorious, joyful life together. I love you with an everlasting and deep love.

Scripture

Arise, shine, for your light has come, and the glory of the LORD rises upon you. (Isaiah 60:1, NIV)

You will seek me and find me when you seek me with all you heart. (Jeremiah 29:13, NIV)

Before I formed you in the womb I knew you, before you were born I set you apart. (Jeremiah 1:5a, NIV)

I will give them a heart to know me, that I am the LORD. They will be my people, and I will be their God, for they will return to me with all their heart. (Jeremiah 24:7, NIV)

You have stolen my heart, my sister, my bride; you have stolen my heart with one glance of your eyes. (Jeremiah 24:7, NIV)

Let's Make It Personal

1. Every victory and every breakthrough begins with a Word from the Lord. Power is released when he speaks, and his Word never returns to him void.
2. He ordains seasons of breakthroughs for you. He promises that he will bring you out of your difficulty. He will rescue you. It does not matter what it is. The season for your breakthrough is upon you. He has heard your cry for help, and he is coming swiftly with answers.
3. Get out the promises the Father has given to you. Revisit them, and as you do, believe that the words are truth and are being fulfilled even now. Do not give up; hold on to the promises. Believe that today God is declaring a new day and a new season in your life.
4. Your Savior Jesus Christ is even now putting Satan under your feet. You can keep him there by the words of your mouth. Mine out scriptures that tell you who you are in Christ; write them down and proclaim them out loud.

Scripture

So is my word that goes out from my mouth: It will not return to me empty, but it will accomplish what I desire and achieve the purpose for which I sent it. (Isaiah 55:11, NIV)

The voice of the LORD is powerful; the
voice of the LORD is majestic.
(Psalm 29:2, NIV)

Now unto him that is able to do exceeding abundantly above all that we ask or think, according to the power that worketh in us. (Ephesians 3:20)

Confession

I have been justified by faith and have peace with God through Jesus Christ. Therefore I will keep my eyes fixed on what lies before me. I will look straight ahead and will know the truth, and it will set me free. (Scripture references: Romans 5:1, ESV; Proverbs 4:25, NLT; John 8:32, NIV)

Helpless

Unable to help oneself; weak or dependent; deprived of strength or power; powerless; incapacitated. (*Dictionary.com*)

Heart's Cry

Helplessness seeps into every fiber of my being. My soul cries out for help. You see the pain. You see the deep needs. You see the need for rescue, yet you remain silent. You are a God of justice. You say, "Justice is mine." Father, bring justice to this situation. Help me breathe again. I am sinking in desperation.

Father Speaks

Child, your need for justice has not gone unnoticed. Your desire to see the wrongs made right is all-consuming you. Are you the one able to correct this? Can you speak peace into something that has gotten so out of control? Do you not need a Savior? One who sees clearly the need at hand. I am the one with the answers to all your hearts cry. I see, I hear, I feel. I am bringing justice swiftly into these situations. You must sit back and rest. I am able to right the wrongs. To stop the destruction. To bring peace and grant heart's desires. Do you trust me, child?

Scripture

Therefore I tell you, whatever you ask in prayer, believe that you have received it, and it will be yours. (Mark 11:24, ESV)

For "Everyone who calls on the name of the LORD will be saved." (Romans 10:13, NLT)

He rescued me from my powerful enemies and from all those who hate me—they were too strong for me. (Psalm 18:17, GNT)

Finally, brothers, whatever is true, whatever is honorable, whatever is just, whatever is pure, whatever is lovely, whatever is commendable, if there is any excellence, if there is anything worthy of praise, think about these things. (Philippians 4:8, ESV)

Let's Make It Personal

1. Have you ever felt lacking in protection or support? Can you journal about that? Journaling will help you see what you are facing. You can get a strategy from God to deal with those issues.
2. Your enemy, Satan, wants you to feel like a victim of your circumstances. You are not! You have the Holy Spirit as your helper. John 14:26 (ESV), "But the Helper, the Holy Spirit, whom the Father will send in my name, he will teach you all thing, and bring to your remembrance all that I have said to you." Journal your feelings.
3. You must know the truth about helpless feelings. The enemy wants to keep you in bondage to those feelings. You may want to read about a psychological condition called "learned helplessness." I won't go into that here. Suffice it to say that a person can begin to associate feeling bad with feeling good.
4. You are NOT helpless because the Lord is with you. He has everything you need to overcome helplessness in a powerful way.

Scripture

For we do not have a high priest who is unable to sympathize with our weaknesses, but one who in every respect has been tempted as we are, yet without sin. (Hebrews 4:15, ESV)
And whatever you do, in word or deed, do everything in the name of the Lord Jesus, giving thanks to God the Father through him. (Colossians 3:17, ESV)
Even before he made the world, God loved us and choose us in Christ to be holy and without fault in his eyes. (Ephesians 1:4, NLT)

Confession

I will trust in my Lord with all of my heart, and I will not lean on my own understanding. Jesus says he is the vine; I am a branch. If I abide in him, and he in me. I will bear much fruit, for apart from him I can do nothing. (Scripture references: Proverbs 3:5, ESV; John 5:15, ESV)

Hidden

Not easy to find. Most people do not know about. (*Cambridge English Dictionary*)

Heart's Cry

I have pursued you, your direction for me. There is excitement inside of me, Father. I know you have placed a call upon my life. Yet I feel so invisible. People recognize and compliment others in their gifts. I am not searching for praise of man, you know that. However, what you are doing inside me begs to come out. I am unsure what it is, or what to do with it. Keep me hidden for as long as it takes to get me prepared, strong and willing to move out with you. I will wait upon you, Father.

Father Speaks

When I say, come walk this way, child, you must heed my words. I have the path cleared out before you. All the briar thorns and pits have been done away with. You are my called, my chosen one, for such a time as this. I died for you; I live for you. You are mine. The walk I have called you to will bring much joy as your see others set free and delivered from the enemy of their souls. I will breathe fire upon the dead branches. I will burn up the dead works. I will set you above and not below. No longer are you hidden. No longer are you invisible. No! You are my glorious prize. I am unwrapping you. I am unveiling you. I am presenting you to my needy world as a clean, unblemished sacrifice. You will go when I say go, do what I do, speak what I speak, touch what I touch, deliver what I deliver. Much power has been given to you, child. Use it wisely. Hear my voice.

Scripture

The LORD of Heaven's Armies has sworn this oath: "It will all happen as I have planned. It will be as I have decided." (Isaiah 14:24, NLT)

The LORD directs the steps of the godly. He delights in every detail of their lives. (Psalm 37:23, NLT)

Now go; I will help you speak and will teach you what to say. (Exodus 4:12, NIV)

You did not choose me, but I chose you and appointed you so that you might go and bear fruit—fruit that will last—and so that whatever you ask in my name the Father will give you. (John 15:16, NIV)

Let's Make It Personal

1. Have you felt "hidden"? In what ways?
2. Ask the Holy Spirit to show you what the Father means when he says he has the path cleared out before you. What dead branches and dead works has he burned up in you? Journal.
3. Father says he is bringing you out; he is unwrapping you. He knows you are ready. Relax in him. He will not let you stumble or miss him.
4. Pray to be a good steward of the gifts he is awakening within you. Journal about them.

Scripture

My child, hold on to your wisdom and insight. Never let them get away from you. They will provide you with life—a pleasant and happy life. You can go safely on your way and never even stumble. (Proverbs 3:21–23, GNT)

As each has received a gift, use it to serve one another, as good stewards of God's varied grace. (1 Peter 4:10, ESV)

Confession

I will not walk in unrighteousness. I walk in your ways; you make the path straight before me. You keep me safe from my foes. (Scripture references: Psalm 5:8, 119:3, NASB)

Hide

Put or keep out of sight. Conceal from the view
or notice of others. (*Online Dictionary*)

Heart's Cry

It is my desire to hide. I want to get away from life. I must find a place for solace and peace in my life. Help me, Father. Wherever I go, there I am. I cannot out run me. This wretched person, I cannot escape. Father, you are my hiding place. Instead of struggling against my problems, I will embrace them, grow in them.

Father Speaks

Why can't you be settled in your current situation, child? Have I not allowed this for a purpose? The sooner you line up with me, the sooner this too shall pass. I have your steps prepared for you. I have gone before you and walked them myself. I walked them to ensure as you walk them no harm will come to you. You will NOT stumble or trip on a stone, for I have angels surrounding you to lift you up. Lift you above the torment, above the chaos. Trust me, child, hear me, obey me. All is well.

Scripture

The LORD himself goes before you and will be
with you; he will never leave you nor forsake you.
Do not be afraid; do not be discouraged.
(Deuteronomy 31:8, NIV)

Walk with the wise and become wise, for a companion
of fools suffers harm. (Proverbs 13:20, NIV)

You are my hiding place; You preserve me from trouble; You
surround me with songs of deliverance. (Psalm 32:7 NASB)

He has told you, O man, what is good; and what does
the LORD require of you but to do justice, and to love
kindness, and to walk humbly with your God?
(Micah 6:8, ESV)

Let's Make It Personal

1. Have you been crying and complaining about what life has dealt to you? That is one way that pain is handled, yet there comes a time you must stop.
2. Is it possible that during the time you were crying and complaining, you were also hiding out from your life? If so, have you been missing all the joy that is possible when you allow the Father to pick you up and set you on a firm foundation?
3. He is aware of your desire to hide away, to close the door on life. Yet he offers you a hand of mercy. He beckons you to come, take his hand, and allow him to bring you out of hiding.
4. He wants you to embrace all the moments of your life because he is right beside you. He wants you to be full of joy that comes from the assurance that you have a powerful Heavenly Father that is watching out for you with a jealous love. Release, let go, he will not let you fall.

Scripture

Let us then approach God's throne of grace with confidence,
so that we may receiver mercy and find grace to help
us in our time of need. (Hebrews 4:16, NIV)
But go and learn what this means: "I desire mercy,
not sacrifice. 'For I have not come to call the
righteous but sinners.'" (Matthew 9:13, NIV)
Do not be anxious about anything, but it every situation,
by prayer and petition, with thanksgiving, present
your requests to God. (Philippians 4:6, NIV)

Confession

I thank you, Father, that you go before me and follow me. You are forgiving and good, abounding in love to me as I call upon you. Thank you for placing your hand of blessing on my head. (Scripture references: Psalm 139:4, NLT; Psalm 86:5, NIV)

Higher

At, in, or to a lofty position, level, or degree. (*The Free Dictionary*)

Heart's Cry

Father, how I love serving your children well. When you tell me to speak a word to them, I am obedient. You know just what they need and when. It is so much fun to watch their faces light up with joy as you reveal yourself to them. You give me wisdom to speak to others that is beyond my human ability.

Father Speaks

This is what I have called you to. You hear me speak. You obey. Come up here, daughter, come up higher with me, for I delight in you. I delight in your willingness to hear my voice, and you know what to do with what you hear. This delights the Father, for I have spoken of your heart and your love of us. My Father has heard your petitions. I have stood in the courtrooms on your behalf. The verdict is NOT GUILTY. Father has decreed a turnaround for you, daughter. No longer will Satan have any rights to you or your family. It has been stopped. Father has spoken.

Scripture

After this I looked, and there before me was a door standing open in heaven. And the voice I had first heard speaking to me like a trumpet said, "Come up here, and I will show you what must take place after this." (Revelation 4:1, NIV)

Samuel said, "Has the LORD as much delight in burnt offerings and sacrifices as in obeying the voice of the LORD? Behold, to obey is better than sacrifice, and to heed than the fat of rams." (1 Samuel 15:22, NAS)

And since we know he hears us when we make our requests, we also know that he will give us what we ask for. (1 John 5:15, NLT)

Let's Make It Personal

1. Has there been a time in your walk with Father that he has given you a message for someone? What did you do with it? Journal about it.
2. After journaling take your writing to Father in prayer, asking him to reveal to you his purpose in sharing his heart with you for someone else.
3. What does scripture have to say about speaking a word in season to someone else? How do you feel about this? Has anyone ever spoken a word to you that you needed? If so, you can understand what Father does with the words he gives you to speak to others. What a blessing it is to them.
4. Do you want more? Ask and you will receive from your Father. He knows your heart desire, for he placed it there.

Scripture

Everyone enjoys a fitting reply; it is wonderful to say the right thing at the right time! (Proverbs 15:23, NLT)
Asking God, the glorious Father of our Lord Jesus Christ, to give you spiritual wisdom and insight so that you might grow in your knowledge of God. (Ephesians 1:17, NLT)

Confession

I will arise and shine because my light has come and the glory of the LORD has risen upon me. I am found not guilty of offending God because I trust in Jesus Christ and in his kindness; he took away my sins. (Scripture references: Isaiah 60:1, NIV; Romans 3:24, NLT)

Holy Spirit

The third person of the Trinity; God as spiritually active in the world. (*Online Dictionary*)

Heart's Cry

You are my dear friend, my Comforter, my protection. Most of all, you are the voice of proclamation of the Father's deep love for me. You give me wisdom when I am praying for others; you speak the Father's will to me. I need you more than the air that I breathe. Help me to know you better. I will find you in the quite place where we meet and commune together. You teach me things about the Trinity; I understand each person better after spending time with you. When I come away from our time, I am stronger and more assured of complete provision for anything I need or ask for.

Father Speaks

As you pray for others, you must believe I hear your prayers, that I hear and I have an answer before you utter your first word in prayer. I guide and direct your prayers by my Holy Spirit. How well do you know him? How close are you walking with him? I desire to take you deeper into an intimate walk with your Comforter, your Counselor, my Holy Spirit. For we are three—don't you know we are three powerful almighty resources for you? Your Father in heaven, yes! Your Father who surrounds you, who protects you, who created light and darkness. Your Savior, yes! The one who loved you unto death and continues to love you and watch over you with a jealous love. Your Comforter, yes! He is as close as the breath from your lips. Call upon him.

Scripture

He hears us whenever we ask him; and since we know this is true, we know also that he gives us what we ask from him. (1 John 5:15, GNT)

Do all this in prayer, asking for God's help. Pray on every occasion, as the Spirit leads. For this reason keep alert and never give up; pray always for all God's people. (Ephesians 6:18, GNT)

For we do not know what prayer to offer nor how to offer it worthily as we ought, but the Spirit Himself goes to meet our supplication and pleads in our behalf with unspeakable yearnings, and groanings too deep for utterance. (Romans 8:26 AMPC)

The amazing grace of the Master, Jesus Christ, the extravagant love of God, the intimate friendship of the Holy Spirit, be with all of you. (2 Corinthians 13:14, MSG)

Let's Make It Personal

1. The Holy Spirit, the third Person in the Godhead, is looking for a walking companion, someone that will heed his call to walk in step with him. God created you for enjoyment. His desire is for companionship, intimacy.
2. Ask the Holy Spirit to fill you up with passion to walk with him. That is prayer you can be sure he will answer when asked with a pure heart.
3. You will come to know the secrets of walking with God and deeper revelation of Jesus Christ because of and through the Spirit which indwells you. Journal.
4. Your desire is to be used to a greater extent by God. Know this then: he will test your fidelity. If you remain close to him through tragedies of life, and disappointments, you qualify as a vessel worthy to be used. He is looking for humility, faithfulness, and loyalty in his walking companions. Examine your heart. Are you ready?

Scripture

He that sows to the Spirit will of the Spirit reap everlasting life. (Galatians 6:8, NKJV)

He who says he abides in Him ought himself also to walk just as He walked. (1 John 2:6, NKJV)

Present your bodies a living sacrifice, holy, acceptable to God, which is your reasonable service. And do not be conformed to this world, but be transformed by the renewing of your mind, that you may prove what is that good and acceptable and perfect will of God. (Romans 12:1–2, NKJV)

Confession

I will search for you, Lord, and I will ask for your strength continually. You will listen to me when I call out to you and come to you in prayer. (Scripture references: 1 Chronicles 16:11, NLT; Jeremiah 29:12, CEB)

Hope

The feeling that what is wanted can be had or that events will turn out for the best. (*Dictionary.com*)

Heart's Cry

I want to hope. I must hope. Where else can I turn but to you, Father? You are my hope. I am encouraged in you. There is nothing that I have requested of you that you are not willing to grant to me. I feel this stirring within me. I do not understand it. I hope something is changing; I will wait for you. In my waiting, I will hope in you. You alone are my Savior and my hope.

Father Speaks

Are you ready? For it has begun. The stirring you have felt was real, and it was sent by me. Examine yourselves; take heed to what you find there. Am I there? Is the world there? Are the cares of life there? I ask again, are you ready? Remember, my children, many are called but few are chosen. I have a call out now, do you perceive it? Those who will those who hear and will heed the call, I say, come, let me show you where we are going. For those who feel as though they cannot heed the call, not because of lack of desire, but because of feelings of unworthiness, I say to you, I make you worthy. It is nothing you do of yourself. If I have called you and you have heard the call, your heart burns within you, then heed my call! Come find your worthiness in me. For those I call, I equip. I don't call the equipped. You must allow me to equip you, to mold you into the vessel I want you to be. This requires placing yourself on my potter's wheel where you will be molded and formed. Then, my dear child, you will go through the refining fires to solidify what I have done within you. It is not an easy road I call you to. It is a road you will walk with the lover of your soul. You will not journey alone. For many others are willing to lay down their life to follow me. I am raising an army, one that has been picked by me, molded, and refined for my good works. Come all who will.

Scripture

Examine yourselves to see if your faith is genuine. Test yourselves. Surely you know that Jesus Christ is among you; if not, you have failed the test of genuine faith. (2 Corinthians 13:5, NLT)

You did not choose me, but I chose you and appointed you so that you might go and bear fruit—fruit that will last—and so that whatever you ask in my name the Father will give you. (John 15:16, NIV)

For this reason we must pay much closer attention to what we have heard, so that we do not drift away from it. (Hebrews 2:1, NASB)

And yet, O LORD, you are our Father. We are the clay, and you are the potter. We all are formed by your hand. (Isaiah 64:8, NLT)

May the God of hope fill you with all joy and peace as you trust in him, so that you may overflow with hope by the power of the Holy Spirit. (Romans 15:13, NIV)

There is surely a future hope for you, and your hope will not be cut off. (Proverbs 23:18, NIV)

Let's Make It Personal

1. When you call upon your Heavenly Father, he is just and faithful to hear your prayers and to answer them.
2. Be encouraged, dear one, he has heard you, and he has an answer. Before time began, he knew you would be calling out to him for hope. He has waited for your call. He wants you to take your place in his army.
3. Are you ready to be used by him; to be part of his army? Journal your thoughts.
4. You can hope again. He needs you. He has called you. He will use you. Arise, shine, for the glory of the Lord has risen upon you.

Scripture

Then he said to his disciples, "The harvest is plentiful, but the laborers are few; therefore pray earnestly to the Lord of the harvest to send out laborers into his harvest. (Matthew 9:37–38, ESV)

Arise, shine, for your light has come, and the glory of the LORD risen upon you. (Isaiah 60:1, NIV)

Return to the stronghold, O prisoners of hope; today I declare that I will restore to you double. (Zechariah 9:12, ESV)

Confession

I will never be put to shame because my hope is in God. I walk by faith, not by sight, casting all my anxieties on him because he cares for me. (Scripture references: Psalm 25:3, NIV; 2 Corinthians 5:7, ESV; 1 Peter 5:7, ESV)

I Am

God, seen as self-sufficient and self-existent. (*YourDictionary*)

Heart's Cry

My Father, at times, in the night hours, I find myself off guard. Yet I know you are with me! I purpose to give my thoughts to you—bring them under your control. I am gaining my strength! Which comes from you and you alone. You delight in blessing your children; therefore I give you my concerns and cares of this world. I am blessed! I am happy in you. Therefore I have joy and favor that comes upon me when I experience your grace in my life!

Father Speaks

Child, have you not heard? Have you not
seen? Your God is an awesome God.

What will it take, my child, for you to believe that I Am? I Am everything you need. I Am everything you desire. I Am the God of the universe, what is too hard for me? Come touch my garment. Come touch my garment with your praises. I will be found in the praises of my children. I am a loving God. Just one look from your eye and I am compelled to move in your behalf. Child, believe that I Am. Is there anything too hard for Me? Is there anything too hard for your Father? No NOTHING. Is there a magic formula you must quote to get my attention? Why do you struggle so, my child?

Scripture

I am the Alpha and the Omega, the beginning and the ending, saith the Lord, which is, and which was, and which is to come, the Almighty. (Revelation 1:8, NJV)

I am the LORD, the God of all mankind. Is anything too hard for me? (Jeremiah 32:27, NIV)

Praise the LORD, all people on earth, praise his glory and might. (1 Chronicles 16:28, GNT)

I will lie down and sleep in peace, for you alone, O Lord, make me dwell in safety. (Psalm 4:8, NIV)

Return to your stronghold, O prisoners of hope; today I declare that I will restore to you double. (Zechariah 9:12, ESV)

Let's Make It Personal

1. Can you really believe in the I Am? That he is everything you could ever dream, desire, or even imagine. He is the I Am. The one and only. Even though he is what he says he is, there are times in life that does not seem to be the case. Have you experienced that? Can you journal about that?
2. Perhaps in the middle of the storm you are in, the I Am comes in the form of peace and strength. Have you experienced him that way?
3. For you to become more convinced of his enduring love and patience, ask the Holy Spirit to guide you to scriptures to stand on.
4. It takes courage to navigate through this life. Courage is found in the pages of God's Word. There you will find encouragement and inspiration to overcome whatever plagues you.

Scripture

All Scripture is God-breathed and is useful for teaching, rebuking, correcting and training in righteousness. (2 Timothy 3:16, NIV)
But those who hope in the LORD will renew their strength.
They will soar on wings like eagles; they will run and not grow weary they will walk and not be faint. (Isaiah 40:31, NIV)

Confession

I am strong in you Lord and in your mighty power. Your unfailing love is priceless. I can take refuge in the shadow of your wings. (Scripture references: Ephesians 6:10, NIV; Psalm 36:7, NIV)

Impatient

Restless or short of temper especially under irritation, delay or opposition. (*Merriam-Webster Dictionary*)

Heart's Cry

Your Word tells me that out of the heart the mouth speaks. I cannot seem to control the words that come out of my mouth. Surely, my heart cannot be as ugly as my speech. Search me and know me; show me how to be kind again. I must learn to be patient if I am to be used by you the way I desire. My life must reflect you. When others see and hear me speak, they must see and hear the Jesus that is in me.

Father Speaks

Child, I have called you here for such a time as this. I desire you to know me. Allow my spirit to mold and make you, for I delight in you. My spirit which indwells you is special, and perfect for you, the child I made you to be. You have requests of me that I delight in giving to you. Look up, child, for your answers are at the door. Look and patiently wait for astonishing things are about to happen. When you see these things, believe, for your Father in heaven is doing them. Ask me now, what is it you would like me to do for you?

Scripture

Many are the plans in a person's heart, but it is the LORD's purpose that prevails. (Proverbs 19:21, NIV)

I, the LORD, have called you to demonstrate my righteousness. I will take you by the hand and guard you. (Isaiah 42:6a, NLT)

But I did not believe these things until I came and saw with my own eyes. Indeed, not even half was told me; in wisdom and wealth you have far exceeded the report I heard. (1 Kings 10:7, NIV)

Ask me, and I will make the nations your inheritance, the ends of the earth your possession. (Psalm 2:8, NIV)

Let's Make It Personal

1. How many times has your mouth gotten out of control? Did you meditate on the issue until it became so large you had to speak it out?
2. What do you think your Father would have done? How would he have had you react?
3. Journal your thoughts. Then go to the Father and ask him how he saw the situation.
4. Be sure to write down what he tells and shows you in his Word. This is a great spiritual growth opportunity.

Scripture

May the God of hope fill you with all joy and peace as you trust in him, so that you may overflow with hope by the power of the Holy Spirit. (Romans 15:13, NIV)

Listen to advice and accept discipline, and at the end you will be counted among the wise. (Proverbs 19:20, NIV)

Confession

Father, I ask that you search me for you know my heart. You know my anxious thoughts and the words of my mouth. I ask that you point out anything that offends you, so that there will be a guard over my mouth. You watch over the door of my lips and lead me along the path of everlasting life. (Scripture references: Psalm 139:23–24, NLT; Psalm 141:3, NIV)

Journey

An act of traveling from one place to another, usually taking a rather long time. (*Dictionary.com*)

Heart's Cry

I wonder, Father, will this emotional moving from one place to another ever quit. I feel stronger one day and the next; I am so overtaken by grief! It is very exhausting for me. Oh, how I want to escape this mental barrage of memories. If I will just keep my eyes upon you!

Father Speaks

Move forward, no looking back. For I have a plan for you, my child. Plans that will prosper you, take you deeper into Me, to use you, to prove you, to make you my own, my own tool. I desire to reach the downtrodden, the outcast, the sad, the happy with my words. Words I will speak through you, for a time such as this. I take you by the hand to guide you, to direct your path so that you will not stumble. Hear the Word of your Father. I am calling you out this day—out of bondage, out of lack, out of sadness, into glorious joy and happiness such as you have never experienced. This day you will begin your new journey with me. Come, let us begin. I am excited for you, my child. We have much to do. Trust me, walk with me. I will open doors, and I say to you, no man will close them. I am taking you higher, deeper than you have ever gone. This new journey is for a time such as this. Come, my beloved child, take hold of my hand. Let us begin.

Scripture

Jesus replied, "No one who puts a hand to the plow and looks back is fit for service in the kingdom of God." (Luke 9:62, NIV)
For I know that plans I have for you, declares the LORD, plans to prosper you and not to harm you, plans to give you a hope and a future. (Jeremiah 29:11, NIV)
You didn't choose me. I chose you. I appointed you to go and produce lasting fruit, so that the Father will give you whatever you ask for, using my name. (John 15:16, NLT)
My eyes will always be fixed on my Lord. He is at my right hand and there is nothing that can shake me. (Psalm 16:8, NIV)
I know your deeds. See, I have placed before you an open door that no one can shut. I know that you have little strength yet you have kept my word and have not denied my name. (Revelation 3:8, NIV)

Let's Make It Personal

1. Have you felt as though you are on a journey that has no end? What does that look like? What does that feel like?
2. Journal your answers. Express your emotions on paper.
3. Take your questions and frustrations to your Father. He will help you navigate through them until you have found peace for the journey.
4. There is much to be thankful for. Open your eyes and your heart to the wonders around you as you walk out the journey you are on. Keep record of the praise-worthy experiences. That will increase your faith and your endurance.

Scripture

I keep my eyes always on the LORD. With him at my right hand, I will not be shaken. (Psalm 16:8, NIV)
In him and through faith in him we may approach God with freedom and confidence. (Ephesians 3:12, NIV)

Confession

How I praise you, Father, that when I walk, nothing will hold me back, and as I run, nothing can cause me to stumble. Truly, I have come to this place for your use at such a time as this. (Scripture references: Proverbs 4:12, NLT; Ester 4:14b, NIV)

Justice

The quality of being just; righteousness, equitableness, or moral rightness: to uphold the justice of a cause. (*Dictionary.com*)

Heart's Cry

Those that desire to see me destroyed seem to be content with their lives, content to see me completely devastated. They lie about me and my family. How can people live life like that and justify the behavior that hurts others? You have spoken to me about justice. You have told me that justice is yours. I will leave that to you, Father. It is not up to me to bring justice; it is up to you. I am confident that as I walk according to your ways and purpose to love others, you will bring justice to my situation. Thank you, Father.

Father Speaks

Have I not told you that I am a just God? Do I not take one down and bring one up? I am a God of justice. Read my Word. Justice is mine, I say. I will move when I move, and I will judge when I judge. For one to say they follow me and act like the heathens do, behave as though I condone their actions, as though no one sees their evil deeds; that is who I will deal with. For I am a just God. I will bring justice to your situation. I will move soon on your behalf. Your prayers have not gone unheard. Your tears have I collected in my bottle. Soon the time will come for my hand to move—justice. It is for the innocent that I raise up a standard. It is for the innocent that my anger is roused when an injustice is carried out. I will deal with those who have acted ungodly, unjustly. I will restore the years the locust has eaten. I will turn the evil planned for you back upon the wicked who wish to carry out their wicked deeds. It is for the young and innocent that I am moving even now. Pray for your enemies.

Scripture

The LORD will work out his plans for my life—for your faithful love, O LORD, endures forever. Don't abandon me, for you made me. (Psalm 138:8, NLT)

You keep track of all my sorrows. You have collected all my tears in your bottle. You have recorded each one in your book. (Psalm 56:8, NLT)

This is what the LORD says about this people: "They greatly love to wander; they do not restrain their feet. So the LORD does not accept them; he will now remember their wickedness and punish them for their sins." (Jeremiah 14:10, NIV)

The ruthless will vanish, the mockers will disappear, and all who have an eye for evil well be cut down—those who with a word make someone out to be guilty, who ensnare the defender in court and with false testimony deprive the innocent of justice. (Isaiah 29:20–21, NIV)

Let's Make It Personal

1. What does justice look like to you? Should it be harsher in certain circumstances than in others? Your Father will act swiftly in your behalf. You will surely see the destruction of your enemy. Therefore, be careful who you call your enemy. Journal your thoughts.
2. Now take those journal entries before the Father. Ask him to speak to you about them.
3. Do not be surprised if he has correction for you. He loves you and wants the best for you in all circumstances. This correction will be for your good, to help you be free of anger and unforgiveness.
4. Be honest with him and yourself. Journal your feelings and his response. This is an opportunity for spiritual growth; don't turn away from it.

Scripture

For the Spirit God gave us does not make us timid, but gives us power, love and self-discipline. (2 Timothy 1:7, NIV)
People who accept discipline are on the pathway to life, but those who ignore correction will go astray. (Proverbs 10:17, NLT)
I tell you, he will see that they get justice, and quickly. However, when the Son of Man comes, will he find faith on the earth? (Luke 18:8, NIV)

Confession

Because I know you, because I am your servant, I am strong and can do good deeds. In your mercy you cut off my enemies and all who would afflict me. (Scripture references: Daniel 11:32b, NLT; Psalm 143:12, NASB)

Launch

To throw forward: to release, catapult or send off; launched an arrow at a target. To begin doing something that is new and very different from what one has been doing. (*Merriam-Webster Dictionary*)

Heart's Cry

Launch. Slingshot. Pulled back tight. What does this mean? Who am I, Father? A bruised, beat-up kid of yours. Dented armor, holes in my shoes. Yet you have sustained me. You have called me out of my life as I see it and into life with you as you see it. What do you see, Father? Help me to see it too. I will be ready when you speak, when you say go.

Father Speaks

Arise! Arise! I have called you here this day. I say to you, arise! I am calling you. Can you hear me? I have called you here for such a time as this. This day I say pick up your sword, pick up your Bible, child! Arise, arise. Believe in my promises. Your Guidebook, the Way book. Pick it up, read it, believe it. Is there anywhere else to go? Where else will you find words of life? Where else will you hear your Father's instructions? Hear me, believe me, child. I am calling those who will. Come follow me. Sell out to me. Don't look back. I hold the keys to your freedom. I will walk this out with you. I need you, my child. For those who will I say come, prepare for launch.

Scripture

All Scripture is breathed out by God and profitable for teaching, for reproof, for correction, and for training in righteousness. (2 Timothy 3:16, ESV)

Arise, shine; for your light has come, and the glory of the LORD has risen upon you. (Isaiah 60:1, NIV)

But you are a chosen race, a royal priesthood, a holy nation, a people for his possession, so that you may proclaim the excellencies of him who called you out of darkness into His marvelous light. (1 Peter 2:9, ESV)

Brothers, I do not consider that I have made it my own. But one thing I do; forgetting what lies behind and straining forward to what lies ahead. (Philippians 3:13, ESV)

Let's Make It Personal

1. Your Father desires to send you out, to get you started in the plan he has for you.
2. Do you have any idea what that might be? Perhaps a new business idea, change in career? Maybe you have felt the call into ministry. Journal what you think it is. Seek the Holy Spirits guidance through the Word for confirmation.
3. Is it time to put your words into action? Can you believe he has the right path for you to follow?
4. Take that first step; he will be there to place your foot on the path he has called you to.

Scripture

Jesus said to them again, "Peace be with you. As the Father has sent Me, even so I am sending you." (John 20:21, NIV)

I press on toward the goal for the prize of the upward call of God in Christ Jesus. (Philippians 3:14, ESV)

Confession

My plans will be established as I commit my work to the Lord. Even though my beginning was insignificant, my end will increase greatly. (Scripture references: Proverbs 16:3, ESV; Job 8:7, NASB)

Listen

To hear what someone has said and understand that it is serious, important, or true. (*Merriam-Webster Dictionary*)

Heart's Cry

Father, you know me right well. You created me the way you desired. I am created the way I am for your purposes. Can I not obey you? Do I desire not to hear? No, Father, I will hear your voice. I will listen to your directives. I will obey. Speak, for your servant is listening.

Father Speaks

Child, you must keep your focus on Me! I have not taken you out of everything; I have placed you where I want you. Here you can be used of me the way I created you to be used. Don't, I tell you again, don't look to the right or the left. Stay in your own lane. I have much for you to accomplish with me. Places I desire to take you. Ways I desire to use you. You know right well I have called you. Who I call I equip. Stop concerning yourself with that which does not concern you.

Scripture

Now may the God of peace make you holy in every way, and may your whole spirit and soul and body be kept blameless until our Lord Jesus Christ come again. God will make this happen, for he who calls you is faithful. (1 Thessalonians 5:23–24, NLT)

Do not turn to the right or the left; keep your foot from evil. (Proverbs 4:27, NIV)

My foot has held fast to his steps; I have kept his way and have not turned aside. (Job 23:11, RSV)

I press on toward the goal to win the prize for which God has called me heavenward in Christ Jesus. (Philippians 3:14, NIV)

Let's Make It Personal

1. Was there a time that you knew Father spoke something to you? Write down what that was and your response to it.
2. If your response was not what you feel Father had called you to, ask him to reveal to you what his direction is concerning your walk with him.
3. Purpose to follow his direction. Write down what that looks like to you. Then prayerfully commit it him.

Scripture

The LORD says, "I will guide you along the best pathway for your life. I will advise you and watch over you." (Psalm 32:8, NLT)

Set your minds on things above, not on earthly things. (Colossians 3:2, NIV)

Confession

In my heart I make plans for the direction of my life, but you, Father, determines what steps I should take. You are working in me, giving me the desire and the power to do what pleases you. (Scripture references: Proverbs 16:9, ESV; Philippians 2:13, NLT)

Loss

Be deprived of or cease to have or retain. Suffer the loss of; no longer have. (*Online Dictionary*)

Heart's Cry

How do I describe my deep heartache? Seems like every step I take is one step forward and several steps backward. I strive to obtain understanding of my situation. My heart desires to be understood, yet I lose in any conversation that takes place. My happiness seems to slip right through my hands. Father, you understand. Help me to understand. Help me to become a better person.

Father Speaks

Child, I am standing guard over your heart. It was and is breaking. I am pouring out healing balm over your heart even now. The words of your mouth must begin to line up with my Word. Do you understand the importance of this, child? Do you? There is more power in my Word than you will ever fully understand. I spoke my Word, and the world was created. I am able to move within you in a powerful and victorious way if you will speak my Word. Believe me, child. Try it and watch, feel, observe the power in it and how it will move the mountains in your life that you are pushing against in your own strength now. Allow me, my Word, out of your mouth to move the mountains, to take you to the other side.

Scripture

But in that coming day no weapon turned against you will succeed. You will silence every voice raised up to accuse you. These benefits are enjoyed by the servants of the LORD; their vindication will come from me. I, the LORD, have spoken! (Isaiah 54:17, NLT)

He replied, "Because you have so little faith. Truly I tell you, if you have faith as small as a mustard seed, you can say to this mountain, 'Move from here to there,' and it will move. Nothing will be impossible for you." (Matthew 17:20, NIV)

May the words of my mouth and the meditation of my heart be pleasing to you, O LORD, my rock and my redeemer. (Psalm 19:14, NLT)

The tongue can bring death or life; those who love to talk will reap the consequences. (Proverbs 18:21, NLT)

In the beginning the Word already existed. The Word was with God, and the Word was God. (John 1:1, NLT)

For by your words you will be acquitted, and by your words you will be condemned. (Matthew 12:37, NIV)

Let's Make It Personal

1. Have or are you dealing with some type of loss? There can be different types of loss, such as loss of health, death of a loved one or a pet, loss of trust in someone. The feelings of loss are very personal. You need to journal about your feelings. It will help you deal with them.
2. It is unfortunate that not everyone understands when someone is feeling deep sadness over a loss they have experienced. You must know and believe that Jesus Christ has experienced every emotion you will ever have. Examine his walk while he was on this earth. He is acquainted with sorrow.
3. Your loss may take you longer to get over than what others may think it should. Your healing process will take whatever time it takes; it is your process, no one else's.
4. No, you are not going crazy. If you have difficulty concentrating, are sad or irritable, anxious or fearful, Jesus understands.

Scripture

Surely he has borne our griefs and carried our sorrows. (Isaiah 53:4a, ESV)

Praise be to the God and Father of our Lord Jesus Christ, the Father of compassion and the God of all comfort, who comforts us in all our troubles, so that we can comfort those in any trouble with the comfort we ourselves received from God. (2 Corinthians 1:3–4, NIV)

When you go through deep waters, I will be with you. When you go through rivers of difficulty, you will not drown. When you walk through the fire of oppression, you will not be burned up; the flames will not consume you. (Isaiah 43:2, NLT)

Confession

Thank you, Father, that your promise revives me; it comforts me in all my troubles. You are my Lord and my God. You light a lamp for me; my darkness is turned to light. (Scripture references: Psalm 119:50, NLT; Psalm 18:28, NIV)

Miracles

An extraordinary event manifesting divine intervention in human affairs the healing miracles described in the Gospels. (*Merriam-Webster Dictionary*)

Heart's Cry

I long to see miracles. To watch the hand of the Almighty God move in behalf of those who wait upon him. I am one of those that is waiting upon you, Father. I believe in miracles! I believe in your desire to show up and show off for those who need a miraculous touch of your hand. I am one of those that needs the touch of your hand. Come, Lord Jesus, I am eagerly waiting for your touch.

Father Speaks

Miracles, miracles! Like you have never seen. This day it begins. This day it is here. Reach out and take what you need. It is all here for you. Nothing shall be held back; it is here, come to the table. Come be fed, be strengthened. This day is the day for you. A new time for you. Come and taste and see that your Father is good. He wishes to give you his blessings. His blessings. What does that look like? What does that feel like? Do you want me? Do you want me? Do you want all that comes with me? Are you ready to pick up your sword and follow me into the battle? I have much for you to do. Much to accomplish. Must to endow to you, to bestow upon you. Blessings upon blessings. Come, let me bless you. Come, allow me to bless you. Come, I say, for it is all ready.

Scripture

Jesus looked at them and said, "With man this is impossible, but not with God; all things are possible with God." (Mark 10:27, NIV)
And my God will meet all your needs according to the riches of his glory in Christ Jesus. (Philippians 4:19, NIV)
When you walk, you won't be held back; when you run, you won't stumble. (Proverbs 4:12, NLT)
LORD, you alone are my portion and my cup; you make my lot secure. The boundary lines have fallen for me in pleasant places; surely I have a delightful inheritance. (Psalm 16:5–6, NIV)

Let's Make It Personal

1. The definition of *endow* from the *Online Dictionary* is "to give or bequeath an income or property to a person." The definition of *bestow* from the *Online Dictionary* is "to honor or gift someone with something."
2. As the Father spoke, it is his desire to provide for you all you need, including money and land. He knows the meditation of your heart.
3. Have you been asking him for something specific? Journal about it, and take it to the Father. Get his Word and direction for you.
4. His will is that nothing be withheld from you. Can you believe?

Scripture

From his abundance we have all received one gracious blessing after another. (John 1:16, NLT)

And God will generously provide all you need. Then you will always have everything you need and plenty left over to share with others. (2 Corinthians 9:8, NLT)

Confession

I can be assured that no word from you, Father, will ever fail. I will give you thanks with all my heart; I will tell all about your wonderful deeds. (Scripture references: Luke 1:37, NIV; Psalm 9:1, NIV)

Mother's Prayer

Your mother is the woman that gave birth
to you. (*Collins English Dictionary*)
Prayer is our communication process that allows
us to talk to God. (*AllAboutPrayer.org*)

Heart's Cry

I know you are not blind to my children's hearts' cries. Tonight I pleaded with you, bargained with you. What do you want from me? What can I do to get you to move in their lives? What do you require of me? The things I ask are not hard, not impossible for you to do. To me it looks like such a gigantic mountain. To you it is not even a grain of sand. You tell me, if I pray according to your will, my prayers will be answered. The mountain must be cast into the sea.

Father Speaks

I have seen the deep pain in your children. I have sat there as they wept. I was as close as a brother, yet time and time again, they would not call upon me. Because I love them, I will rescue them and set them above the storm. Because a mother's prayer is one of the most important and powerful things in the universe.

Scripture

Then Jesus told his disciples a parable to show them that they should always pray and not give up. (Luke 18:1, NIV)
Then they cried to the LORD in their trouble, and he delivered them from their distress. (Psalm 107:19, ESV)
I tell you the truth, you can say to this mountain, "May you be lifted up and thrown into the sea," and it will happen. But you must really believe it will happen and have no doubt in your heart. (Mark 11:23, NLT)

Let's Make It Personal

1. Do you think a mother can be defined by her unselfish generosity and unconditional giving to her family?
2. What does the unconditional giving mean to you? Describe from a mother's and a child's viewpoint. Journal your thoughts.
3. Do you believe that God's love radiates through a mother? If so, what does that look like to you?
4. God wove himself into a mother's heart in such a way that it denies description. Take a look at the following scriptures. You can sense the nurturing love of a mother.

Scripture

How often I have wanted to gather your children together as a hen protects her chicks beneath her wings… (Matthew 23:37b, NLT)

With his love, he will calm all your fears. He will rejoice over you with joyful songs. (Zephaniah 3:17b, NLT)

Confession

You are a good God, a strong refuge when trouble comes. I trust in your name, and you rescue and protect me. (Scripture references: Psalm 91:14, NLT; Nahum 1:7, NLT)

Mountain

A landmass that projects conspicuously above its surrounding. (*Merriam-Webster Dictionary*)

Heart's Cry

Climbing another one, another mountain. Will I ever find a smooth place to rest for a while? You have told me that I can speak to the mountains in my way and they must move. Perhaps I am not speaking correctly as it seems as though this mountain does not want to move. I am trusting you to help me deal with this. Thank you, Father, for showing me the way through.

Father Speaks

Let's talk about getting real, daughter. Not what do you want from me, not what you need from me. What am I giving to you? What are you looking for? Do you know me? Do you understand me? Do you want to know me better? Can you simply be still, rest, and watch me move the mountains in your way? I am able to lift them up and remove them. Remove them from your presence. The mountain in your way is all in your mind, your emotions. Look! Look again! There is no longer any trace of those mountains. The sea has opened its mouth and swallowed them. They no longer exist. Child, they are no longer. It is time you believe. Step into the supernatural with me. Your most unique and powerful ministry has begun. You don't fully recognize it. Not yet. I will open your eyes. It is not just the mountains that have moved; nothing is left standing in your way. As I spoke to you a few years ago, it is a very unique and powerful walk I have called you to. Only you can do this, only you are equipped to step out into the life I have called you to. It is time to be all I made you for. You must have strength; I have strengthened you. You must be courageous; I have given you courage. You need power; I filled you with power. My precious daughter. Come, it is now time. Trust me.

Scripture

Therefore I tell you, do not worry about your life, what you will eat or drink; or about your body, what you will wear. Is not life more than food, and the body more than clothes? (Matthew 6:25, NIV)

It is God who removes the mountains, they know not how, when He overturns them in His anger. (Job 9:5, NASB)

I tell you the truth, you can say to this mountain, "May you be lifted up and thrown into the sea," and it will happen. But you must really believe it will happen and have no doubt in your heart. (Mark 11:23, NLT)

Having the eyes of your hearts enlightened, that you may know what is the hope to which he has called you, what are the riches of his glorious inheritance in the saints. (Ephesians 1:18, ESV)

And these whom He predestined, He also called; and these whom He called, He also justified; and these whom He justified, He also glorified. (Romans 8:30, NASB)

Let's Make It Personal

1. If you want to move the mountain in your life, you must pray out loud to your Father in heaven, using the scriptures you are standing on. Speak to your mountain, believing it must move. You can declare a thing, releasing positive thoughts out of your mouth. For example, declare your day to be full of God's blessings, your marriage to be restored, your body to be healed.
2. In Mark 11:23, Jesus says that whatever you say will come to pass.
3. Scripture tells us that death and life are in the power of the tongue. When it comes to using your authority and speaking out loud to the spiritual atmosphere, to your Father in heaven, you must believe that there is the power of death and life in the tongue.
4. You can call forth what you want to have done. It must line up with scripture.

Scripture

He says, "Be still, and know that I am God; I will be exalted among the nations, I will be exalted in the earth." (Psalm 46:10, NIV)
The tongue has the power of life and death, and those who love it will eat its fruit. (Proverbs 18:21, NIV)
Look, I have given you authority over all the power of the enemy, and you can walk among snakes and scorpions and crush them. Nothing will injure you. (Luke 10:19, NLT)
You will also decree a thing, and it will be established for you; and light will shine on your ways. (Job 22:28, NASB)

Confession

When I walk, I will not be held back, and when I run, I will not stumble because you go before me and level the mountains; you break down gates of bronze and cut through bars of iron. (Scripture references: Proverbs 4:12, NLT; Isaiah 45:2, NIV)

Need

Require (something) because it is essential or very important. (*Oxford Dictionary*)

Heart's Cry

Oh, how I need you, Father. My heart cries out in the night hours, searching for you. I must hear from you and sense your presence. My need for you is all-consuming, and you are my Rescuer in these times I am living in. My spirit longs for more of you. What is it that you would have me do, Father? You are a good Father, and you meet every need I have. You have spoken to me that you need me, that you have a purpose for me. Show me, and I will do as you direct. Lead me, Father, and I will go.

Father Speaks

This is a new day! A new beginning, child. Have I not called you for such a time as this? Have you not heard my voice? You get sidetracked easily. This is not my desire for you. Your focus must ever be upon me. For in me you shall live and have your being. If I desire for you to turn this way or that, I will be sure you recognize my voice. For I have a purpose and a call on your life. You are what I need for such a time as this. Before time began, I called you into this place. I formed you and put specific tools within your person, before you were formed in your mother's womb. Those tools have been residing within you for such a time as this. I am now waking those tools up, calling them forth and sharpening them for my work. Child! Do not look back, for there is nothing there for you. Do not look beside you, for there is much to draw you away from me. I say to you, look forward. Look up, for your Father is smiling down upon you. He is dripping his anointing upon you. With each drip you become more powerful and equipped for my use. Drip, drip...can you not feel the anointing? Drip, drip... Daughter, let this oil fill in all the dry spots in your spirit. It shall fill to overflowing. Then as you have prayed for, my anointing and joy will flow forth from you to others in a might way. You will carry with and inside you my power. So much power that it, that I, must flow forth from you on to others. Is this not your heart's greatest desire?

Scripture

And who knows but that you have come to your royal position for such a time as this? (Ester 4:14b, NIV)
You have anointed me with the finest oil. (Psalm 92:10b, NLT)
"Is not My word like fire?" declares the LORD, "and like a hammer which shatters rock?" (Jeremiah 23:29, NASB)
Fear not, for I have redeemed you; I have called you by name, you are mine. (Isaiah 43:1b, ESV)
He has saved us and called us to a holy life—not because of anything we have done but because of his own purpose and grace. This grace was given us in Christ Jesus before the beginning of time. (2 Timothy 1:9, NIV)

Let's Make It Personal

1. Do you need the Father? In what way? Journal about this.
2. Keeping things to yourself does not keep them from your Father.
3. Speaking out loud to him about your desires can clarify them. You can sort through them verbally, knowing he is listening. This will help you focus. Journal.
4. He wants you to know that he has need of you, and he is ready to instruct you. Are you ready to obey him?

Scripture

I press on toward the goal for the prize of the upward call of God in Christ Jesus. (Philippians 3:14, ESV)
For we are his workmanship, created in Christ Jesus for good works, which God prepared beforehand, that we should walk in them. (Ephesians 2:10, ESV)

Confession

I give you praise, Father, for you grant me my heart's desire and fulfill all my plans; you establish my steps. (Scripture references: Psalm 20:4, ESV; Proverbs 16:9, ESV)

New Beginning

When moving forward means leaving the past behind. (*Elements Behavioral Health*)

Heart's Cry

Oh, how I long for a new beginning in my life. Something fresh and alive. I feel change is coming, yet I do not fully understand. You are in this, I know. I can sense this is a good thing. Something that I have sensed and anticipated is now on its way. You are never late with your purpose. Keep me close to you, Father. Here I am, send me.

Father Speaks

Tonight there will be a new beginning. What has been felt and sensed in the spirit is beginning to play itself out. Listen, listen, children can you hear it? Can you hear the rumbling of a mighty army being assembled? This night I ask you, are you for me or against me? For I tell you, those who are called and say yes to the call are now being called up higher. Gird yourself, children, prepare for a mighty breakthrough. One such as you have never seen before. One that you have only hoped could happen. Come those that will. I am ready, and I am willing to pour myself into and upon you in such a way that those around you will say, "Surely, they have been in the presence of a mighty and powerful God." For those that will I say, "Come," I am waiting.

Scripture

Forget the former things; do not dwell on the past. See, I am doing a new thing! Now it springs up; do you not perceive it? I am making a way in the wilderness and streams in the wasteland. (Isaiah 43:18–19, NIV)

The LORD thunders at the head of his army; his forces are beyond number, and mighty is the army that obeys his command. The day of the LORD is great; it is dreadful. Who can endure it? (Joel 2:11, NIV)

Whoever is not with me is against me, and whoever does not gather with me scatters. (Matthew 12:30, NIV)

The one who calls you is faithful, and he will do it. (1 Thessalonians 5:24, NIV)

I thank him who has given me strength, Christ Jesus our Lord, because he judged me faithful, appointing me to his service. (1 Timothy 1:12, ESV)

Let's Make It Personal

1. Have you sensed something different in your time with the Father?
2. Ask him to reveal his heart to you regarding the changes coming. Some of those changes coming to you are because you have said, "Here I am, Lord."
3. Stay close to him and in his Word. Get prepared for his move in your life.
4. Journal your feelings. Pray about them. Record what the Father is speaking to you.

Scripture

May he equip you with all you need for doing his will. May he produce in you, through the power of Jesus Christ, every good thing that is pleasing to him. All glory to him forever and ever! Amen. (Hebrews 13:21, NLT)

So then, prepare your hearts and minds for action! Stay alert and fix your hope firmly on the marvelous grace that is coming to you. For when Jesus Christ is unveiled, a greater measure of grace will be released to you. (1 Peter 1:13, TPT)

Confession

I am not consumed because of your great love for me. Many will see what you have done and put their trust in you. Your mercy and compassion never fail me. They are there for me every morning. You are so faithful to me. I choose to wait upon you for direction. While I wait, I will sing praises to you, my God. (Scripture references: Lamentations 3:22, NLT; Psalm 40:3, ESV)

New Season

A time characterized by a particular circumstance.
(*Merriam-Webster Dictionary*)

Heart's Cry

Yes! I sense something is changing. I seem to understand you and your Word better, Father. It feels like you are much closer to me. What is this? Something is happening inside of me. I have a confidence that I have not had before. I trust the you in me now. No longer will I question your voice or your direction. It is time for me to step into what you have for me. What is it? Show me. Speak to me.

Father Speaks

You are walking into a new season. In this season I will be walking very close to you. You will feel my presence like never before. There are things you will see, things you will hear that will cause you to ponder. I tell you, it is me in the midst of the situations. It is me in the midst of your world. Seek me. I will be found by you, for I am as close as your breath. The coming days will require eyes to see. Spiritual eyes that see beyond the veil into the deep things my Spirit is doing. I am calling you out on to the waters. You will surely walk and not faint. For what you see with your spiritual eyes will tell you a different story than what you see in the natural. Time is short. I need you. Come follow me.

Scripture

For everything there is a season, a time for every activity under heaven. (Ecclesiastes 3:1, NLT)

But from there you will search again for the LORD your God. And if you search for him with all your heart and soul, you will find him. (Deuteronomy 4:29, NLT)

Open my eyes, that I may behold wondrous things out of your law. (Psalm 119:18, ESV)

But those who trust in the LORD will find new strength. They will soar high on wings like eagles. They will run and not grow weary. They will walk and not faint. (Isaiah 40:31, NLT)

Let's Make It Personal

1. Have you been feeling like the Father is closer than he used to be? Can you describe that? Journal your thoughts.
2. Does it seem like you have stepped from sure footing onto shaky ground? You have stepped into your new season. Do you know what that is?
3. Ask Father to confirm to you through his Word what it is that you sense he is doing.
4. Trust that what he tells you is truth and a new direction for your life.

Scripture

Seek the LORD and his strength; see his presence continually! (1 Chronicles 16:11, ESV)

But as for me, how good is it to be near God! I have made the Sovereign LORD my shelter, and I will tell everyone about the wonderful things you do. (Psalm 73:28, NLT)

Confession

I will let God transform me by the renewing of my mind as he lives with me. He takes delight in me; he is my mighty Savior. My fears are all calmed down because of his love. Therefore, I will not conform to the patterns of this world. Because I will renew my mind, I will be able to test and approve what God's perfect will is for me. (Scripture references: Romans 12:2, NLT; Zephaniah 3:17, NLT)

Offense

Annoyance or resentment brought about by a perceived insult to or disregard for oneself or one's standards or principles. (*Online Dictionary*)

Heart's Cry

No one seems to care about what is right. I do not want to take offense to things; however, I find myself doing just that. The pressure from others, the demands from them, is making me angry. I respond in anger rather than in love. Forgive me, Father. Help me to keep my gaze set upon you and your Word, and I will walk in love.

Father Speaks

I desire to take you on a journey with me. To places you have never been before. I desire to use you in ways you have never been used before. Your heart must be completely mine, sold out to your Master. I am building an army. Yes! An army of people who want to see me. Who want to do my will. Who want to go forth and conquer the enemy. An army of people who will walk in love. Taking no offense. No offense. For the enemy will bring much offense. You will conquer in love. Come, let me empower you.

Scripture

Then He said to the disciples, "It is impossible that no offenses should come, but woe to him through whom they do come!" (Luke 17:1, NKJV)

Do not gloat when your enemy falls; when they stumble, do not let your heart rejoice. (Proverbs 24:17, NIV)

Search me, O God, and know my heart; try me, and know my anxieties; and see if there is any wicked way in me, and lead me in the way everlasting. (Psalm 139:23–24, NKJV)

Let's Make It Personal

1. Are you dealing with offense right now? If so, how are you handling it?
2. Have you spoken to your Father about this? He understands exactly how you are feeling. Remember, Jesus experienced all the emotions we have while he was on the earth.
3. It becomes an act of our will to walk in love as scripture tells us we are to do.
4. List ways in which you will purposely walk in love from this day forward. Commit to Father, and allow the Holy Spirit to guide you. Be sure to journal.

Scripture

A new command I give to you: Love one another. As I have loved you, so you must love one another. (John 13:34, NIV)
Let the morning bring me word of your unfailing love, for I have put my trust in you. Show me the way I should go, for to you I entrust my life. (Psalm 143:8, NIV)

Confession

It is my desire to give you my heart and to delight in you. Because of that, I will not conform to the way of this world. I will be transformed by renewing my mind. Then I will be able to understand what God's good, pleasing, and perfect will is for me. (Scripture references: Romans 12:2, NLT; Proverbs 23:26, NLT)

Open Door

A recognized right of admittance: freedom of access. (*Merriam-Webster Dictionary*)

Heart's Cry

How I long to see your hand move in my behalf. Father, I will follow you. I will obey you. Open the door you want me to walk through. Help me to hear your voice clear and precise. Because I am your child, I have the right to ask you for these things.

Father Speaks

From this day forward, there will be great victories to be seen. You have labored and toiled long enough. It is time for repayment. Greater shall be your latter days than your former. The King of Kings goes before you. He tears down gates of iron. Gates that have been erected within you. Within others. No more. The gates have lost their power. The door is now open. The gateway is revealed. Walk this way, not that. Keep your eyes upon me. Do you desire to see the gates of hell crumble? It is time for victory. The doorway is open. Those who will come, come walk through them. Those who will will see clearer and hear better than before. Nothing will stand in the way of those who will. Are you ready?

Scripture

But thanks be to God! He gives us the victory through our Lord Jesus Christ. (1 Corinthians 15:57, NIV)

I will go before you and will level the mountains; I will break down gates of bronze and cut through bars of iron. (Isaiah 45:2, NIV)

I know your works. See, I have set before you an open door, and no one can shut it; for you have a little strength, have kept my word, and have not denied my name. (Revelation 3:8, NIV)

Let's Make It Personal

1. List times you have felt powerless. Examine yourself to find out why you felt that way. Journal your thoughts.
2. Now take your Bible and find scriptures that speak on strength. There are many that you can find that will strengthen you.
3. Write them down on a three-by-five card and begin speaking them out loud over yourself. By doing this, you are preparing yourself for the open door.
4. Are you one that hears, one that will? Father is looking for you. He has a plan for your life. He has opened the door for you. Keep your eyes on him and walk through the door.

Scripture

Examine yourselves to see whether you are in the faith;
test yourselves. Do you not realize that Christ Jesus
is in you—unless, of course, you fail the test?
(2 Corinthians 13:5, NLT)
The LORD is my strength and my shield; my heart
trusts in him, and he helps me. My heart leaps for joy,
and with my song I praise him. (Psalm 28:7, NIV)

Confession

I heard your voice call saying, "Whom shall I send?" And I said to you, "Here I am, send me!" For you my Lord and my God, go with me to fight against my enemies, and you give me victory. (Scripture references: Isaiah 6:8, NIV; Deuteronomy 20:4, NIV)

Overcomer

A person who overcomes something: one who succeeds in dealing with or gaining control of some problem of difficulty. (*Merriam-Webster Dictionary*)

Heart's Cry

I must be an overcomer. In order for me to find my way, I have to ask you for something, Father. I am asking for forgiveness. Things in my life must be set straight with you. What do you want me to do? Holy Spirit, come be my Counselor, my Guide, as I tread through these deep waters. Come Father, Son, and Holy Spirit, rescue me. I will serve you all the days of my life in a new way. Forgiveness sets me free to be the overcomer you have called me to be. From this day forward, I will be about my Father's business. Thank you, Father, I am an overcomer in Jesus Christ!

Father Speaks

My child, my child, many things concern you. You are on a journey to find the ONE thing that you should concern yourself with. That is me and our relationship. Have I not told you we have much to do? You and I. I have a plan for you, to be used by me. I do not take away callings; they may be delayed, but never withdrawn. These things that trouble you are in your past. Have I not heard the deep sorrow, the cries of your heart, your very soul crying out to me? Yes, I have gathered every tear you have shed. I placed them in a bottle and will strengthen you and provide for you. No tear has gone unseen by me. Forgiveness has been extended to you. My grace has been given to you. I will repair the broken places, and I will repay what Satan took from you. This I will do for you, child. Do you not perceive it? Have you not heard, your Father is a good Father? He repays from the beginning of time. He sees his children. He knows how to fix broken things. Allow me, child, allow me to do what I have come to do in your life.

Scripture

No one will be able to stand against you as long as you live. For I will be with you as I was with Moses. I will not fail you or abandon you. (Joshua 1:5–6, NLT)

May he equip you with all you need for doing his will. May he produce in you, through the power of Jesus Christ, every good thing that is pleasing to him. All glory to him forever and ever! Amen. (Hebrews 13:21, NLT)

You keep track of all my sorrows. You have collected all my tears in your bottle. You have recorded each one in your book. (Psalm 56:8, NLT)

I, even I, am he who blots out your transgressions, for my own sake, and remembers your sins no more. (Isaiah 43:25, NIV)

But in all these things we overwhelmingly conquer through him who loved us. (Romans 8:37, NASB)

Let's Make It Personal

1. The word *overcomer* can mean "conquering," "prevailing," or "winning a victory." Do those words resonate within your soul? They should; that is who you are in Christ.
2. Scripture, found in 1 John 5:4, tells us that whatever is born of God overcomes the world.
3. If things in your past keep nagging at you, remind yourself that there is nothing you can do to change the past. Remind Satan that you have been forgiven, and don't partner with those thoughts again. You do not want to continue replaying the past because you will be forfeiting your present. God needs you in the present with him.
4. Are you ready to allow God to do what he desires with your life? There is a great plan ready for you to step into with him.

Scripture

You see, every child of God overcomes the world, for our faith is the victorious power that triumphs over the world. (1 John 5:4, TPT)
I have been crucified with Christ and I no longer live, but Christ lives in me. The life I now live in the body, I live by faith in the Son of God, who loved me and gave himself for me. (Galatians 2:20, NIV)

Confession

My God will never leave me or abandon me. He has healed up my broken heart and has bound up my wounds. (Scripture references: Hebrews 13:5b, NLT; Psalm 147:3, NIV)

Peace

Freedom from disturbance; tranquility. (*Oxford Dictionary*)

Heart's Cry

So many call upon me for help. I want to help others, Father, but how? There is such unrest in me. Peace evades me; there is a war in my mind. I am not sure what peace looks like Father. What does it feel like? Help me find a way to settle my spirit, my mind. I know you are here with me. Speak, Father, I am listening.

Father Speaks

Peace, peace, I give to you. Not your kind of peace. Not because you have it all figured out, but because I Am is giving you peace. Take this offering from me, child. Allow my peace to envelop you. Don't take the care of this world upon yourself. You were not made to carry the burdens of this life. You were made to speak for me to others that desperately need to hear my message of peace. Be still, child. You cannot hear in a cacophony of sounds. Be still and listen for my voice. It will break through the chaos in your soul. It will bring you peace that passes all understanding. Then and only then will you hear me as you desire to hear me. I am waiting for you. Come sit with me and be at peace.

Scripture

Peace I leave with you; my peace I give to you. Not as the world gives do I give to you. Let not your hearts be troubled, neither let them be afraid. (John 14:27, ESV)

Cast your burden on the LORD, and he will sustain you; he will never permit the righteous to be moved. (Psalm 55:22, ESV)

And the peace of God, which transcends all understanding, will guard your hearts and your minds in Christ Jesus. (Philippians 4:7, NIV)

The LORD gives strength to his people; the LORD blesses his people with peace. (Psalm 29:11, NIV)

Let's Make It Personal

1. Oftentimes, no matter how hard we try, peace escapes us. Is there a war in your mind causing peace to be elusive? Can you journal about that?
2. Getting it out on paper may help you get a clearer understanding of the source of the problem that is troubling you.
3. You must know that God has not abandoned you. Jesus is the prince of peace.
4. Still yourself before your Father. Allow him to fill you with the peace that passes all understanding. Only he can do that. It is nothing we can do on our own.

Scripture

You will keep in perfect peace those whose minds are steadfast, because they trust in you. (Isaiah 26:3, NIV)
And he will be called: Wonderful Counselor, Mighty God, Everlasting Father, Prince of Peace. (Isaiah 9:6b, NLT)

Confession

I thank you, Father, that I am a peacemaker, and because I sow peace, I will reap a harvest of righteousness. You call me your child. Because I am your child, I can cast all my anxiety on you because you care for me.
(Scripture references: Matthew 5:9, NIV; James 3:18, NIV; 1 Peter 5:7, NIV)

Perfect

Being entirely without fault or defect: flawless.
(*Merriam-Webster Dictionary*)

Heart's Cry

You are the perfect one, Father. Perfect in all your ways. Your love for me is perfect. I am not perfect. I need you to perfect that which concerns me. You have called me out, yet I feel so inadequate. You tell me you need me, but it is I who need you. Show me how you see me, see us. My heart cries out to know you better.

Father Speaks

Do you believe I am perfect in all my ways? In all that concerns you? In the things that tear at your heart? Child, do you believe I am perfect in all of my ways? The thing I have called you to is not something you thought of yourself. I called you to it. I am the author and finisher of it! I planned it with great expectation and joy. You and I doing this thing together. You showing me off through you. I have so much to do through you. So many to reach, so many to touch. It has been allowed—this trying time. Without it you would not be equipped to reach the many that need you. That need of me in you. You cannot do this alone. For it is I who placed it all in your spirit. It is I who has been calling you forth. It is I that have awakened from your slumber. We have much to do. We have a wonderful time ahead of us. For I walk with you and in you. You can feel my presence. I know you can. I am the air that you breathe. That for which you asked me for. Oh, child, if I could just show you what is ahead for you and me. Yet I cannot, for you would not be able to bear it. It would be to wonderful for your humanness to comprehend. We must walk this out together. We have begun.

Scripture

And those he predestined, he also called; those he called, he also justified; those he justified, he also glorified. (Romans 8:30, NIV)

Looking unto Jesus the author and finisher of our faith. (Hebrews 12:2, KJVa)

And do this, understanding the present time: The hour has already come for you to wake up from your slumber, because our salvation is nearer now than when we first believed. (Romans 13:11, NIV)

But you are a chosen people, a royal priesthood, a holy nation, God's special possession, that you may declare the praises of him who called you out of darkness into his wonderful light. (1 Peter 2:9, NIV)

For he is sent by God. He speaks God's words, for God gives him the Spirit without limits. (John 3:34, NLT)

Let's Make It Personal

1. Do you believe your Father in heaven is perfect?
2. If so, is there anything too hard for him? Journal your thoughts.
3. You have desires in your heart that you have waited to see fulfilled. Can a perfect Father grant you those desires? If so, what does that look like to you?
4. We all have different ways that we "expect" our Lord to answer our prayers. However, we need to seek him and find his perfect will for us, then we can pray accordingly and believe that he has heard us and will answer.

Scripture

I am the LORD, the God of all mankind. Is anything too hard for me? (Jeremiah 32:27, NIV)
Seek the LORD and his strength; seek his presence continually! (1 Chronicles 16:11, ESV)

Confession

You are giving me the desires of my heart because I look for my happiness in you. I remain in you, and as I search your Word, I have assurance that I can ask for anything and you will grant it to me. (Scripture references: Psalm 37:4, GNT; John 15:7, GNT)

Pieces

Into which a thing is destructively divided
or broken. (*Dictionary.com*)

Heart's Cry

I have caused pain. I have been caused pain. Is there a solution? If so, what? I know the solution is you. My heart is in pieces, and I try to carry on like I am okay. If I could only come to you. There are times I so wish you would take me home to be with you. This suffering would come to an end. I know that is selfish of me. I know you are not done with me here on this earth. When I come through this, I will be equipped to help others. I need you. I must have your intervention.

Father Speaks

Child, during the times things look the worse, and during the dark, desolate times in your life you must know, I am right here beside you. I see the tears; I hear the cries of your heart. I hold the broken pieces of your soul. I am the great Healer. It is my desire to put you back together again. This time you will be better than ever. As I put each piece into place, I seal it with my purpose, my plan for you. Nothing will stand in your way, child. It is your Father's goodwill to make you complete and whole, ready for every good work I call you to. The pain will subside as you keep your gaze upon me, the lover of your soul. Let me weep with you, let me strengthen you. Soon you will see the purpose for all this.

Scripture

I know the LORD is always with me. I will not be shaken, for he is right beside me. (Psalm 16:8, NIV)

A joyful heart is good medicine, but a crushed spirit dries up the bones. (Proverbs 17:22, NIV)

O LORD, if you heal me, I will be truly healed; if you save me, I will be truly saved. My praises are for you alone! (Jeremiah 17:14, NLT)

God uses it to prepare and equip his people to do every good work. (2 Timothy 3:17, NLT)

Let's Make It Personal

1. Suffering should not take us by surprise. Scripture tells us that in this life there will be trial and tribulations. Yet when it happens to us, that scripture holds little comfort. Are you suffering right now?
2. Please know that none of these things are random or without purpose. You are in a battle for your soul. Father is in this with you. He knows the purpose for it all. Ask him.
3. Journal your thoughts and take them before the Father. Invite him into your pain. He will comfort you. He will direct you. He will bring you through.
4. When you come through your trials, you will understand that God is true to his Word and has a purpose for your pain. Do you trust him? Lean into him. He will bring you through; He will do it.

Scripture

I cry out to God Most High, to God who
fulfills his purpose for me.
(Psalm 57:2, ESV)

We are hard pressed on every side, but not crushed;
perplexed, but not in despair, persecuted, but not
abandoned; struck down, but not destroyed.
(2 Corinthians 4:8–9, NIV)

Confession

You go with me, LORD my God, to fight for me against
my enemies and give me victory. I am strong in you
and in your mighty power. (Scripture references:
Ephesians 6:10, NIV; Deuteronomy 20:4, NLV)

Poor Choices

A wrong action attributable to bad judgment
or ignorance or inattention.
(*Word Magic English-Spanish Dictionary*)

Heart's Cry

It seems like I am not choosing what you have for my life. I live on the fringes. I am realizing that my choices, my poor choices, have taken the best years of my life. Who has been damaged in the wake of my choices? Father, forgive me. Help and heal those I have wounded with my poor choices. Help and heal me.

Father Speaks

My precious daughter. Do not punish yourself like you do. I have not given you the right to do so. I am not a punishing God. I am a forgiving God. Much more will be accomplished for me and for my kingdom if you will stop wallowing around in your own self-destruction. When I died, I died for your sins—past, future, and present. Present, child, do you understand what I am saying? How am I to use you when your focus is on what you have or have not done? I have so many things to share with you. So much for you to accomplish with me. It is time now for you to ask and to receive forgiveness. Come, child, loose the tethers that you are binding yourself with. Let me have them. They will be thrown into the sea of forgetfulness, never to be remembered again. Can you trust me with this? I must have your attention.

Scripture

For by that one offering he forever made perfect those who are being made holy. (Hebrews 10:14, NLT)

You have searched me, LORD, and you know me. You know when I sit and when I rise; you perceive my thoughts from afar. You discern my going out and my lying down; you are familiar with all my ways. Before a word is on my tongue you, LORD, know it completely. You hem me in behind and before, and you lay your hand upon me. (Psalm 139:1–5, NIV)

If we confess our sins, he is faithful and just to forgive us our sins and to cleanse us from all unrighteousness. (1 John 1:9, ESV)

So whoever know the right thing to do and fails to do it, for him it is sin. (James 4:17, ESV)

You will again have compassion on us; you will tread our sins underfoot and hurl all our iniquities into the depths of the sea. (Micah 7:19, NIV)

Let's Make It Personal

1. Are you still replaying the poor choices you have made? Can you find anywhere in scripture where you are given permission to do that? If Christ does not condemn you, why do you condemn yourself? Journal your thoughts.
2. Yes, there are consequences for your bad choices. That is not called punishment; it is called discipline. While your Father does not punish or count your sins against you, there is still the consequences of your actions. He forgives, and he desires to help you through whatever you are facing. He is a good Father. He wants the best for you.
3. Perhaps the next time you are faced with the opportunity to make poor choices, you will remember and choose a different attitude or response.
4. God knows everything about you. He knew the choice you were going to make before you made it. There is nothing hidden from him. While he was there to help you avoid the poor choice, he remains there to forgive you and help you find forgiveness for yourself. He knows your weakness and uses it for his glory!

Scripture

For by a single offering he has perfected for all time those who are being sanctified. Where there is forgiveness of these, there is no longer any offering for sin. (Hebrews 10:14, 18, ESV)

And Jesus said, "Neither do I. Go and sin no more—" (John 8:11a NLT)

Confession

My heart does not condemn me; therefore, I have confidence before God that because of Jesus Christ, I will not receive condemnation. (Scripture references: 1 John 3:21, NIV; Romans 8:1, NIV)

Powerful

Having the ability to control or influence people or things. Having a strong effect on someone or something. (*Merriam-Webster Dictionary*)

Heart's Cry

Father, I am becoming more powerful in you every day. I felt so distant from you for such a long time. I withdrew from life for a period. Now my walk with you is strengthening. I have a burning desire to know you, to experience your presence in my life as never before. You have told me to ask and you will answer. Now is the time for me to ask of you. Now is the time for you to answer. I am your child, Father, and you delight in me.

Father Speaks

Yes, my child! Yes! I am your Father! I love you deeply, child. I will take you from glory to glory. For it is my greatest delight to move through you! This time has been good for you. I have your attention again. Come, beloved child, come to me. Sit on my lap. I will so fill you that you will not be able to help pouring me out upon others. As you pour me out, others will be healed, set free, delivered from the enemy of their souls. As you move in me, you will grow in power. For my delight is to move you from glory to glory. Come up higher! Child, I am calling you out and up NOW, this very minute. Come, child. Trust me. I am your Father! I can and will do it! Everything you can imagine or desire is prepared for you and MORE! MUCH MORE! You must believe me, child. Believe and leave the rest to me. No more toiling, no more struggle. Come, let us begin your new life. I am bringing you out of hiding. Now is the time.

Scripture

But we all, with open face beholding as in a glass the glory of the Lord, are changed into the same image from glory to glory, even as by the Spirit of the Lord. (2 Corinthians 3:18, KJV)

God poured out the Holy Spirit abundantly on us through Jesus Christ our Savior. (Titus 3:6, GNT)

Arise, shine, for your light has come, and the glory of the LORD rises upon you. (Isaiah 60:1, NIV)

Now faith is confidence in what we hope for and assurance about what we do not see. And without faith it is impossible to please God, because anyone who comes to him must believe that he exists and that he rewards those who earnestly seek him. (Hebrews 11:1, 6, NIV)

Let's Make It Personal

1. Are you becoming stronger, more powerful in your walk with the Father?
2. Why do you think this is happening? Journal your thoughts.
3. Now put into practical application what you are experiencing. What does that look like to you?
4. If Father is calling you up higher, are you willing to go where he calls you? Examine your heart.

Scripture

Test me, LORD, and try me, examine my heart and my mind. (Psalm 26:2, NIV)

But he said to me, "My grace is sufficient for you, for my power is made perfect in weakness.: Therefore I will boast all the more gladly about my weaknesses, so that Christ's power may rest on me. (2 Corinthians12:9, NIV)

Confession

I thank you, Father, that I am able to share in the glory of my Lord Jesus Christ because you have told me that there is nothing I cannot do in your strength. You have called me, and you are faithful to do it. (Scripture references: 2 Thessalonians 2:14, NIV; Philippians 4:13, NIV)

Prepared

Made at an earlier time for later use: made ready in advance. Made ready for some activity, purpose, use, etc. (*Merriam-Webster Dictionary*)

Heart's Cry

Father, you bid me come walk with you. I have no desire to follow another. You alone do I seek; you alone do I desire. You fill me up with love and sustaining power. You truly love me. Your love is true and unconditional. I feel blessed by you. What is to come, Father? I am sure it is good. Thank you.

Father Speaks

Can you not feel something? Something is changing. Listen for my voice, seek me this day, and I will be found by you. For I have many unexpected blessings in store for you. The hours of pain, the days of pain, the months of pain, shall come to an end. For I decree it to be so. I have gone before you. Yes, I was there at the beginning of time. I have watched you, cried with you, rejoiced with you, and most of all, I have hoped with you. Open yourself to me. Allow me to come in and visit with you, to tell you things you do not understand just yet. The time is short, and I choose to prepare you for what is to come. My delight will be in using you, a willing vessel. We have much to do, many to reach. Come take my hand, child, let us begin. Welcome to your new journey with me, your Savior, Teacher, Guide, lover, Healer, and your God. Child, you shall walk this way and not that way. You will hear a voice behind you directing your path. You must believe this.

Scripture

Do not be afraid or discouraged, for the LORD will personally go ahead of you. He will be with you; he will neither fail you nor abandon you. (Deuteronomy 31:8, NLT)

Then the LORD said: "I am making a covenant with you. Before all your people I will do wonders never before done in any nation in all the world. The people you live among will see how awesome is the work that I, the LORD, will do for you." (Exodus 34:10, NIV)

So teach us to number our days, that we may present to You a heart of wisdom. (Psalm 90:12, NASB)

You own ears will hear him. Right behind you a voice will say, "This is the way you should go," whether to the right or to the left. (Isaiah 30:21, NLT)

Let's Make It Personal

1. The Father is waiting to bring you into all he has for you. Are you ready to find out what that is?
2. You have called out to him, and he has heard your cry. Journal what you feel he has spoken to you about your situation.
3. Listen closely to his voice, for he will tell you the direction for you to move in.
4. He has gone before you; therefore, you need not concern yourself about the details. Keep your eyes on him. Do you trust your Father? Examine yourself.

Scripture

For when God made a promise to Abraham, because He could vow by no one greater, He vowed by Himself, saying, "Surely I will bless you, and surely I will multiply you." (Hebrews 6:13–14, MEV)

And I am certain that God, who began the good work within you, will continue his work until it is finally finished on the day when Christ Jesus returns. (Philippians 1:6, NLT)

Confession

I have the assurance that if I seek your will in everything I do, the God of hope will fill me with joy and peace. He will show me which path I am to take so that I may overflow with the power of the Holy Spirit.
(Scripture references: Romans 15:13, NIV; Proverbs 3:6, NLT)

Problems

A matter or situation regarded as unwelcome or harmful and needing to be dealt with and overcome. (*Online Dictionary*)

Heart's Cry

Problem after problem. What am I to do, Father? I want to run away from them. They seem to chase me down and find me. Where can I go to find relief from these problems? Show me what to do, Father, and I will do it. I will overcome.

Father Speaks

My child, cast your care. I have this. I have had it. I will continue to HAVE IT! I can handle these things much better than you can. Child, believe me! I care for what troubles you. I knew this day would come. I have great plans for you from today forward if you will let me have it. I will take you on a journey you will not be able to comprehend. Yes! It is I, your Father. I call you forward; I call you out. Come, child, come walk on the water with me. You will not drown, for I have called you.

Scripture

Do not let your hearts be troubled. You believe in God; believe also in me. (John 14:1, NIV)

Seek his will in all you do, and he will show you which path to take. (Proverbs 3:6, NLT)

But when he saw the wind, he was afraid and, beginning to sink, cried out, 'Lord, save me!" Immediately Jesus reached out his hand and caught him. (Matthew 14:30–31a, NIV)

Let's Make It Personal

1. Have you found that it is easier to avoid problems than to face them?
2. Should life always be fair? Our Father is a just God, and he treats everyone equally. He shows no favoritism.
3. Is it always right just because you feel that it is right? What do you do with those feelings? Journal about them.
4. Are you waiting for everything to line up for you before you can be happy? Fill in the blank, I can't be happy until ___. Write your answer down and take it to the Father. Listen for his answer and direction.

Scripture

Again I looked throughout the earth and saw that the swiftest person does not always win the race, nor the strongest man the battle, and that wise men are not necessarily famous. (Ecclesiastes 9:11, TLB)

Those who trust their own insight are foolish, but anyone who walks in wisdom is safe. (Proverbs 28:26, NLT)

Confession

I am so grateful that fairness is part of your character. You long to be gracious to me, and you show me your compassion. For you are clothed with fairness and with truth. Blessed are all who wait for you.
(Scripture references: Isaiah 11:5 TLB; Isaiah 30:18, NIV)

Puzzle

To feel confused because they cannot understand or make sense of something. A problem designed to test ingenuity or knowledge. (*Online Dictionary*)

Heart's Cry

I feel like the puzzle piece that does not fit. The last piece that people are trying to force into a space that it was not created to fit in. In the process I have become broken. Where do I fit, Father? I am standing outside looking in. What do I do with me? Where DO I fit? Surely, you know and will show me.

Father Speaks

Child, you are not too broken. I AM the puzzle piece you need. All other pieces will come together as you focus on me and my power within you. You are not too broken. I am the glue, the glue that holds all the pieces of you together. You are my masterpiece. You have been called, broken, and glued back together by me. Now, child, come, for it is time to live out the picture you see as you gaze at your puzzle. The puzzle your Father created. The puzzle that I AM has put back together and glued with my blood. Blessed are you child, for I AM has called you. You will be the puzzle piece glue for others. For this is my will for you. Many need who I am in you. Come, child, refresh yourself at my feet.

Scripture

He is before all things, and in him all things hold together. (Colossians 1:17, NIV)

For we are God's masterpiece. He has created us anew in Christ Jesus, so we can do the good things he planned for us long ago. (Ephesians 2:10, NLT)

God, picked up the pieces. Put me back together again, You are my praise! (Jeremiah 17:14, MSG)

I will refresh the weary and satisfy the faint. (Jeremiah 31:25, NIV)

Let's Make It Personal

1. Jesus is the glue that holds your life together. Can you feel his holding power in you?
2. When you think of the word *hold*, you can believe that the Father has got his hold on you and has given you a place to stand strong.
3. In Christ everything is held together, even the smallest atom; every sound is held together because of Christ. Will he not hold you together more tightly because you are his child? He gave his life for you.
4. Spend some time journaling about the wonder of the glue your Father holds you together with, the very blood of his Son, Jesus Christ.

Scripture

The Son radiates God's own glory and expresses the very character of God, and he sustains everything by the might power of his command. When he had cleansed us from our sins, he sat down in the place of honor at the right hand of the majestic God in heaven. (Hebrews 1:3, NLT)
"From eternity to eternity I am God. No one can snatch anyone out of my hand. No one can undo what I have done." The LORD's Promise of Victory. (Isaiah 43:13, NLT)

Confession

You are all around me. Thank you, Father, for being behind me and in front of me. I can stand up tall in your presence so I can see you eye to eye. You know me inside and out, and you hold me together by your power. (Scripture references: Psalm 139:5, NIRV; Psalm 41:12, MSG)

Redeemer

A person who brings goodness, honor, etc., to something again: a person who redeems something. (*Merriam-Webster Dictionary*)

Heart's Cry

So many tears I have cried. Darkness has so surrounded me that I struggle with things of daily life. I feel as though I am locked in my own prison of grief and sadness. Surely, there is light to be found in my situation. You, Father, have promised to never leave me. Help me find you in this fog I am living in.

Father Speaks

I am your Redeemer, your Deliverer, the one who sets the captive free. The one who has collected your tears, your fears and your doubts in a basket. A woven basket made of the purest gold. I am the one that is even now pouring out upon you all that I have collected. Pouring out upon you blessings, answers, and hope to replace all the sadness and sorrow in your life. I am the Life-giver. I come swiftly with my blessings pouring them out upon you. I tell you, my child, there will not be room enough for you to take it all in. Let them pour on to others. Be my vehicle of blessing to those around you.

Scripture

And God is able to bless you abundantly, so that in all things at all times, having all that you need, you will abound in every good work. (2 Corinthians 9:11, NIV)
The righteous cry out, and the LORD hears them; he delivers them from all their troubles. (Psalm 34:17, NIV)
The thief comes only to steal and kill and destroy. I came that they may have life and have it abundantly. (John 10:10, ESV)
I have swept away your offenses like a cloud, your sins like the morning mist. Return to me, for I have redeemed you. (Isaiah 44:22, NIV)
Turn your ear to listen to me; rescue me quickly. Be my rock of protection, a fortress where I will be safe. (Psalm 31:2, NLT)
Praise be to the God and Father of our Lord Jesus Christ, who has blessed us in the heavenly realms with every spiritual blessing in Christ. (Ephesians 1:3, NIV)

Let's Make It Personal

1. Are you able to see the Father as your Redeemer? The one that lifts you up out of the pain and sorrow you find yourself in?
2. Did you know that when you weep, it is your soul's way of releasing sorrow? Somehow tears have a way of flushing it out of our system. God is in the middle of the pain you're are feeling; he is consoling you as only he can. His protection comes in the form of peace and strength in the middle of your sorrow.
3. As he consoles you, remember that death and life are in the power of your tongue. You want his blessings; you must speak his Word. Read Proverbs 18:21.
4. Jesus promises victory in the midst of our trials. He overcame everything you are experiencing. Be encouraged to press on knowing that you are an overcomer!

Scripture

This is what the LORD says—your Redeemer, the Holy One of Israel: "I am you LORD your God, who teaches you what is good for you and leads you along the paths you should follow." (Isaiah 48:17, NLT)

In his kindness God called you to share in his eternal glory by means of Christ Jesus. So after you have suffered a little while, he will restore, support, and strengthen you, and he will place you on a firm foundation. (1 Peter 5:10, NLT)

Worry weighs a person down; an encouraging word cheers a person up. (Proverbs 12:25, NLT)

These things I have spoken to you, so that in Me you may have peace in the world you have tribulation, but take courage; I have overcome the world. (John 16:33, NASB)

Confession

The Spirit of my God made me, and his breath gives me life. You are my fountain of life; you are the light by which I see. (Scripture references: Job 33:4, NIV; Psalm 36:9, NLT)

Refuge

A place that provides shelter or protection. Something to which one has recourse in difficulty. (*Merriam-Webster Dictionary*)

Heart's Cry

Where can I go, Father? Who can help me? I want to run to a place of solitude; however, the provision would have to come from someone that would not be good for me to be around. This mental game. Where is peace? It is found in my Savior, Jesus Christ. I will seek his face. He will speak to me. I must come away with him. To that solid rock I will cling. To you, Father, I will look, for my redemption comes from none other.

Father Speaks

Oh, my child! Hear my voice! For I am calling you to be apart. I desire to set you apart with me for a period. I am watching for those whose hearts are completely mine. For I delight in having a powerful, moving army. One that looks only to me for guidance. Seeking my face, my will in everything you do. I am not a God of the big happening only. Oh no! I am the God of the very small things in your life. Listen, do you hear my voice? Seek me in everything, in everything.

Scripture

I will say of the LORD, "He is my refuge and my fortress, my God, in whom I trust." (Psalm 91:2, NIV)
But my eyes are upon You, O GOD the Lord: In You I take refuge; do not leave me destitute. (Psalm, 141:8 NKJV)
The LORD says, "I will guide you along the best pathway for your life. I will advise you and watch over you." (Psalm 32:8, NLT)
God is our refuge and strength, a very present help in trouble. (Psalm 46:1, ESV)

Let's Make It Personal

1. Wanting to seek refuge from the storm is a normal response. Where do you go?
2. You will not find the refuge you are looking for unless you are looking to your Father. Grab your Bible and mine out scriptures to stand on. Write them in your journal and claim those promises out loud every day.
3. Call upon him now. Cry out to him now. Pray without ceasing. He has a way through for you.
4. God delights in hearing thanksgiving in the midst of your storms. As you praise and thank him, you are reminded of the goodness of God, and that strengthens your faith.

Scripture

Show me your unfailing love in wonderful ways.
By your might power you rescue those who seek
refuge from their enemies. (Psalm 17:7, NIV)
And since we know he hears us when we make our requests, we
also know that he will give us what we ask for. (1 John 5:15, NLT)
Don't worry about anything; instead, pray about everything.
Tell God what you need, and thank him for all he has done.
Then you will experience God's peace, which exceeds anything
we can understand. His peace will guard your hearts and
minds as you live in Christ Jesus. (Philippians 4:6–7, NLT)

Confession

You keep me safe in your dwelling in the day of trouble.
From a sea of troubles, I can cry out to you. You hide me
in your sanctuary and set me high upon a rock. (Scripture
references: Psalm 27:5, NIV; Psalm 130:1, CEV)

Rescuer

To free from confinement, danger, or evil: save, deliver. (*Merriam-Webster Dictionary*)

Heart's Cry

I am so tired, Father, so weary. Deeply disturbed in my heart, to my very soul. When will this cease? When will I find peace and reconciliation within myself? My tongue set on fire by hell in my life. I hurt many. Forgive me, Father. No one understands. No one cares to understand. How long will I be so alone? I know you are here, or I would have perished by now. Waves and torrents of memories wash over and over me. Demons in hell riding those waves. Yet you sit enthroned over the flood. You tell me you are my Rescuer. Yes, you rescue me from the arrows that fly by night. You rescue me from the pestilence and the assault of the enemy. In you I trust. To you I turn my gaze. I say to you, "Father, I trust you." Help me.

Father Speaks

Child, you are walking a very troublesome path right now. I have allowed it. It is for my purpose you are needing me so desperately. Caution, my child. The enemy of your soul wishes to not just sift you; he wishes to destroy you, who you are in me. I am right beside you. I am holding your hand. I am supporting you and infusing you with my power and strength. You have felt surges of my presence. Little breakthroughs of happiness. Soon the clouds will part. Oh, child, soon this will end.

Scripture

Yet I am always with you; you hold me by my right hand. (Psalm 73:23, NIV)

Simon, Simon, behold, Satan demanded to have you, that he might sift you like wheat, but I have prayed for you that your faith may not fail. And when you have turned again, strengthen your brothers. (Luke 22:31–32, ESV)

For I hold you by your right hand—I, the LORD your God. And I say to you, "Don't be afraid. I am here to help you." (Isaiah 41:13, NLT)

Be strong and courageous. Do not be afraid or terrified because of them, for the LORD your God goes with you; he will never leave you nor forsake you. (Deuteronomy 31:6, NIV)

Let's Make It Personal

1. Do you recall a time the enemy came to sift you? Are you still being sifted? Can you journal about that? Journaling can be painful sometimes. Yet getting your feeling down on paper seems to take some of the emotional "power" out of the situation.
2. Please know that while the enemy demanded to have you, to sift you, your Father did not permit him full access to you. If you need to repent of some things, do so now.
3. Father is in control of the circumstances that the enemy levels at you. He changes them in your behalf. Father uses everything that has or is happening in your life to mold you into something beautiful.
4. You are coming through this. The Lord has spoken; you are coming out.

Scripture

God is our refuge and strength, an ever-present help in trouble. (Psalm 46:1, NIV)

So be truly glad. There is wonderful joy ahead, even though you must endure many trials for a little while. (1 Peter 1:6, NLT)

The righteous person may have many troubles, but the LORD delivers him from them all. (Psalm 34:19, NIV)

Confession

The wise choices I make will watch over me, and my understanding will keep me safe. Because you are a faithful God, you strengthen me and guard me from the evil one. (Scripture references: 2 Thessalonians 3:3, NLT; Proverbs 2:11, NLT)

Rest

Cease work or movement in order to relax, sleep, or recover strength. (*Oxford Dictionary*)

Heart's Cry

Why! Why am I so weary? I want to sleep all the time, Father. My body is fatigued. My mind is fatigued. My flesh is so weak right now. I know this crushing need to rest is not from you, Father. You desire that I rest; you have told me to rest. Perhaps this weariness is because I did not rest when I should have. The rest I seek is rest in you. I will resist the enemy. His intent is to take me away from time with you, from listening to you, Father. Rest. I will obey you. You will fortify me, and I will rise up strengthened.

Father Speaks

Yes, rest is what I have called you into. Think it not strange when you feel the need to lie down and rest. Your thoughts must be stayed on me. I desire rest for you. The time to come will require you to be well rested. I have spoken to you that I have a grand plan for you. You have caught a glimpse of it. Yet it is far more marvelous than you have suspected. I will do great and mighty things with and through you. For now, you are strengthening yourself though you know it not. Child, you must give it all to me during this time, for the enemy would take you off track into a great delay. There will be no delay. I spoke it. No delay. We have waited a long time for you, child. My Father, Jesus, and I we need you. And very soon you will be ready. For now, do as I have said. Rest, rest in me. Leave everything else, yes, everything—family, finances, health—to me, for I have a perfect plan, and even now it is being played out. Hold on to me, child, my precious child. For I will not allow you to stumble or fall. My grace holds you. My grace is sufficient. *Amen.*

Scripture

The LORD replied, "My Presence will go with you, and I will give you rest." (Exodus 33:14, NIV)

Call to me and I will answer you, I'll tell you marvelous and wondrous things that you could never figure out on your own. (Jeremiah 33:3, MSG)

But you, LORD, do not be far from me. You are my strength; come quickly to help me. (Psalm 22:19, NIV)

Therefore the LORD longs to be gracious to you, and therefore He waits on high to have compassion on you for the LORD is a God of justice; how blessed are all those who long for Him. (Isaiah 30:18, NASB)

Yes, my soul, find rest in God; my hope comes from him. Truly he is my rock and my salvation; he is my fortress, I will not be shaken. (Psalm 62:6–7, NIV)

Let's Make It Personal

1. Grab your journal. Write about your weariness, your bone-tired weariness. You feel like shutting down? Life can cause one to feel chronically fatigued, too many heavy burdens.
2. The believer is encouraged to enter into God's rest. He has called you to this; it will be for refreshing. He calls out to you "Come to me, all of you who are weary and carry heavy burdens, and I will give you rest" (Matthew 11:28, NLT).
3. Tell your Father what you need during this time. Listen to his guidance. Be sure to journal.
4. Believe that he has a perfect plan for your life and he is ready and willing to share that with you.

Scripture

He gives strength to the weary and increases the power of the weak.
(Isaiah 40:29, NIV)

Take my yoke upon you. Let me teach you, because I am humble and gentle at heart, and you will find rest for your souls. For my yoke is easy to bear; and the burden I give you is light. (Matthew 11:29–31, NLT)

In all your ways submit to him, and he will make your paths straight.
(Proverbs 3:6, NIV)

The heart of man plans his way, but the LORD establishes his steps.
(Proverbs 16:9, ESV)

Confession

I am so thankful to you, Father, that you make it possible for me to lie down and rest in the safety you have provided for me. You have told me that your presence goes with me wherever I go and you provide the rest I need. (Scripture references: Psalm 4:8, NLT; Exodus 33:14, NIV)

Restless Heart

Showing inability to remain at rest: a restless mood: unquiet or uneasy. (*Dictionary.com*)

Heart's Cry

Father, I know I need to seek you out when my heart feels so restless. I could go to my friends and ask for advice, but only you, Father, see my heart. You are the only one that knows the reason for my restless feelings. I feel that something must need fixed or changed in my life, Father. Help me understand what it is, how you see it. I will hear from you and obey your directions. For only you know the why behind these feelings. Only you know how to help me.

Father Speaks

Child, child, why are your thoughts so restless? A mind stayed on me is a mind at peace. A mind at peace can hear my voice. If you hear my voice, you will be able to receive direction. If you are able to receive direction, you will know which path to take, what direction to walk in. My way is easy, walk with me. Come, let us begin. Keep in step with me. Relax, know that I am guiding you. Do you trust me, child? It is your choice. Ask, and it shall be given to you. Do you believe?

Scripture

Do not be anxious about anything, but in every situation, by prayer and petition, with thanksgiving, present your requests to God. And the peace of God, which transcends all understanding, will guard your hearts and your minds in Christ Jesus. (Philippians 4:6–7, NIV)

I will also walk among you and be your God, and you shall be My people. (Leviticus 26:12, NASB)

For I have stayed on God's paths; I have followed his ways and not turned aside. (Job 23:11, NLT)

Let's Make It Personal

1. Restlessness is something all of us have dealt with one time in our lives. It can be all-consuming as we make vain attempts at satisfaction. List some things you have done in an attempt to calm your restlessness.
2. Know that your Father is not the author of this malady. Is it a direct assault from the enemy? Or is it coming from your soul? Do you feel like you are not productive unless you are constantly doing something?
3. Do not chastise yourself for this. The Holy Spirit is the Comforter and wants to help you navigate through to victory.
4. Pray and seek God's view. Journal what he tells you. Ask for scriptures that will help you overcome the need or compulsion to be "busy" all the time. Seek out a trusted friend to help you, hold you accountable.

Scripture

And we know that God causes everything to work together for the good of those who love God and are called according to his purpose for them. (Romans 8:28, NLT)

Those who seek the LORD lack no good thing. (Psalm 34 :10b, NIV)

Confession

I will give you all my anxieties because you care about me. I cannot add a single hour to my life by being anxious. (Scripture references: 1 Peter 5:7, NLT; Matthew 6:27, ESV)

Revelation

An act of revealing or communicating divine truth. Something that is revealed by God to humans. (*Merriam-Webster Dictionary*)

Heart's Cry

I must find you, Father. Where are you? I search for you and cannot find you. Show yourself to me. Speak to me. Your Word promises me that if I seek for you, I will find you. I know you will never leave or forsake me. Thank you, Father, for sending your Word to me. It is my strength and my salvation. On you I will wait, and in the waiting I will be strengthened.

Father Speaks

Revelation, revelation is here. Do you perceive it? I have a message for you. Listen, listen, child, for I am speaking. It is revealing time. Are you ready? Revealing me as only you can for, I have taken you down a road only you could walk with me. There were times you felt so alone. I was there. There were times you felt so lost. I was there. There were times you searched for me. I was there. I revealed myself to you as you were ready to accept me. Strong you are. Stronger, daughter. From here we will go from strength to strength. For I AM is here.

Scripture

So that the God of our Lord Jesus Christ, the Father of glory, may give you the Spirit of wisdom and revelation in the knowledge of Him. (Ephesians 1:17, ESV)

Moreover, I will make My dwelling among you and My soul will not reject you. (Leviticus 26:11, NASB)

For flesh and blood has not revealed this to you, but my Father who is in heaven. (Matthew 16:17, ESV)

They go from strength to strength. (Psalm 84:7, NIVa)

Let's Make It Personal

1. Can you remember a time that you searched for the Father and it did not seem like he was near?
2. Were you searching for him in his Word? I can promise you that if you seek him in his Word, he will be found by you. His Word is life to you.
3. Journal your feelings about sensing a distance from the Father. There will be nothing you can say that he is not aware of. Be honest, be bold as you come before his throne with your concerns.
4. Please know that during the quiet times, Father is trusting you to come close to him and to seek him. He wants to reveal himself to you, to be found by you. You will grow from those times. Always journal your experiences.

Scripture

If you look for me wholeheartedly, you will find me. (Jeremiah 29:13, NLT)

Those who know Your name will put their trust in You, for You, LORD, have not forsaken those who seek You. (Psalm 9:10, ESV)

Confession

I will seek you with all my heart, for you have made me glad with the joy of your presence. I am blessed continually. (Scripture references: Jeremiah 19:13, NIV; Psalm 21:6, ESV)

Revive

To restore to life, consciousness or strength. To give new strength or energy to. (*Merriam-Webster Dictionary*)

Heart's Cry

My Father, at times, in the night hours, I find myself off guard. Yet I know you are with me! I purpose to give my thoughts to you, bring them under control. I am gaining my strength! Which comes from you and you alone. You delight in blessing your children. I give you my concerns and cares of this world. I am blessed! I am happy in YOU! Therefore, I have joy and favor that comes upon me when I experience your grace in my life!

Father Speaks

Child, today is a day of new beginnings. Can you not feel something? Something is changing. Listen for my voice, seek me this day and I will be found by you. For I have many unexpected blessings in store for you. The hours of pain, the days of pain, the months of pain shall come to an end. I decree it to be so. I have gone before you. Yea I was there at the beginning of time. I have watched you, cried with you, rejoiced with you and most of all I have hope with you. Open yourself to me, allow me to come in and visit with you, to tell you things you do not understand; just yet. The time is short and I choose to prepare you for what is to come. My delight will be in using you, a willing vessel. We have much to do, many to reach. Come take my hand child let us begin. Welcome to your new journey with me your Savior, teacher, guide, lover, healer and your God. Child you shall walk this way and not that way. You will hear a voice behind you directing your path. You must believe this.

Scripture

Do you not know? Have you not heard? Has it not been told you from the beginning? Have you not understood since the earth was founded? (Isaiah 40:21, NIV)

"You are my witnesses," declares the Lord, and my servant whom I have chosen, that you may know and believe me and understand that I am he. Before me there was no god formed, nor shall there be any after me. I, I am the LORD, and besides me there is no savior. (Isaiah 43:10–11, ESV)

"I am the Alpha and the Omega," says the Lord God, "who is and who was and who is to come, the Almighty." (Revelation 1:8, ESV)

I am the LORD, the God of all mankind. Is anything too hard for me? (Jeremiah 32:27, NIV)

Sing to the Lord, praise the LORD, for he has rescued the needy from the clutches of evildoers. (Jeremiah 20:13, CEB)

Let's Make It Personal

1. When life is hard, do you find it hard to have peace even though you have faith? Can you process your thoughts and journal about that?
2. During your life, have you thought that it is easier to avoid your problems than face them?
3. Your Father in heaven is the great I Am. He is everything you could ever have need of.
4. You can trust God to be what he says he is. That should bring you peace and happiness even during the storms of life.

Scripture

I will call out to my Lord and He will answer me.
He will show me great and mighty things that I do
not understand yet. (Jeremiah 33:3, NKJV)
For I am the Lord! If I say it, it will happen. (Ezekiel 12:25, NIV)
For I am the LORD who heals you. (Exodus 15:26b, NLT)
I am merciful. (Exodus 22:27b, NLT)

Confession

I lie down and sleep in peace, for you alone, O Lord, makes
me dwell in safety. You are "I Am," and you do not change.
(Scripture references: Psalm 4:8, NIV; Malachi 3:6, NIV)

See

To notice or become aware of someone or something.
(*Merriam-Webster Dictionary*)

Heart's Cry

Am I missing you, Father? What am I not seeing? You desire to dwell with me and speak to me. I want that too. Not only do I think I may not be seeing you correctly, I believe that others do not see me either. Not that I want to be noticed, no! However, the gift you have given me to write and to share your Word, I do want others to accept. It is from you not me. Perhaps others are focused on hearing from you and do not perceive you have something to speak to them through me. Whatever it is, I am okay with it. You are the one that will reveal me if you want others to see me, the you in me. Thank you, Father, that I can rest in you. It is not about me. It is all about you.

Father Speaks

There will be a day of revelation. Others will see you as I see you. They will understand a bit better the call upon your life that I place there before the beginning of time. Yes, daughter, there has been a mighty call upon your life since the beginning of time. You are just now beginning to understand. Seeing in a light dimly, what path I have set out for you, what race I have planned for you, what direction I have you walking in. You will hear the still, small voice behind you reassuring you to walk in my ways, my direction, the path I have set up for you. I will deflect the enemy's arrows. He desires to stop such a force as you. He derailed you for a period of time. He will not have you again. You have done well, daughter. I have taken such delight in you. I am the lover of your soul. Is there anything too difficult for me to do for you? Walk my way, listen for my voice. We will have a grand journey together. Come, let us begin.

Scripture

Now we see things imperfectly, like puzzling reflections in a mirror, but then we will see everything with perfect clarity. All that I know now is partial and incomplete, but then I will know everything completely, just as God now knows me completely. (1 Corinthians 13:12, NLT)

Therefore, since we are surrounded by such a huge crowd of witnesses to the life of faith, let us strip off every weight that slows us down, especially the sin that so easily trips us up. And let us run with endurance the race God has set before us. (Hebrews 12:1, NLT)

Your own ears will hear him. Right behind you a voice will say. "This is the way you should go," whether to the right or to the left. (Isaiah 30:21, NLT)

I am the LORD, the God of all mankind. Is anything too hard for me? (Jeremiah 32:27, NIV)

Let's Make It Personal

1. Have you ever felt as though no one sees you? Perhaps you're in a small group and you feel as though no one sees you. Can you journal about your feelings?
2. Know this: you are not invisible. Your Father sees you, and he is so very pleased with you. Sometimes all you can do is remind yourself of that fact. It hurts sometimes, to feel like no one even cares enough to "see" you.
3. There has been a specific call placed on your life; perhaps walking through this "invisible" time is just what he wants you to understand to be a tool for his use in the future. Know that he who has called you will be faithful to bring it all to pass.
4. The ones he has placed a powerful call on must walk through the valley, be purged and refined for his use. Hold on, light is breaking forth, soon you will see clearly.

Scripture

Lift up your eyes and look to the heavens: Who created all these stars? He who bring out the starry host one by one and calls forth each of them by name. Because of his great power and might strength, not one of them is missing. (Isaiah 40:26, NIV)

You have searched me, LORD, and you know me. You know when I sit and when I rise; you perceive my thoughts from afar. (Psalm 139:1–2, NIV)

Where can I go from your Spirit? Where can I flee from your presence? If I go up to the heavens, you are there; if I make my bed in the depths, you are there. If I rise on the wings of the dawn, if I settle on the far side of the sea, even there your hand will guide me, your right hand will hold me fast. (Psalm 139:7–10, NIV)

Confession

He gives me strength, and I can do all things. He goes before me and will level mountains. He will break down gates of bronze and cut through bars of iron for me. (Scripture references: Philippians 4:13, NIV; Isaiah 45:2, NIV)

Seeking

To try to find by searching; look for to seek a solution, to try to obtain or acquire. (*Dictionary.com*)

Heart's Cry

How I long to come closer to you, Father. My heart aches for you. I do not ever want to be the same after encountering you. Create in me a heart that longs for you. Cause me to draw closer to you. Call me, and I will come. Speak to me, and I will listen. Touch me, and I will be forever changed.

Father Speaks

I need you. Therefore, I am drawing you. This will be a time that I will release a new seeking draw upon your life. You will begin to seek me and long for me. You will begin to say, "I must have intervention, I must have a breaking-in of God's presence and his life." I am going to draw you, and you will seek me in a way you haven't sought me. You will know me in a way you haven't known me. Feel the drawing, and submit to the drawing. Watch your new level of seeking begin. I will draw you into that which you have been longing to experience.

Scripture

Create in me a clean heart, O God; and renew a right spirit within me. (Psalm 51:10, KJV)

Blessed (happy, fortunate, to be envied) is the man whom You choose and cause to come near, that he may dwell in Your courts! We shall be satisfied with the goodness of Your house, Your holy temple. (Psalm 65:4, AMP)

God looks down from heaven on the entire human race; he looks to see if anyone is truly wise, if anyone seeks God. (Psalm 53:2, NLT)

Sow for yourselves righteousness; reap steadfast love; break up your fallow ground, for it is the time to seek the LORD, that he may come and rain righteousness upon you. (Hosea 10:12, ESV)

Let's Make It Personal

1. Are you seeking his face? You desire a closer walk with him. Journal about that. Write about your feelings and how you are seeking him.
2. He is always with you, yet there are times you do not feel his presence with you. The Bible tells us that we are to seek the Lord's presence continually even when his evident, mindful presence is not your constant companion.
3. Could it be because at times he is neglected and no thought has been given to him?
4. Mental choice is what seeking is all about. You must direct your heart toward God as is stated in 2 Thessalonians 3:5 (ESV), "May the LORD direct your hearts to the love of God and to the steadfastness of Christ."

Scripture

Now set your mind and heart to seek the LORD your God.
(1 Chronicles 22:19a ESV)
Seek the LORD and his strength; seek his presence continually!
(Psalm 105:4, ESV)
Ask, and it will be given to you; seek, and you will find;
knock, and it will be opened to you. For everyone who
asks receives, and the one who seeks finds, and to the one
who knocks it will be opened. (Matthew 7:7–8, ESV)
You have said, "Seek my face." My heart says to you,
"Your face, LORD, do I seek." (Psalm 27:8, ESV)
And without faith it is impossible to please him, for whoever
would draw near to God must believe that he exists and that
he rewards those who seek him. (Hebrews 11:6, ESV)

Confession

I will search for the Lord and for his strength continually. You love me, and because I diligently seek you, I find you. (Scripture references: 1 Chronicles 16:11, NLT; Proverbs 8:17, ESV)

Serve

Perform duties or services for another person or organization.
(*Oxford Dictionaries*)

Heart's Cry

When I awake from sleep, my soul is yearning for you. Father, how I long to go deeper in you during my quiet times with you. Yet my flesh is such a nuisance. It does not want to settle down. Therefore, I must train it to desire time with you as I desire time with you. Guide and direct me, Father. You are the one and only God. You are my Father in heaven. I love you, Father. I want to be used by you as never before. You are my God in whom I trust. Speak to me, and I will listen to you. Guide me, lead me, and I will follow.

Father Speaks

I would say to you this day shall be like no other day. For this is the day your Lord has made. My people must choose to rejoice and be glad in it for I am in it. I am here. One must pray for eyes to see me, ears to hear me, and a heart that desires me. My eyes are roaming to and fro across the earth, seeking one who would serve me. One whose heart is mine, one whom I can move in and through. I have much to get accomplished in this world, and I must have ready and willing workers. Seek me, seek my voice in your daily activities so that I may work through you. I have so many I desire to reach. The harvest is ripe, yet I have so few who would stand up and say, "Send me, my Lord." To serve me with abandon means to know me and to seek to walk in a deeper walk with me. To desire me and my presence above all else—above all else—above all that calls and demands your attention. I must be more important than all else. Search yourself, my child, see if there be any wicked way in you. For I desire a spotless bride. Where the spirit of the Lord is, there is not room for imposters. For I offer a refining fire. I desire you to be the vessel I created you to be—cleansed, purified, strengthened in all power and ready for your master's work. Come now, child.

Scripture

For the eyes of the LORD run to and fro throughout the whole earth, to give strong support to those whose heart is blameless toward him. (2 Chronicles 16:9a, ESV)

For we are God's fellow workers. You are God's field, God's building. According to the grace of God given to me, like a skilled master builder I laid a foundation, and someone else is building upon it. Let each one take care how he builds upon it. For no one can lay a foundation other than that which is laid, which is Jesus Christ. (1 Corinthians 3:9–11, ESV)

How much more then, will the blood of Christ, who through the eternal Spirit offered himself unblemished to God, cleanse our consciences from acts that lead to death, so that we may serve a living God! (Hebrews 9:14, NIV)

He told them, "The harvest is plentiful, but the workers are few. Ask the Lord of the harvest, therefore, to send out workers into his harvest field. (Luke 10:2, NIV)

Let's Make It Personal

1. You must realize this, keep it tucked away in your heart: God is never in a hurry, and he is never too late. He knows the perfect time to bring about what you have asked of him. He knows right well the call he has placed upon you.
2. Do you consider yourself to have come a long way in your walk with the Father? Do you think he has brought you this far to leave you? Journal your thoughts.
3. Your life may be difficult right now, and you could be facing tough issues; you must believe that your God would NEVER abandon you.
4. He has called you to serve him and the struggles you are facing could very well be the enemy of your soul attempting to keep you from moving forward in the calling upon your life.
5. It could be your flesh that is the problem. Are you are going through the refiner's fire? Ask the Father to show you and give you a plan to overcome those obstacles. You have a call to fulfill. You desire to serve the God of the universe, and nothing because of him will be too difficult for you.

Scripture

And we know that for those who love God all things work together for good, for those who are called according to his purpose. (Romans 8:28, ESV)

Have I not commanded you? Be strong and courageous. Do not be afraid; do not be discouraged, for the LORD your God will be with you wherever you go. (Joshua 1:9, NIV)

Behold, I have refined you, but not as silver; I have tried you in the furnace of affliction. (Isaiah 48:10, ESV)

I am the LORD, the God of all people.
Nothing is too difficult for me.

Confession

I will press on toward the prize for which God has called me to in Christ Jesus. He has commanded me to be strong and courageous not to be discouraged because he goes with me wherever I go. (Scripture references: Philippians 3:14, NIV; Joshua 1:9, NIV)

Snare

A position or situation from which it is difficult to escape. (*Merriam-Webster Dictionary*)

Heart's Cry

Those that call themselves my enemies have plotted to bring me to ruin by damaging my family. It is my very being they desire to extinguish. Assaulting my loved ones and relentlessly pursuing them and pointing their accusing finger. But, GOD! You are my Redeemer and the vindicator of my family. For you know we have done no evil. We have inflicted pain on no one. You have seen it all, and you speak vindication over us. You have created a snare for my enemies, and soon they will be caught in it.

Father Speaks

This is just the beginning, child. For now, I have opened the door; no man will shut it. I have declared a blessing be upon you and your family. This is just the beginning. For your eyes will see the deliverance of your Lord. Deliverance from your enemies. Those who would see you destroyed will themselves eat of that bitter fruit. The snare has been set. You have done well, my child, I am pleased with you. Keep calling out to me. Keep desiring me in your life. Keep desiring my friendship. Continue walking forward step by step; I have this. For I delight in you. Come, child, let the journey begin.

Scripture

Keep me from the snares they have laid for me, and from the traps of the workers of iniquity. Let the wicked fall into their own nets, while I escape safely. (Psalm 141:9–10, NKJV)

I know what you do. I have put before you an open door that no one can close. I know you are weak, but you have followed my teaching. You were not afraid to speak my name. (Revelation 3:8, ERV)

Likewise, David said, "Let their bountiful table become a snare, a trap that makes them think all is well. Let their blessings cause them to stumble, and let them get what they deserve." (Romans 11:9, NLT)

Let's Make It Personal

1. Have you experienced relentless attacks from others? Maybe you are still walking through some tough stuff. Can you express how you feel? Journal about it.
2. Do you believe that the Father was/is walking through the trouble waters with you?
3. Be encouraged! The Father has set a snare for your enemies! Soon you will see the deliverance of the Lord!
4. He has the way for you to walk through this. Journal what he tells you and obey.

Scripture

If you forgive others the wrongs they have done to you, your Father in heaven will also forgive you. (Matthew 6:14, GNT)
When you go through deep waters, I will be with you. When you go through rivers of difficulty, you will not drown. When you walk through the fire of oppression, you will not be burned up; the flames will not consume you. (Isaiah 43:2, NLT)

Confession

I rejoice because I will not have to fight my battles. I will call out to you, and you will answer me and tell me great things. You have instructed me to stand still and watch the LORD's victory, for he is with me. (Scripture references: 2 Chronicles 20:17a, NLT; Jeremiah 33:3, NIV)

Soon

As in a short time, in the near future or quickly. (*YourDictionary*)

Heart's Cry

Come quickly, Lord Jesus! How long, oh, Lord? There are things changing in the spirit realm. I can sense them. I will listen and obey your direction, for the time is short, and you have many to reach. Speak, and I will obey you, Father. You have called many for such a time as this. It is my prayer that those you have called have answered. Much is needed to be done. Show me which way to walk. Tell me what to say.

Father Speaks

Tell my children I am coming soon. I will come on a day, at a time they know not. I bring my glory with me. All of heaven is on alert. Can you not hear the rejoicing, the laughter? For my day is appointed; it shall not tarry. Many are seeking my face. I will be found by many. Rejoice, for your redemption draweth nigh. Gird yourself, child. Put on the armor I have provided for you. Walk out! Walk out! Walk forward into the battle. I declare to you no harm shall befall you. I have a call, and I have a purpose for you. Come, child, I am waiting. I am excited. I am ready. I am ready to fill you up to overflowing with me. I will fill your spirit; I will fill your heart; I will fill your mouth. Come! I can hardly wait. Come with me, child; let us begin the magnificent journey. For I have called. I created you; I formed you in your mother's womb for such a time as this. Pick up your sword! Pick up your pen! Pick up your books, let us begin!

Scripture

I will be found by you, declares the LORD. (Jeremiah 29:14a)
Look, I am coming soon! My reward is with me,
and I will give to each person according to what
they have done. (Revelation 22:12, NIV)
Finally, be strong in the Lord and in his mighty
power. Put on the full armor of God, so that you can
take your stand against the devil's schemes.
(Ephesians 6:10–11, NIV)
The one who calls you is faithful, and he will
do it. (1 Thessalonians 5:24, NIV)
No harm will overtake you, no disaster will come near your tent.
(Psalm 91:10, NIV)
Before I formed you in the womb I knew you, before
you were born I set you apart. (Jeremiah 1:5a, NIV)

Let's Make It Personal

1. Do you hear the Father calling? He is calling you to be united with him in every aspect of your life. What is he saying to you?
2. Are you fearful of these last days? Is it because you don't trust him or because of all the uncertainties? Journal about that.
3. Perhaps you are excited. Ready to move with the Lord. Are you putting on the whole armor of God so that you can stand against the enemy?
4. How can you get better prepared for what Father has called you to do?

Scripture

Have I not commanded you? Be strong and courageous. Do not be afraid; do not be discouraged, for the LORD your God will be with you wherever you go. (Joshua 1:9, NIV)

No one can come to me unless the Father who sent me draws them, and I will raise them up at the last day. (John 6:44, NIV)

Confession

If I seek you with all my heart, your Word tells me I will find you. You will equip me to do your will and work out in me everything that is pleasing to you. This will all be to your glory. (Scripture references: Jeremiah 19:13, NIV; Hebrews 13:21, NIV)

Sorrow

A feeling of deep distress caused by loss, disappointment, or other misfortune suffered by oneself or others. (*Oxford Dictionaries*)

Heart's Cry

Such sorrow consumes me. I cannot see beyond it. When will this sadness relinquish its hold on me? I am very weary of this sadness. Help me, Father, for surely, he (Jesus) carried my sorrows. I must give them to him; come swiftly to help me.

Father Speaks

Some are called to walk a harder road than others, my precious child. You cannot move and manifest me the way I desire to use you without having experienced some of what I call sorrow. I will allow only that which will make you, will prove you, will set you apart for an intimate close fellowship with me, the one acquainted with sorrow. I will carry you lest you hit your foot against a stone, lest you become to weary and want to lay your sword down. I will strengthen you. I am even now strengthening you.

Scripture

Be glad about this, even though it may now be necessary for you to be sad for a while because of the many kinds of trials you suffer. (1 Peter 1:6, GNT)

For I am convinced that neither death nor life, neither angels nor demons, neither the present nor the future, not any power, neither height nor depth, nor anything else in all creation, will be able to separate us from the love of God that is in Christ Jesus our Lord. (Romans 8:38–39, NIV)

Blessed by the God and Father of our Lord Jesus Christ, the Father of mercies and God of all comfort, who comforts us is all our afflictions, so that we may be able to comfort those who are in any affliction, with the comfort with which we ourselves are comforted by God. (2 Corinthians 1:3–4, ESV)

Let's Make It Personal

1. No! Your sorrow will not last forever. That is a lie of the enemy. You are deeply loved and needed by your family and friends! Please remember the enemy wants to destroy you. John 10:10a (NIV), "The thief comes only to steal and kill and destroy. But GOD! He comes to give life and give it abundantly."
2. The enemy of your soul has great timing. He knows what to say and when to say it. It is all lies! John 8:44b (NIV), "He was a murderer from the beginning," Jesus also said of Satan, "not holding to the truth, for there is no truth in him." When he lies, he speaks his native language, for he is a liar and the father of lies.
3. I know that the sadness that Jesus went through is something you will never have to encounter. In the Garden of Gethsemane, he spoke the words found in Matthew 26:38 (NIV), "My soul is overwhelmed with sorrow to the point of death."
4. Jesus endured it all for you. He will reach down and take your hand and show you the way through your sorrow. Open his Word, and journal what he shows you.

Scripture

Is anyone crying for help? God is listening, ready to rescue you. If your heart is broken, you'll find God right there; if you're kicked in the gut, He'll help you catch your breath. (Psalm 34:17–18, MSG)

So do not fear, for I am with you; do not be dismayed,
for I am your God. I will strengthen you and help you;
I will uphold you with my righteous right hand.
(Isaiah 41:10, NIV)

Confession

My God is my refuge and my strength; he is a very present help in trouble. He goes before me and will be with me; he will never leave me or forsake me. I will not be afraid or discouraged. (Scripture references: Psalm 46:1, ESV; Deuteronomy 31:8, NIV)

Sound

Something that you can hear or that can be heard. (*Cambridge English Dictionary*)

Heart's Cry

Father, I know hard times are on the way. However, I also know your protection is all over your kids, those of us who answered the call who listened to the new sound to follow you.

Father Speaks

The enemy is gathering his troops for a full-out assault on my children. He has already lost the battle. Yet my people act as though he is still the roaring lion seeking someone to devour. It is true, and sad, that many of my children are believing the bad reports. They are seeing the enemy's destruction in their own life and in the lives of others. Their focus must be on ME. Therein lies the crossroad. Believe in me and my power. Complete, perfect belief, or believe in what the enemy of their soul is doing. Choices in this dark hour. Many believe this is the darkest hour for America and the world. I say to you, this is the finest hour to be alive! For I am surely doing a new thing! There is a new sound! My people who are called by my name must rise above the troubles of this world. Their focus must be fixed on me. Hear me, hear the new sound. Believe, children. For I am your Deliverer from all things. All things! You shall walk through the fire and not get burned. I declare to you this day, no harm will come to my beloved. They are kept under the shadow of my almighty wings.

Scripture

But the Lord stood by me and strengthened me, so that through me the message might be fully proclaimed and all the Gentiles might hear it. So I was rescued from the lion's mouth. (2 Timothy 4:17, ESV)

The Lord said to his people: "You are standing at the crossroads. So consider your path. Ask where the old, reliable paths are. Ask where the path that leads to blessing and follow it. If you do, you will find rest for your soul." But they say, "We will not follow it." (Jeremiah 6:16, NET)

See, I am doing a new thing! Now it springs up; do you not perceive it? I am making a way in the wilderness and streams in the wasteland. (Isaiah 43:19, NIV)

When you go through the deep waters, I will be with you. When you go through rivers of difficulty, you will not drown. When you walk through the fire of oppression, you will not be burned up; the flames will not consume you. (Isaiah 43:2, NLT)

Let's Make It Personal

1. Have you been feeling like there is something different in the spirit? Can you describe it?
2. Journal everything you feel is changing. Are you believing the bad reports?
3. Are you one that hears the sound and will obey the Father?
4. What does that look like to you in your current situation? Are you ready to hear and obey the Father?

Scripture

Why are you down in the dumps, dear soul? Why are you crying the blues? Fix my eyes on God. Soon I'll be praising again. He puts a smile on my face. He's my God. (Psalm 42:5, MSG)

Do your best to present yourself to God as one approved, a worker who has no need to be ashamed, rightly handling the word of truth. (2 Timothy 2:15, ESV)

Confession

You answered me and delivered me from all of my fears because I let my eyes look straight ahead and kept my gaze directly upon you. (Scripture references: Psalm 34:4, NLT; Proverbs 4:25, NIV)

Speak

Say something in order to convey information or to express a feeling, talk to in order to reprove or advise. (*Oxford Dictionaries*)

Heart's Cry

Lately I have been seeking you, and it seems like you are very quiet. I remind myself of the things you have spoken to me. I must find you and hear from you to walk in the way you have shown me. You have told me that I am to speak to others for you. If that is what you desire for me, you will have to fill my mouth with your words. Will I be able to express your heart to others? Am I the one you want? If you lead, I will follow; when you speak, I will speak. I know that you will never let me down. It is my greatest heart's desire to be used by you and to bring glory to your name. I will keep my eyes on you and my heart in tune with yours. Thank you, Father, for trusting me.

Father Speaks

I will speak with you. You have sought me, looked for me, desired me. Yet it seemed to you that I was hiding from you. Child, look at me, seek me. I will be found by you, greater than you can imagine, more powerful and mighty than you have thought. I am an awesome God. A fearful God. Those who seek me must seek me with a pure heart, a heart open to my spirit. For I desire to use you, child, in a much more powerful way. For those who see my anointed shall say, "There is one who loves the Lord and is called according to his purpose." My walk for you is great. I desire to be revealed to those around you, through you. Those that have an ear will hear. Those that can see will see. Those who can feel will experience me in a new and magnificent way. You are called to open the eyes of the blind, to lead and direct them to me, the lover of their souls. For only at my feet will they find what they have been seeking. Speak as I direct. Lead where

I direct. Show others the love of the Father through you. Let your light so shine before man that they will surely find me.

Scripture

And we know that God causes everything to work together for the good of those who love God and are called according to his purpose for them. (Romans 8:28, NLT)

In the same way, let your light shine before others, that they may see your good deeds and glorify your Father in heaven. (Matthew 5:16, NIV)

My heart says of you, "Seek his face!" Your face, LORD, I will seek. (Psalm 27:8, NIV)

For the LORD your God is the God of gods and Lord of lords. He is the great God, the mighty and awesome God, who show no partiality and cannot be bribed. (Deuteronomy 10:17, NLT)

Whoever has ears, let them hear. (Matthew 11:15, NIV)

You will open the eyes of the blind. You will free the captives from prison, releasing those who sit in dark dungeons. (Isaiah 42:7, NLT)

Let's Make It Personal

1. God speaks in a still, small voice which prompts your spirit to do or speak.
2. How do you know it is him speaking to you? Does what your heard line up with scripture? Have you sought good counsel about what you believe he has spoken?
3. Your ability to understand spiritual things come from a relationship with the Holy Spirit. He will teach you, reveal to you what the Word says. God will instruct you through his Word. You will never discover truth; truth is revealed to you by the Holy Spirit. As you search the Word, you will have an encounter with God.
4. When he shows you what he wants of you, be quick to obey. Review with the Holy Spirit what you heard. If you are hearing him, you must respond to his voice. To neglect the call a time could come where you will find yourself in a famine of hearing the Lord speak to you.

Scripture

I will stand on my guard post and station myself on the rampart; and I will keep watch to see what He will speak to me, and how I may reply when I am reproved. (Habakkuk 2:1–2, NASB)
I will instruct you and teach you in the way which you should go; I will counsel you with My eye upon you. (Psalm 32:8, NIV)
Your word is a lamp to my feet and a light to my path. (Psalm 119:105, NASB)
The spirit of man is the lamp of the LORD, searching all the innermost parts of his being. (Proverbs 20:27, NASB)

Confession

I will call out to my Father, and he will answer me and tell me great and hidden things that I have not known before. I am blessed because I hear the Word of God and I keep it. (Scripture references: Jeremiah 33:3 NASB; Luke 11:28, NASB)

Stand in the Breach

Stepping in to the breach is to take the place of someone who is suddenly unable to do a job or task. To stand in the breach is to bear the brunt of attack when other defenses have failed. (*The Free Dictionary*)

Heart's Cry

What am I feeling, Father? Such an urgency to pray, to reach out to others. So many are lost or sitting on the fence (lukewarm), and so many people have become disillusioned in their walk with you. Tell me, Father, how am I to help? What have I to offer? Speak and guide me. I will obey your call.

Father Speaks

I am in the midst of all the hustle and bustle around you. Let not your heart be troubled, neither let it be afraid. I hear the cries of the hearts in the people around you. Oh, if they would only turn to me for comfort. I would answer their hearts cry. So many people, so many without me. Can you sense my yearning for those lost? Those who know not of my salvation. Those who choose to know not of me. My heart yearns for them. I call and they do not heed the call. I knock, and they do not answer. Yet for a short time my patience will linger. I am now and will forever remain hopeful. The harvest is ripe. There are too few workers. Out of those workers, I have called them all; few have answered. Pray, my child, pray for those lost that they will find the way home before it is too late. To the lukewarm, I say, soon you will no longer hear my call, I will give you over to your own demise. To those on fire, I say to you, your fire will be stoked hotter and hotter for there is much to do. There is little time. Sound the alarm, daughter! Stand in the breach!

Scripture

And I sought for a man among them who should build up the wall and stand in the breach before me for the land, that I should not destroy it, but I found none. (Ezekiel 22:30, ESV)

Then he said to his disciples, "The harvest is plentiful but the workers are few." (Matthew 9:37, NIV)

For many are called, but few are chosen. (Matthew 22:14, NIV)

Then I heard the voice of the Lord saying, "Whom shall I send? And who will go for us?" And I said, "Here am I. Send me!" (Isaiah 6:8, NIV)

Let's Make It Personal

1. Have you ever felt an urgency to tell others about Jesus Christ? Did you?
2. Journal your thoughts and your concerns.
3. Now take those to the Father in prayer. Ask him how you are to reach out to the lost. Life-changing transformation is the purpose of God's calling upon your life.
4. Journal what he tells you, and be willing and obedient to do what he says.
5. He will not leave you by yourself; he will walk every step with you, and he will give you the words to speak to others.

Scripture

Pray also for me, that whenever I speak, words may be given me so that I will fearlessly make known to them the mystery of the gospel. (Ephesians 6:19, NIV)

Don't worry or surrender to your fear. For you've believed in God, now trust and believe in me also. (John 14:1, TPT)

Confession

I thank you, Father; you are so faithful to me. You have called me, and you will bring it to pass as I call out to you in truth. (Scripture references: 1 Thessalonians 5:24, NASB; Psalm 145:18, NASB)

Steadfast

Resolutely or dutifully firm and unwavering. (*Online Dictionary*)

Heart's Cry

I must tell you, Father. I love you so! Yet I do not show it enough. For that I am saddened. I want you to fill me up! I want to be who you created me to be. My desire is to get deeper into you. The cares of this world interfere. Cares about money, job, survival—these scream at me demanding my attention. I do not want that! Help me, Father, to believe you have everything under control. Help me in my unbelief. I must be steadfast in what and who you are in and to me. Thank you, Father, for rescuing me.

Father Speaks

How far are you willing to walk with me? Is there any limit I place upon myself? Why should you limit me? Have you not been told that you are limitless? Have people not spoken into your life regarding where I want to take you? Check you heart, child. What is the true desire that resides there? Who put that desire there? Did I? If you search yourself and realize that the desire is tucked away in me, with me, then I will be able to move mightily in your life. We shall walk together to build your heart's desire as long as you keep your eyes upon me. Keep snuggled in close with me, resting in me, in my direction for your life. For I am well able to accomplish more than you could ever imagine or think in and for you. It is my heart's desire to help you find the desire, to nurture that desire, to cause you to arise and shine in me. Nothing do I choose to keep from you. Can you dream with me, child? Dream your Father's dream. I am here to bring it all to pass in your life. For what is tucked away in your heart was planted there by me; I delight in watching you unwrap treasures in your life that have been given to you by me, the lover of your soul.

Scripture

God blesses those whose hearts are pure, for they will see God. (Matthew 5:8, NLT)

I keep my eyes always on the LORD. With him at my right hand, I will not be shaken. (Psalm 16:8, NIV)

May he grant you your heart's desire and fulfill all your plans! (Psalm 20:4, ESV)

And I am sure of this, that he who began a good work in you will bring it to completion at the day of Jesus Christ. (Philippians 1:6, ESV)

Now all glory to God, who is able, through his mighty power at work within us, to accomplish infinitely more than we might as or think. (Ephesians 3:20, NLT)

Let's Make It Personal

1. Have you put God in a box and limited him? When things did not work out, or just did not look right to you, did you limit God? Journal your thoughts.
2. Your Father in heaven is unlimited in power and knowledge. He is full of compassion and grace. He knows what is best and he wants that for you.
3. Has someone told you what they think the call is on your life? Did it resonate with you? Why or why not? Your calling comes from the Father, and it must be confirmed through him and his Word.
4. You can live the desires of your heart. Finding God's purpose for you and then mining out scriptures to confess over yourself on a daily basis will lead you in victory!

Scripture

The Lord is now slow to fulfill his promise as some count slowness, but is patient toward you, not wishing that any should perish, but that all should reach repentance. (2 Peter 3:9, ESV)

So faith cometh by hearing, and hearing by the word of God. (Romans 10:17, KJV)

For I know the plan I have for you, says the Lord. They are plans for good and not for disaster, to give you a future and a hope. (Jeremiah 29:11, NLT)

Confession

Before God made the world, he chose me. I have been called by him to fulfill the dreams he has given to me. I am worthy of the calling; my purpose is to please him in every way. My faith is strong, and I will live out my dreams. Because I am growing in the knowledge of God, I am continually hearing the voice of the Father. (Scripture references: Ephesians 1:4, NIV; Romans 10:17, NLT; Colossians 1:10, NIV)

Strengthen

To become stronger, more forceful, more effective. (*Merriam-Webster Dictionary*)

Heart's Cry

I do not understand, Jesus. Something is happening or is going to happen? I must have your strength. I am weary, Jesus. It is my belief that you told me that you were angry at the assault against me and that you have prayed for me. That you are strengthening me. Strengthen me, Father, and I will overcome. I must have more of you, more of your power within me.

Father Speaks

From this day you shall walk in stronger authority. In power and might. For I have called you. I equip those I call. I have risen you above. Strengthen, strengthen, child. I have equipped you for the things to come. I have prepared you so that they will not take you by surprise. I am so near you, child. I reside within you! All my power resides within you. Step out, I say step out! Look up! For I will sustain you! I will strengthen you! Step into the journey with me, I delight in you.

Scripture

Do not fear, for I am with you; do not anxiously look about you, for I am your God. I will strengthen you, surely, I will help you. Surely I will uphold you with My righteous right hand. (Isaiah 41:10, NASB)

Everyone must submit to governing authorities. For all authority comes from God, and those in positions of authority have been place there by God. (Romans 13:1, NLT)

The LORD is my strength and my defense; he has become my salvation. He is my God, and I will praise him, my father's God, and I will exalt him. (Exodus 15:2, NIV)

Let's Make It Personal

1. When was the last time you ask Father to strengthen you? Did He? How?
2. Journal about the way in which he strengthens you. Be specific.
3. Are you ready for the things Father has planned for you? What do you think he meant by the things to come?
4. If you will not be taken by surprise, how have you prepared yourself? Scripture holds all the answers. Call upon him, and he will answer you.

Scripture

He gives strength to the weary and increases the power of the weak. (Isaiah 40:29, NIV)

This is all the more urgent, for you know how late it is; time is running out. Wake up, for our salvation is nearer now than when we first believed. (Romans 13:11, NLT)

Be thankful in all circumstances, for this is God's will for you who belong to Christ Jesus. (1 Thessalonians 5:18, NLT)

Confession

I will skip and dance all the day long, because you are near to me as I call upon you. At daybreak you surprise me with your love because I am searching for you. I can do all things through Jesus Christ, who gives me strength. (Scripture references: Psalm 90:14, MSG; Psalm 145:18, NIV; Philippians 4 :13, NIV)

Strong

Able to withstand great force or pressure. (*Online Dictionary*)

Heart's Cry

Am I strong enough for this walk? So many others seem to have it together. Their walk with you seems to be so grounded and powerful. When I look at myself, I see weakness. I want to be strong in you. It must come from the you inside of me. As I seek your face and abide in your Word, I know you are perfecting that which is in me. You are burning out the dross in me with your Word and your Spirit. Thank you, Father, for making me into what you have called me to be.

Father Speaks

Stay in your own lane, daughter. I planted gifts in you that are for you only. Time is not yet. Abide in me. I will abide in you and strengthen you for the journey we have ahead of us. Let there be no comparisons. You are wonderfully made. You were made in my image. All is well. Say all is well. Shout all is well. For I hold your day in the palm of my hand. I hold your future, daughter. Allow me to move in you, to breathe in you, to conquer in you. Amen and amen, your Father declares it. It is so.

Scripture

Have I not commanded you? Be strong and courageous. Do not be afraid; do not be discouraged, for the LORD your God will be with you wherever you go. (Joshua 1:9, NIV)

Pay careful attention to your own work, for then you will get the satisfaction of a job well done, and you won't need to compare yourself to anyone else. For we are each responsible for our own conduct. (Galatians 6:4–5, NLT)

Let's Make It Personal

1. Are you sensing that you are not as strong in your walk as others are? How does that make you feel? Remember, you are to keep your focus on the path he has put you on. No other.
2. Do you think your Father wants you to walk out the strength he has placed in you? He has specific people that need the strength he is in you. These people will be able to identify with you and what you have to offer them. There is where your ministry is.
3. Are you uncertain about the gifts he has planted in you? If so, confess that to him and ask him to help you find your way.
4. He has a good and perfect direction for your life. You are the only one that can do what he has called you to do. His calling upon you is irrevocable. Rejoice in that!

Scripture

For God's gifts and his call can never be
withdrawn. (Romans 11:29, NLT)
Seek his will in all you do, and he will make your paths straight.
(Proverbs 3:6, NLT)

Confession

You have commanded, called, and commissioned me
to do it and will be sure to help me out in it. I will be
strong and courageous when I am in the way of duty,
for my God goes ahead of me and he won't fail me.
(Scripture references: Joshua 1:9, NLT; Deuteronomy 31:6, NLT)

Surprise

Something that surprises. The feeling caused by something unexpected or unusual. (*Merriam-Webster Dictionary*)

Heart's Cry

What is it, Father? I have such anticipation. Is there something unusual happening? You have told me that in your time things would change for me, for my situation. Is the time now? Should I be expecting you? Are you calling me to see and hear clearer? I am listening for your voice. Speak.

Father Speaks

For this time has come for you to see clearer, much clearer into what I am doing with you, with and in those around you. With the hearts of my children. Be wise with the revelation I share with you. Some will be for public pronouncement, others for you and I to know. For you to pray about. For me to work out in you. For yes, I have a plan for you. It began long ago. It has lain dormant. Now it has been awakened. I am calling it forth. You have heard the call, the beginnings of it. Oh, my precious child, you are now ready to walk with me, your father. Such great plans I have for you. Many, many blessings will be falling upon you from my hand.

Scripture

May he equip you with all you need for doing his will. May he produce in you, through the power of Jesus Christ, every good ting that is pleasing to him. All glory to him forever and ever! Amen. (Hebrews 13:21, NLT)

The one who calls you is faithful, and he will do it. (1 Thessalonians 5:24, NIV)

The unfolding of your words gives light; it imparts understanding to the simple. (Psalm 119:130, ESV)

The godly offer good counsel; they teach right from wrong. (Psalm 37:30, NLT)

Faithful is He who calls you, and He also will bring it to pass. (1 Thessalonians 5:24, NASB)

Let's Make It Personal

1. Have you ever anticipated something good coming from the Father?
2. What did that feel like? Were you expecting good things? Were you hoping for good things? Did you tell him about it?
3. Journal about that. Find scripture to confirm what the Father has been doing. Trust that you are able to hear his voice clearly.
4. Now look to him with joy in your heart, for surely, he is up to something good. He delights in surprising his children.

Scripture

Delight yourself in the LORD, and he will give you the desires of your heart. (Psalm 37:4, ESV)

But as for me, I watch in hope for the LORD, I wait for God my Savior, my God will hear me. (Micah 7:7, NIV)

Confession

I will see the way of life because you grant me the joy of your presence and pleasure of living with you forever. Each morning I am filled with your unfailing love. (Scripture references: Psalm 16:11, NLT; Psalm 90:14, NIV)

Sustain

Strengthen or support physically or mentally. (*Online Dictionary*)

Heart's Cry

Father, some days deep sadness overwhelms me. I know you are here with me. I know I need to cry out to you. You will help me. My help comes from you, Father. In the deep, broken places, I know you reside there with me. You have never left me. You will never forsake me. You have placed a call upon my life. I feel as though the enemy of my soul has robbed me of walking into what you have for me. But, GOD! You would never leave me on my own. He who called me is able.

Father Speaks

Give it all to me and leave it with me, child. I am quite able to bring you through this. I am so near you, child. I reside within you. All my power resides within you. I who placed a call upon you am able, am faithful to bring it to fruition. Need you doubt me? Step out, I say, step out! Take the step out of the boat; don't look down. Look up! The one who called you is able. I am able. I placed the call upon your life. I will do it! I will sustain you. I will strengthen you. Step into the journey with me. I delight in you.

Scripture

But when God, who set me apart from my mother's womb and called me by his grace, was pleased to reveal his Son in me. (Galatians 1:15–16a, NIV)

I am he who will sustain you. I have made you and I will carry you; I will sustain you and I will rescue you. (Isaiah 46:4, NIV)

God will strengthen you with his own great power so that you will not give up when troubles come, but you will be patient. (Colossians 1:11, NAS)

Let's Make It Personal

1. Are you at the point of giving up? Grab your journal and write about those feelings.
2. Take those feelings to the Father. Remember, nothing will take him by surprise.
3. Do you believe he can sustain you?
4. What do you need from the Father in order to feel his sustaining power? Tell him what you need, what you want from him. Believe that he has heard and he has the answer you seek.

Scripture

Cast your burden on the LORD, and he will sustain you; he will never permit the righteous to be moved. (Psalm 55:22, ESV)

And we know that for those who love God all things work together for good, for those who are called according to his purpose. (Romans 8:28, ESV)

Confession

You Father are so good. You are a stronghold in the day of my trouble. I can cast all my cares upon you because you care for me. I can take refuge in you. (Scripture references: Nahum 1:7, ESV; 1 Peter 5:7, ESV)

Terror

A state of intense fear. (*Merriam-Webster Dictionary*)

Heart's Cry

In the night hours the replay of the accident fills me with terror. The enemy replays the entire thing in my mind. His accusations, so brutal. You were always there, as close as the mention of your name. When I cried out for peace in my mind, you came to my rescue. You took my thoughts captive. In your mercy you rose up inside of me with your power to cause the enemy to flee. Thank you, Father, for being a safe place for me.

Father Speaks

There are times in our lives that tragedy hits, sorrow comes, disbelief tries to set in. I have come to set you free of troublesome times. I AM the answer to your sorrows. I AM the answer to your questions. When the enemy comes in, like a flood my presence will lift up a standard against him. This I do for you, child. Take hold of my hand and hold tight. Listen to the sound of my spirit within you. For it is speaking, singing, making beautiful sounds within you. Ask me, and I will open your ears, that you will hear better what is happening in the spirit. I will open your eyes, and I will show you amazing things that you know not of right now. Come, let us reason together, child.

Scripture

Then you will call, and the LORD will answer; you will cry for help, and he will say: Here am I. (Isaiah 58:9a, NIV)

The hearing ear and the seeing eye, the
LORD has made them both.
(Proverbs 20:12, ESV)

So shall they fear the name of the LORD from the west, and his glory from the rising of the sun. When the enemy shall come in like a flood the Spirit of the LORD shall lift up a standard against him. (Isaiah 59:19, KJV)

Let's Make It Personal

1. List a time when the enemy of your soul caused terror in your mind.
2. How did you handle that? Did you call upon the Father for help?
3. If you did, how did he help you? Journal about it.
4. Write down all the positive things you can about your experience with the Father and how he came to your rescue.

Scripture

In righteousness you shall be established; you shall be far from oppression, for you shall not fear, and from terror, for it shall not come near you. Indeed they shall surely assail you fiercely, but not from Me, whoever assails you shall fall for your sake. (Isaiah 54:14–15, MEV)

God is our refuge and strength, always ready to help in trouble. (Psalm 46:1, NLT)

Confession

I give you all the glory, Father, for when I am in trouble and call out for you, you come to my rescue. If you are for me, Father, who can be against me? (Scripture references: Psalm 50:15, NLT; Romans 8:31, NIV)

The Call

A cry made as a summons or to attract someone's attention. (*Online Dictionary*)

Heart's Cry

Oh, that I would hear your voice again. Is that you that I hear calling me? Surely it must be, for I will not heed the voice of another. Speak to me, Father, I will listen.

Father's Word

There is a time coming soon, yes, it is at the door. Those who are mine will heed the call. I am calling those that will. Come arm yourself with love and peace. Learn from me. Look to my example. I did not come to bring peace but a sword. What does that mean? Search what does that mean? I walked in perfect love, and I carried a powerful sword. I knew my Father, and he knew me. It was his will that I came to you, that I brought love, peace, and a sword. I submitted to my Father. This you to must do! Is he everything to you? Are you ready to allow him to have his will? Arm yourself. Pick up your sword, walk in love, bring peace to those around you. The world is in a desperate place. The world needs me. You are me to this world. Shout aloud; proclaim Jesus to the world. I have called you; will you answer the call?

Scripture

For the word of God is alive and powerful. It is sharper than the sharpest two-edged sword, cutting between soul and spirit, between joint and marrow. It exposes our innermost thoughts and desires. (Hebrews 4:12, NLT)

Do not suppose that I have come to bring peace to the earth. I did not come to bring peace, but a sword. (Matthew 10:34, NIV)

God is not a man, that He should lie, nor a son of man, that He should repent. Has He spoken, and will He not do it? Or has He spoken, and will He not make it good? (Numbers 23:19, MEV)

God is faithful, who has called you into fellowship with his Son, Jesus Christ our Lord. (1 Corinthians 1:9, NIV)

Let's Make It Personal

1. Have you heard the Father call you? Did your heart burn inside of you when you heard him speak?
2. Was it in the still, small voice? His Word?
3. Are you prepared to count the cost of serving Jesus? To truly follow Christ, he must become everything to you.
4. What do you think "everything" means? Once you have listed some of them, open the Word, and get his understanding of what your call looks like.

Scripture

They said to each other, "Didn't our hearts burn within us as he talked with us on the road and explained the Scriptures to us?" (Luke 24:32, NLT)

For the gifts and the calling of God are irrevocable. (Romans 11:29, ESV)

For many are called, but few are chosen. (Matthew 22:14, ESV)

Confession

I know you are near to me as I call upon you in truth. You will make things happen for me because you are faithful. I love you, Lord, with all my heart, my soul, my mind, and my strength. (Scripture references: 1 Thessalonians 5:24, NLT; Psalm 145:18, NIV; Mark 12:30, NLT)

Tragedy

An event causing great suffering, destruction, and distress, such as a serious accident. (*Oxford Dictionaries*)

Heart's Cry

Why was I not more aware of what was happening? Because of my neglect tragedy struck. You saw it coming, Father. I could ask you why you did not warn me so that I could have stopped it. Yet I will not ask that. I will ask that you help me, heal me, and enable me to leave it in the past where it belongs. This is going to take some time. A lot of time for me to heal. For my family to heal. However, it is your will that we all come through this healed and set free from the trauma. Thank you, Father, for caring for me and my family.

Father Speaks

I was there; I was there when tragedy struck. I never left you. I was there to help you. I was there to help you breathe. I walked every step with you. At times it was me that carried you. I saw to it that you survived. You are still here. You are overcoming. Keep your eyes on me, hold tight to my hand. We will walk through this together, child. I will never leave you.

Scripture

Even though I walk through the darkest valley, I will fear no evil, for you are with me; your rod and your staff they comfort me. (Psalm 23:4, NIV)

Even to your old age I am he, and to gray hairs I will carry you. I have made, and I will bear; I will carry and will save. (Isaiah 46:4, ESV)

Let's Make It Personal

1. Has something tragic happened to you? Did you wonder where the Father was?
2. Can you believe he was right there with you?
3. Did you reach out for his help during that time?
4. Journal your thoughts and feelings. Take them to the Father. Ask him to help you with any unanswered questions. Trust that he will be truthful with you and you will find solace.

Scripture

Come to me, all who labor and are heavy laden, and I will give you rest. (Matthew 11:28, ESV)
Do not be afraid or discouraged, for the LORD will personally go ahead of you. He will be with you; he will neither fail you nor abandon you. (Deuteronomy 31:8, NLT)

Confession

I will experience God's peace, which exceeds anything I can understand. The angel of the LORD defends me. His peace guards my heart and mind as I live in Christ Jesus. (Scripture references: Philippians 4:7, NLT; Psalm 34:7, NLT)

Transition

The process or a period of changing from one state or condition to another. (*Online Dictionary*)

Heart's Cry

I know it is time. It is time for breakthrough, for transitioning from the old to the new. You truly are a good, good Father! Thank you for loving me. You are my wonderful Counselor, Prince of my Peace. You are God above all gods. You are my Healer. Nothing can withstand your power and intention. You are my Comforter, my Guidance, my Salvation; you are my Peace. The cares of this world diminish in the light of your Word. For your Word is a light unto my path. You direct my steps. I shall not stumble. I will hear your voice behind me saying, "This is the way, walk in it." You go before me, walk beside me, and are my rear guard. I know that you have decreed an eternal plan for my life; it is for your glory. You have foreordained everything, and it will come to pass as you have willed.

Father Speaks

I decree and declare that from this day forward—those hearts that are crying out to me for more, more shall you have. I seek a heart that is open and hungry for me. Come, child, come. I delight in you. Oh, child, come, I desire to gather you under my wings as a mother hen gathers her chicks. I desire to fill you, to grant you the desire of your heart. When your desire is for me, you shall have that which you pray for. This day, child, be filled to overflowing with my spirit. For those who will, the spirit says come. Come to the fountain of life. Come to the lover of your soul. Come to me. I desire you. I love you. Can you even begin to comprehend that love?

Scripture

See, I am doing a new thing! Now it springs up; do you not perceive it? I am making a way in the wilderness and streams in the wasteland. (Isaiah 43:19, NIV)

I know that you are pleased with me, for my enemy does not triumph over me. In my integrity you uphold me and set me in your presence forever. (Psalm 41:11–13, NIV)

For he satisfies the longing soul, and the hungry soul he fills with good things. (Psalm 107:9, ESV)

For with you is the fountain of life; in your light we see light. (Psalm 36:9, NIV)

For I am God, and there is no other; I am God, and there is not one like me, declaring the end for the beginning and from ancient times things not yet done, saying, "My purpose shall stand, and I will fulfill my intention." (Isaiah 46:9–10, KJV)

Let's Make It Personal

1. Have you called out to God to fill you up with him? He loves you so much he sent the Holy Spirit to indwell you. The Holy Spirit will fill you up with peace and his presence. As you vacate, God occupies!
2. God is eager to satisfy the thirsty and fill up the hungry with all good things.
3. Call upon him to fill up all your empty places. It is time to move on from what was in the past. God has a new day for you, a new future.
4. From this day forward, it will not be what you say but who you represent that others will be drawn to. Others will see the Jesus Christ in you and want to know him.

Scripture

O God, you are my God; I earnestly search for you. My soul thirst for you; my whole-body longs for you in this parched and weary land where there is no water. (Psalm 63:1, NLT)
Blessed are those who hunger and thirst for righteousness, for they will be filled. (Matthew 5:6, NIV)
He fills my life with good things. My youth is renewed like the eagle's!
(Psalm 103:5, NLT)
For the kingdom of God does not consist in talk but in power.
(1 Corinthians 4:20, ESV)

Confession

Because I am in Christ, I am a new creation; the old has gone, and the new is here. Now I will let my light shine before others that they may see my good works and glorify my Father in heaven.
(Scripture references: 2 Corinthians 5:17, NIV; Matthew 5:16, NIV)

Trauma

A deeply distressing or disturbing experience. Overwhelms the individual's ability to cope. Includes helplessness, pain, confusion, loss. (*Online Dictionary*)

Heart's Cry

I could have prevented this! My soul screams, wails, feels as though it is torn in two! I feel as though the very air has been sucked out of my lungs. OH, MY FATHER IN HEAVEN! FORGIVE ME! WHAT AM I GOING TO DO? HOW AM I GOING TO MANAGE LIVING WITH ME? During those times I wondered where you were, Father. You were there. You saw it all. In your compassion you did not allow me to be destroyed. I do not understand the "whys" behind this traumatic ordeal. Only you, my Father in heaven, know the answers.

Father Speaks

My dearest child, I was there. I held you up with my arms wrapped around you. You did not sense me at that time. That is okay. I never left your side. The devils in hell tried to get you that day; they wanted to destroy you. But I AM was there to protect you. I AM sheltered you with my wings and sang songs of deliverance over you. My precious child, I knew that was going to happen; it did not take me by surprise. I was ready for it. I was ready and able to carry you through. You did not walk through that alone. You must trust me. No, I did not stop that from happening, but I had a plan. You went through a fiery trail and came out victorious; you don't even smell like smoke. Because of that trauma in your life, you have become stronger than ever. Nothing you have gone through have I not used for your good and for my glory. It has been difficult, I know. Allow me to use the pain and sorrow that hangs on to this day, for it is not designed to hurt you but to mold you into the vessel fit for the potter's hand—my hand. You have been through the refining fire; you are as pure gold.

Scripture

You are my hiding place; you protect me from trouble and surround me with songs of deliverance. (Psalm 32:7, NIV)

But you, O God, are both tender and kind, not easily angered, immense in love, and you never quit! So look me in the eye and show kindness, give your servant the strength to go on, save your dear, dear child! (Psalm 86:15–16, MSG)

He reached down from on high and took hold of me; he drew me out of deep waters. He rescued me from my powerful enemy, from my foes, who were too strong for me. (Psalm 18: 16–17, NIV)

But they who wait for the Lord shall renew their strength; they shall mount up with wings like eagles; they shall run and not be weary; they shall walk and not faint. (Isaiah 40:31, ESV)

Let's Make It Personal

1. Our brains want to reply the traumatic event over and over as if looking for a way to make sense of it. When these events happen, it can take a while to get over the pain and feel safe again. You will feel better. However, from time to time, that event will pop up in your memory. You need to tuck in close to your Father. He will comfort you during those times.
2. Understand, there is no right or wrong way to think, feel, or respond to others. Don't judge yourself. Your reactions are normal. You are reacting to something abnormal in your life.
3. Take time to do nice things for yourself. Yes, even if you don't feel you deserve it. Find a quiet place, pray, and receive comfort from the Holy Spirit. Your Father will never let you down; he will never leave you. You are never alone.
4. At some point you may need to confront situations that are associated with the trauma. Remember you do not have to do this alone. God is with you. Seek out a trusted friend that can be there to walk through this with you.

Scripture

Don't fret or worry. Instead of worrying, pray. Let petitions and praises shape your worries into prayers, letting God know your concerns. (Philippians 4:6, MSG)

Guard your heart above all else, for it determines the course of your life. (Proverbs 4:23, NLT)

All praises belong to the God and Father of our Lord Jesus Christ. For he is the Father of tender mercy and the God of endless comfort. (2 Corinthians 1:3, TPT)

And those who know Your name will put their trust in You, for You, O LORD, have not forsaken those who seek You. (Psalm 9:10, NASB)

And I will bring the third part through the fire, refine them as silver is refined, and test them as gold is tested.

They will call on My name, and I will listen and answer them; I will say, "They are My people," and they will say, "The LORD is my God." (Zechariah 13:9, AMP)

Confession

In my distress I called out for you, Lord; to you, my God, I called. From your temple you heard my voice, and my cry came to your ears. I was confronted in the day of my disaster, but my Lord was my support. You brought me out into a spacious place; you rescued me because you delight in me. (Scripture references: 2 Samuel 22:7, ESV; Psalm 18:18–19, NIV)

Trial

To test quality, value, or usefulness. Difficult experiences and problems. (*Merriam-Webster Dictionary*)

Heart's Cry

One after another. Day after day. When will this end? Am I getting stronger and don't realize it? I feel like one more thing, and I will be down for the count. I am getting weary, Father. I know you have this. I need to see some breakthrough. Help me, strengthen me, and I will come through this trial.

Father Speaks

Child, you have been delivered from a dark scheme sent out against you. During the trial you remained faithful to me. You sought my face. I saw your pain; I heard your cries in the night. I felt your sorrow. I commanded it to stop. It stopped. This day I delivered you from the fowlers snare. I protected you as you navigated through the land mines Satan had planted for you. He has chosen those you love to harm you. This has stopped. The attacks will continue, but I have given you a mighty shield to deflect the arrows sent out against you. You shall walk through the fire, and it shall not harm you. You shall walk through walls and they will crumble before you. The plans and schemes of the enemy hold no power over you. I will deal with those that will to hurt you. I have declared that you are my child in whom I am well pleased. All the demons in hell shall not prevail against you. Those who dare to hurt you will surely hurt themselves. The plots against you are even now being turned against your accusers. I will deal with your enemies. They shall become your footstool. Keep your eyes on me in the coming days and months. To overcome, you must keep your gaze upon me. Lift up your head. Your redemption is drawing nigh.

Scripture

Look to the LORD and his strength; seek his face always. (1 Chronicles 16:11, NIV)

For he will deliver you from the snare of the fowler and from deadly pestilence. (Psalm 91:3, ESV)

He is my loving God and my fortress, my stronghold and my deliverer, my shield, in who I take refuge, who subdues peoples under me. (Psalm 144:2, NIV)

until I make your enemies a footstool for your feet. (Luke 20:43, NIV)

When these things begin to take place, stand up and lift up your heads, because your redemption is drawing near. (Luke 21:28, NIV)

Consider it pure joy, my brothers and sisters, whenever you face trials of many kinds, because you know that the testing of your faith produces perseverance. Let perseverance finish its work so that you may be mature and complete, not lacking anything. (James 1:2–4, NIV)

Let's Make It Personal

1. Be careful when going through trials not to question God or his motives for the trial. When you question, Satan will try to attack you by telling you that God really does not care, that God really does not love you or he would not let you go through this.
2. He will tell you that unbelievers are not going through such adversities. Be quick to turn away from the thoughts he puts in your mind. Turn to scripture to anchor your mind and your heart in Jesus.
3. Trials teach you what you are, what you are made of. Prayer and speaking scripture out loud are the best way to fight against trials.
4. Walking with the Father does not prevent you from facing the darkness; however, it teaches you how to use that darkness as a tool for your growth.

Scripture

The LORD is my light and my salvation—so why should I be afraid? The LORD is my fortress, protecting me from danger, so why should I tremble? (Psalm 27:1, NLT)

For I am the LORD your God who takes hold of your right hand and say to you, do not fear; I will help you. (Isaiah 41:13, NIV)

God blesses those who patiently endure testing and temptation. Afterward they will receive the crown of life that God has promised to those who love him. (James 1:12, NLT)

Confession

I will cast all of my anxiety on my God because he cares for me. And I can do all things through my God who strengthens me. (Scripture references: 1 Peter 5:7, NIV; Philippians 4:13, NKJV)

Tumultuous

Making an uproar or loud, confused noise. (*Oxford Dictionary*)

Heart's Cry

Oh, Father! How can someone be so out of control? Show me the way, Father. I feel like a battering ram used and assaulted by the enemy's waves tossing me this way and then that. But wait! You have always been my safe harbor. I am getting stronger at your feet! It is my mind, Father, this organ, this muscle you placed in my cranial vault; it betrays me. It delights in thinking the worst. It delights in relentlessly harassing me, attempting to conquer me. It is driven by devils from hell. They know me, Father; they know the most painful vulnerable spots to attack me, bring me to my knees. Yes, bring me to my knees before YOU! At the foot of the cross. They cannot win if I do not allow them to win.

Father Speaks

Daughter, the coming days will be tumultuous. The enemy wants to sift you more. I tell you, if you keep your eyes fixed on me and my Word, you will soar above the chaos as an eagle soars above the storm. There will be those who become frustrated that their onslaught against you is not working. I am and I will continue to deal with those that desire to hurt you. The precious ones that just came to your mind—know, you must know that I have them covered and protected. I have heard your prayers. I am a God who answers. From this day forward you will not walk in defeat. Victory is yours in me. Demons shall flee from you as you walk through their schemes. You will tear down gates of bronze, walk through walls of steel. For today receive from me a fresh, new anointing. Power is yours this day. More power is bestowed upon you, child. All you have to do is receive.

Scripture

The Lord is your mighty defender, perfect and just in all his ways; your god is faithful and true; he does what is right and fair. (Deuteronomy 32:4, GNT)
So humble yourselves before God. Resist the devil, and he will flee from you. (James 4:7, NLT)
Indeed, the LORD is the one who will keep on walking in front of you. He'll be with you and won't leave you or abandon you, so never be afraid and never be dismayed. (Deuteronomy 31:8, ISV)
The Lord replies: I have seen violence done to the helpless and I have heard the groans of the poor, now I will rise up to rescue them as they have longed for me to do. (Psalm 12:5, NLT)
I will go before you and will level the mountains; I will break down gates of bronze and cut through bars of iron. (Isaiah 45:2, NIV)
But those who trust in the LORD will find new strength. They will soar high on wings like eagles. They will run and not grow weary. They will walk and not faint. (Isaiah 40:31, NLT)
As for you, the anointing you received from him remains in you, and you do not need anyone to teach you. But as his anointing teaches you about all things and as that anointing is real, not counterfeit—just as it has taught you, remain in him. (1 John 2:17, NIV)

Let's Make It Personal

1. Even in the midst of painful times your Father will be faithful to you. Do you believe that? Why or why not? Journal your thoughts.
2. Read 2 Corinthians 1:3–7, NIV. What word do you read repeated several times?
3. Can you praise God in your troubles? A sacrifice of praise lifted up to the only One who can help you. At times that praise gets wedged in your throat, praise anyway.
4. Suffering is unavoidable, and loss comes. How do you cope during those times? Where do you find hope? Are you committed to follow Jesus even in tumultuous times? Journal about this, and ask the Holy Spirit to guide your time in the Word.

Scripture

Through Jesus, therefore, let us continually offer to God a sacrifice of praise—the fruit of lips that openly profess his name. (Hebrews 13:15, NIV)

Also to you, Lord, belongs gracious love, because you reward each person according to what he does. (Psalm 62:12, NIV)

When you go through deep waters, I will be with you. When you go through rivers of difficulty, you will not drown. When you walk through the fire of oppression, you will not be burned up; the flames will not consume you. (Isaiah 43:2, NLT)

Confession

My hope is in you is not shaken because I know that you share in my sufferings and you share in my comfort. I will give thanks always and for everything to God the Father in the name of my Lord Jesus Christ.
(Scripture references: 2 Corinthians 1:7, ESV; Ephesians 5:20, ESV)

Unveiling

To remove a veil or covering from. To make public. (*Merriam-Webster Dictionary*)

Heart's Cry

Father, something is changing. I can sense a change within me. There is no describing what is happening within me. The atmosphere has changed. I believe you are causing things in my life to line up with your will. While I don't understand what is happening, I say to you, "Have your way with me, Father, where you lead, I will follow."

Father Speaks

Now, this moment unveiling has begun. Can you sense it? Power and more power is yours. Take it, claim it, proclaim it. Now is the time. Now is the presentation. Are you ready? I Am is ready. I Am will do it. Keep your eyes fixed on me now.

Scripture

Call to me and I will answer you. I'll tell you marvelous and wondrous things that you could never figure out on your own. (Jeremiah 33:3, MSG)

Who would have had faith in the word which has come to our ears, and to whom had the arm of the Lord been unveiled. (Isaiah 53:1, BBE)

Let's Make It Personal

1. What has been occurring in your life that leads you to believe that change is coming? There is something happening… Maybe it is on the fringes of your mind, but you can sense something shifting.
2. Journal about it. Seek the scripture to support what you are experiencing.
3. Guard and keep close what he reveals to you. People can be discouraging because they do not understand the call upon your life. The Holy Spirit does, and he is with you to help you.
4. It is possible that you are to keep what you are hearing from the Father between the two of you and a pastor or mentor you trust. Discouragement is something that you want to avoid if at all possible; guard your heart.

Scripture

Above all else, guard you heart, for everything you do flows from it. (Proverbs 4:23, NIV)

I keep asking that the God of our Lord Jesus Christ, the glorious Father, may give you the Spirit of wisdom and revelation, so that you may know him better. (Ephesians 1:17, NIV)

He gives strength to the weary and increases the power of the weak. (Isaiah 40:29, NIV)

Confession

Because your Word is a lamp for my feet and a light on my path, you show me the way of life. You grant me the joy of your presence, and I have the pleasure of living with you forever. (Scripture references: Psalm 16:11, NLT)

Valley

A low point or condition. (*Merriam-Webster Dictionary*)

Heart's Cry

Father, right now I feel like a waste of human flesh just taking up space on this earth. When, when will I come back to who I used to be, who I so want to be again? They say wounded people wound people. How about destroyed people? Do we destroy people? I pray not. I do not want to hurt others. I want to be doing what you called me to do. Today, this day, the struggle is wearing me out. I know for a short time I can pull aside and rest in you. I will be a better version of me when I get through this valley. You would never leave me as I was or as I am. When I come out the other side, when I make it up this mountain, when I overcome, I will be the version of me you called me to be. I will PRAISE you in this storm because I know the trying of my faith is working out great things within me.

Father Speaks

How can I express my love of you, my child? I have given my most precious gift to you, my Son. My one and only Son. Part of the Godhead. Sent to earth because of the deep yearning desire to save you. He came willing, obedient unto death. For you, child. What can I do to show you how much I love you? I will rescue you, my daughter. I am a God of justice. I will say this again. I am a God of justice, and my will, will be done in this situation. Yes, child, I have seen you, watched you as others have tried to take the life from you. They sit in their ivory towers declaring who shall be blessed and who shall not. I declare to you, daughter, I never gave them that authority! For the time has come for justice. I have heard your cries. I have seen your heart. I know your inward thoughts, child. I know how you desire to do my will. You have done well. While others have railed and ranted against you, you found shelter in me.

Scripture

For the Father himself loves you. He loves you because you love me and have believed that I came from God. (John 16:27, GNT)

Vindicate me, O God, and defend my cause against an ungodly people, from the deceitful and unjust man deliver me! (Psalm 43:1, ESV)

And hath given him authority to execute judgement also, because he is the Son of man. (John 5:27, NASB)

He sent from on high, he took me; he drew me out of many waters. He rescued me from my strong enemy, from those who hated me, for they were too mighty for me. They confronted me in the day of my calamity, but the Lord was my support. He brought me out into a broad place; he rescued me, because he delighted in me. (2 Samuel 22:17–20, ESV)

For the mountains may depart and the hills be removed, but my steadfast love shall not depart from you, and my covenant of peace shall not be removed. Says the LORD, who has compassion on you. (Isaiah 54:10, ESV)

Let's Make It Personal

1. Have you walked through the valley? Perhaps you are there now. Encourage yourself with the knowing that God knows exactly what to do, even if you don't. Ask him to guide you through.
2. Valley experiences are a part of life. I am sure you wonder why you have to walk through them. Can you journal your feelings?
3. Your valley will be different than someone else's. God knows what will mature you and strengthen you in him. Valleys can be looked at as a time of pressing into God and coming out the other side more equipped for the road he has put you on.
4. You will be more equipped to extend the hand of hope to someone once you have come through.

Scripture

Lord, even when your path takes me through the valley of deepest darkness, fear will never conquer me, for you already have! You remain close to me and lead me through it all the way. Your authority is my strength and my peace. The comfort of your love takes away my fear. I'll never be lonely, for you are near. (Psalm 23:4, TPT)

After you have suffered for a little while, the God of all grace, the one who called you into his eternal glory in Christ Jesus, will himself restore, empower, strengthen, and establish you. (1 Peter 5:10, CEB)

Confession

I cried out to the Lord, and he answered me and delivered me from all my enemies. In his righteousness he rescued me; he inclined his ear to me and saved me. (Scripture references: Psalm 34:4, 71:2, ESV)

Victory

The overcoming of an enemy or antagonist: achievement of mastery or success in a struggle or endeavor against odds or difficulties. (*Merriam-Webster Dictionary*)

Heart's Cry

I am feeling so much stronger now, Father. What has changed? You have sent your Spirit to comfort me, to strengthen me, to carry me through the deep waters. This is a good feeling, Father! I feel more awake and aware. I am so much more aware of you. Even though I am not fully aware of what you are doing with and in me, I am so at peace that I now can feel you and hear you again. Thank you, Father.

Father Speaks

Child, today is the first day of the rest of your life in me. Think not is strange these feelings you have, for I am in them. I call upon you to pick up your sword and fight the good fight. You will see clearly from this day forward. Obstacles in your way must fall away as you walk forward. Gates of bronze will crumble before you. No demon in hell can stand before you ever again! The power of the enemy in your life and walk is broken. Open your mouth and I will fill it with words of victory. Warfare words shall come forth from your lips. Yes! You shall be a victorious warrior for me from this day forward. I have anointed your lips; I have anointed your eyes to see beyond the veil! Come up higher, child! Now is the day; now is the time I have prepared you, dressed you in my glory, wrapped you in my blood for NO weapon formed against you shall prosper. It is done!

Scripture

Fight the good fight of faith; take hold of the eternal life
to which you were called… (1 Timothy 6:12, NASB)
I will go before you and will level the mountains; I will break down
gates of bronze and cut through bars of iron. (Isaiah 45:2, NIV)
Arise, LORD! Deliver me, my GOD! Strike all my enemies
on the jaw; break the teeth of the wicked. (Psalm 3:7, NIV)
But thanks be to God! He gives us the victory
through our Lord Jesus Christ.
(1 Corinthians 15:57, NIV)
The Spirit of the Sovereign LORD is on me, because the LORD
has anointed me to proclaim good news to the poor. He has sent me
to bind up the brokenhearted, to proclaim freedom for the captives
and release from darkness for the prisoners. (Isaiah 61:1, NIV)
No weapon formed against you shall prosper, and you will
refute every tongue that accuses you. (Isaiah 54:17a, NASB)

Let's Make It Personal

1. Are you sensing your strength coming back to you? In what ways?
2. Do you feel that something has changed in your walk with the Father? Why or why not?
3. Victory is yours! In what ways and what places are you feeling more victorious?
4. Journal what you are sensing. Take it to Father and allow him to speak into your life.

Scripture

For the LORD your God is the one who goes with you to fight for you against your enemies to give you victory. (Deuteronomy 20:4, NIV)
Clap your hands, all ye people! Shout unto God with the voice of triumph. (Psalm 47:1, KJV)

Confession

I will be strong in my Lord and in his mighty power. I boldly say that God is for me and no one can be against me. (Scripture references: Ephesians 6:10, NIV; Romans 8:31b, NIV)

Vision

The faculty or state of being able to see, the ability to think about or plan the future with imagination or wisdom. (*Oxford Dictionary*)

Heart's Cry

There seems to be nothing good in my future. Yet there is that word—*vision*. Vision is a look at what the future holds for me. Father, what is the vision you have for me? You are assembling an army. Those who choose to pick up their sword, walk in peace, and follow you. Those who will stay in their own lane and not compare their gifts to others. You are raising up an army that will have victory in Jesus as their vision. This is the vision you have called me to.

Father's Word

I am raising up an army that will pick up their sword and walk in love and peace into the battle in which they are called. Each one, if willing, will come into the position in this army that I have called them to. There are no better positions than another for each is designed for their gift. The gift I placed in them before the beginning of time. I knew before time began who would stand up and say, "Here am I, send me." You feel the gifting stirring you up. I say to you pick up your sword, walk in peace and love. Come take your place in God's army. Let us walk arm in arm defeating the enemies that come with the word of your testimony and power of the Holy Spirit. The time is now.

Scripture

For the vision is yet for the appointed time; it hastens toward the goal and it will not fail. Though it tarries, wait for it; For it will certainly come, it will not delay. (Habakkuk 2:3, NASB)

Then I heard the Lord asking, "Whom should I send as a messenger to this people? Who will go for us?" I said, "Here I am. Send me." (Isaiah 6:8, NLT)

But in fact God has placed the parts in the body, every one of them, just as he wanted them to be. (1 Corinthians 12:18, NIV)

Let's Make It Personal

1. Do you have a vision? Do you sense a stirring up of gifts within you? Do you know what they are? Have you asked the Father about them?
2. God-given gifts are revealed to us. Some gifts are obvious to others, some are not. That does not mean you are not carrying the gifts he has given to you. You have a specific vision that Father has placed within your spirit.
3. When you are working with your gifts, you struggle less and are happier. The key here is to operate in them consistently. Do not seek after someone else's gift, someone else's vision.
4. Give thanks daily for the gifts you know you have been given. Do a comprehensive study about the gifts that are yours. Practice, practice, practice using your gifts.

Scripture

And the Lord answered me: Write the vision; make it plain on tablets so he may run who reads it. For still the vision awaits its appointed time; it hastens to the end—it will not lie. If it seems slow, wait for it; it will surely come; it will not delay. (Habakkuk 2:2–3, ESV)

Through the power of the Holy Spirit who lives within us, carefully guard the precious truth that has been entrusted to you. (2 Timothy 1:14, NLT)

For we are God's handiwork, created in Christ Jesus to do good works, which God prepared in advance for us to do. (Ephesians 2:10, ESV)

Confession

My Father has not given me a spirit of fear, but of power, love, and a sound mind. So I will stir up the gift he has given me. For he has good plans for me, not disasters. I have a future and a hope in him. (Scripture references: 2 Timothy 1:6–7 NKJV; Jeremiah 29:11, NLT)

Wanted

To have a strong feeling to have; wish; desire greatly. (*The Free Dictionary*)

Heart's Cry

There are times that I have wondered if I am or have ever been wanted. It seems as though others would rather not have me around. Not seeing me makes things easier for them. They don't have to try to help me, to understand me. While I know my situation is difficult for them, it is not too difficult for you, Father. You tell me I was wanted before time began. That you knew me and you formed me in my mother's womb. I am not only wanted by you; you desired me so much you call me the apple of your eye.

Father Speaks

There are so many of my children who still do not know who they are. Who are you? Whose are you? If I am your Father, that makes you my child. You were bought with the blood of my Son, Jesus Christ. If you are my child, then you are seated in the heavenlies with your Savior. Is there anything I do not do for my Son? Are you my child? Have you not heard that everything your Savior Jesus Christ has is yours? What is stopping you from taking your rightful seat next to him? Who told you, you were not worthy? Who told you, you cannot hear me speak to you? You are my child. Does a child not know their Father's voice? When I call, answer me, child. For surely it is I speaking to you. Ask and I will empower you to hear my voice clearer. The counterfeit you will not listen to. It will be like clanging cymbals in your ear. My Spirit, the Spirit, that indwells you will drown out the voice of another. It is time you begin to believe. I need you to hear me. I have much to tell you. You must listen for my voice; the voice of another you will not heed. Come to me. Don't make this hard. I am not the burden-giver; I am the burden-taker. My yoke is light;

my yoke is easy. I am giving you what you ask of me this night. Now it is time, you are under an open heaven. Can you hear me call you? Believe there is nothing I will withhold from you.

Scripture

For you are all children of God through faith in Christ Jesus. (Galatians 3:26, NLT)

He is so rich in kindness and grace that he purchased our freedom with the blood of his Son and forgave our sins. (Ephesians 1:7, NLT)

Do not be conformed to this world, but be transformed by the renewal of your mind, that by testing you may discern what is the will of God, what is good and acceptable and perfect. (Romans 12:2, ESV)

Then Jesus said, "Come to me, all of you who are weary and carry heavy burdens, and I will give you rest." (Matthew 11:28, NLT)

Oh, that you would burst from the heavens and come down! How the mountains would quake in your presence! (Isaiah 64:1, NLT)

Let's Make It Personal

1. God wants you to hear his voice. A. W. Tozer said, "It's the nature of God to speak."
2. Your Father wants to have fellowship with you; he wants you to hear him!
3. Once you learn to tune into his voice, you will experience him every day. Jesus says in the Word, "He who has ears to hear, let him hear."
4. You don't have to go through your life making decisions on your own. He will fellowship with you; you will learn what the Spirit is saying to you. The following are a few scriptures for you. God will not scream and yell at you. He always speaks to you in a still, small voice. You must tune into it and listen carefully.

Scripture

And you will seek for Me and find Me, when you search for me with all your heart. (Jeremiah 29:13, NKJV)
At God's command amazing things happen, wonderful things that we can't understand. (Job 37:5, GNT)
I have been crucified with Christ. It is no longer I who live, but Christ who lives in me. and the life I now live in the flesh I live by faith in the Son of God, who loved me and gave himself for me. (Galatians 2:20, ESV)

Confession

I have ears to hear what you are saying; I will listen and understand. You are just like me; you are my companion, my close friend. (Scripture references: Matthew 11:15, NLT; Psalm 55:13, NIV)

Warfare

Warfare is engagement in violent conflict, or the activities involved with violent conflict. (*YourDictionary*)

Heart's Cry

Father, I am so weary of this spiritual battle. As soon as I think I have overcome the torrent of sadness and hopelessness, it seems to have just begun. Will I ever rise above this raging battle in my soul? Your Word tells me that you have fought the battle for me. That I am to trust you and move forward prepared for victory. Help me strengthen myself in you. Then I will be an overcomer in this warfare that rages on within me.

Father Speaks

Blackness is turned to light. It is over, child; the heavenlies have declared the war is over. You have won. Father heard your prayers before you spoke them. He felt your heart ache before the war began. I tell you, my child, the war has been won. The battle in the heavenlies is over. It is overcome by the word of your testimony. The courtroom of heaven has declared the battle is over. You have won. Your Father has the final Word. It is over. Now rejoice and be glad, for the redemption you seek is nigh to your visual eye, to your reality. Open your eyes, child, open your heart. For I have overcome for you. Victory is yours. Now speak victory.

Scripture

The light shines in the darkness, and the darkness has not overcome it.
(John 1:5, NLT)

And they have conquered him by the blood of the Lamb and by the word of their testimony, for they loved not their lives even unto death.
(Revelation 12:11, ESV)

When Jesus spoke again to the people, he said, "I am the light of the world. If you follow me, you won't have to walk in darkness, because you will have the light that leads to life." (John 8:12, NIV)

When these things begin to take place, stand up and lift up your heads, because your redemption is drawing near. (Luke 21:28, NIV)

You will not need to fight in this battle. Stand firm, hold your position, and see the salvation of the LORD on your behalf… (2 Chronicles 20:17, ESV)

Let's Make It Personal

1. What battle have you been engaged in lately? What have your thoughts been during this time? Remind yourself that you are an overcomer in him!
2. Ask Father how he sees it. What does he want to be to you in this? What does he want you to be in this?
3. He is wanting to give you a strategy for this battle.
4. As you wait upon him, journal the directives he gives to you and put them to work in your life. Victory is yours.

Scripture

In the morning, LORD, you hear my voice; in the morning, I lay my requests before you and wait expectantly. (Psalm 5:3, NIV)
Brothers and sisters, I do not consider myself yet to have taken hold of it. But one thing I do: Forgetting what is behind and straining toward what is ahead, I press on toward the goal to win the prize for which God has called me heavenward in Christ Jesus. (Philippians 3:13–14, NIV)

Confession

My Father is the one that goes with me into battle. He is the one that fights for me. Victory is mine. In him I have overcome because greater is he that is in me than he who is in this world. (Scripture references: Deuteronomy 20:4, NLT; 1 John 4:4, NLT)

Weapon

Something used to injure, defeat, or destroy. A means of contending against another. (*Merriam-Webster Dictionary*)

Heart's Cry

The condemning things being said about me, my family. The finger pointing. The mocking of who I am. Father, I have done nothing. I choose to not respond. I choose to pray for those who are using verbal and spiritual weapons against me. Strengthen me, Father, lest I be destroyed. Hear my prayers and comfort me. Guide me in the right direction.

Father Speaks

The enemy has come at you from many directions. I have come at you from ALL directions. Nothing has been allowed to hit its target. I sit in the heavens and laugh at the enemy and his devices he has set up against you. I enjoy, I take great delight in defeating him for you. You are well trained for this battle. Your mouth is power. I put the words inside your mouth to speak to the assaults. Now speak. All is well. No weapon formed against you will prevail. Your prayers are heard. I am honoring them, child. Trust me in this. Those you love are cherished by me. Woe be unto anyone that attempts to bring them harm. I tell you, daughter. I have heard your pleas; I have felt your heart; I have answered.

Scripture

But the one who rules in heaven laughs. The Lord scoffs at them. (Psalm 2:4, NLT)

No weapon formed against you shall prosper, and every tongue which rises against you in judgement you shall condemn. This is the heritage of the servants of the LORD, and their righteousness is from Me, says the LORD. (Isaiah 54:17, NKJV)

So they will fear the name of the LORD from the west and His glory from the rising of the sun. For He will come in like a narrow, rushing stream which the breath of the LORD drives [overwhelming the enemy]. (Isaiah 59:19, AMP)

I have given you authority to trample on snakes and scorpions and to overcome all the power of the enemy; nothing will harm you. (Luke 10:19, NIV)

Let's Make It Personal

1. Have you experienced verbal attacks against you or someone you love?
2. Journal about your feelings during that time. Did you want to seek revenge?
3. If so, you can tell Father about those feelings. He already knows them anyway. Nothing can be hidden from him. He is a forgiving Father, a comforting Father, an accepting Father. He will help you navigate through.
4. Quiet yourself, close your eyes, and seek his face. Ask him where he was during those times. Listen and watch for his response to you. Be sure to journal about what he says and shows you.

Scripture

Do not take revenge, my dear friends, but leave room for God's wrath, for it is written: "It is mine to avenge; I will repay." says the Lord. (Romans 12:19, NIV)

You are of God, little children, and have overcome them, because He who is in you is greater than he who is in the world. (1 John 4:4, MEV)

I can never escape from your Spirit! I can never get away from your presence! (Psalm 139:7, NLT)

Confession

You, Father, are my mighty Defender and Protector. You are perfect in all you do, and you do what is right and fair. You defend and protect me; I put my hope in your promises. (Scripture references: Deuteronomy 32:4, GNT; Psalm 119:114, GNT)

Weariness

Extreme tiredness; fatigue, reluctance to see or experience any more of something. (*Oxford Dictionary*)

Heart's Cry

Father, I am so tired, so sleepy. At times I have to push through my day by sheer willpower. I desire to lie down and sleep. This cannot be your will for me. I cannot endure anymore bad news. I cannot be the strong one any longer. I must find strength for myself. Extend your hand to me, and I will be strengthened. If not for you, I would surely perish.

Father's Word

You are most weary with the concerns of this life. Much has come against you, yet I have brought you through. You must remember to listen for my voice in the storm. Heed my direction, for surely, I say to you, you will hear my voice behind you saying, this is the way, walk ye in it. There is no room for doubt or discouragement. You must believe that I am who I say I am, and I will accomplish what I declare. Have I not told you I have a plan for your life? Though you see it not, I am bringing it to pass. I speak, you listen and declare boldly the things I speak to you in the quiet. You will discern my voice more clearly every day. Purpose to talk with me every day. Purpose to draw close to me each day, for I have wonderful things to share with you. Treasure in my Word for you to find. Great revelation for the life you walk in and with me. I am leveling the paths before you so that you shall not stumble. You have my power residing in you. Just remember to speak my name, Jesus.

Scripture

Brothers and sisters, I do not consider myself yet to have taken hold of it. But one thing I do: Forgetting what is behind and straining toward what is ahead, I press on toward the goal to win the prize for which God has called me heavenward in Christ Jesus. (Philippians 3:13–14, NIV)

For you have been a stronghold to the poor, a stronghold to the needy in his distress, a shelter from the storm and a shade from the heat; for the breath of the ruthless is like a storm against a wall. (Isaiah 25:4, ESV)

For I know the plans I have for you, declares the LORD, plans to prosper you and not to harm you, plans to give you hope and a future. You will seek me and find me when you seek me with all your heart. (Jeremiah 29:11, 13, NIV)

So is my word that goes out from my mouth: It will not return to me empty, but will accomplish what I desire and achieve the purpose for which I sent it. (Isaiah 55:11, NIV)

Let's Make It Personal

1. Are you overwhelmed with the concerns of this life? Weary to the point of mental exhaustion? Good news! You are in the perfect place to see the deliverance you so desire.
2. He has seen it all. He says "no more doubt" only believe. Believe in him and what he can and will do for you.
3. Your Father loves you with an everlasting love and he is swift with deliverance when he hears his child cry out. In his Word you will find everything you need.
4. Ask anything according to his will and he will do it. He desires to fill you with joy.

Scripture

Therefore, since we are surrounded by such a great cloud of witnesses, let us throw off everything that hinders and the sin that so easily entangles. And let us run with perseverance the race marked out for us. (Hebrews 12:1, NIV)

But they who wait for the LORD shall renew their strength; they shall mount up with wings like eagles; they shall run and not be weary; they shall walk and not faint. (Isaiah 40:31, ESV)

This is the confidence we have in approaching God: that if we ask anything according to his will, he hears us. (1 John 5:14, NIV)

Confession

I will not let my heart be troubled because I trust in God and in Jesus Christ. I commit my way to the LORD; I trust him, and he will act. (Scripture references: John 14:1, NIV; Psalm 37:5, ESV)

Wilderness

An uncultivated, uninhabited, and inhospitable region. (*Online Dictionary*)

Heart's Cry

Father, what can I do? Things have been so difficult for me. I don't want to confess that, but it is truth. When will I come out of this wilderness? I feel so useless, lost in this place called life. You tell me I have a purpose. I don't understand why I have to battel so much. Seems like every time I am awake, I am getting pummeled by memories, my mind. I will call it like it is. It is the enemy of my soul. I need help, Father. When will the breakthrough you have promised come? When will I see life again?

Father Speaks

Child, listen to me, listen to my Word for you. New things are coming. Yes, they have begun. You will no longer walk in the wilderness. I have opened a way for you. Look and see what your Lord has done.

Scripture

For I am about to do something new. See, I have already begun! Do you not see it? I will make a pathway through the wilderness. I will create rivers in the dry wasteland. (Isaiah 43:19, NLT)

This is the confidence we have in approaching God: that if we ask anything according to his will, he hears us. (1 John 5:14, NIV)

Seek his will in all you do, and he will show you which path to take. (Proverbs 3:6, NLT)

The steps of a man are established by the LORD, and he delights in his way. (Psalm 37:23, NASB)

Let's Make It Personal

1. The wilderness is a tough time in which trials are endured and pleasant things of life are absent. Spiritual attacks and temptations occur.
2. This time can be viewed as ordained testing, not a sign that you have sinned.
3. During these times, you are compelled to wait upon the Lord. Find God's peace and even joy in the midst of the wilderness. You will mature in your walk with the Lord; you will be strengthened.
4. Remember that the God who created all good things also created the wilderness. His grace will sustain you, and you will make it through.

Scripture

Then you will call on me and come and pray to me,
and I will listen to you. (Jeremiah 29:12, NIV)
Wait patiently for the LORD. Be brave and courageous.
Yes, wait patiently for the LORD. (Psalm 27:14, NLT)
Count it all joy, my brothers, when you meet trials of
various kinds, for you know that the testing of your
faith produces steadfastness. (James 1:2–3, ESV)

Confession

I am blessed because I hear the Word of God; I
do not merely listen to it; and I obey it.
(Scripture references: James 1:19, NIV; Luke 11:28, NIV)

Wisdom

The quality or state of being wise; knowledge of what is true or right coupled with just judgment; discernment or insight. (*Dictionary.com*)

Heart's Cry

Today hear my cry. Today hear my heart. Father, there are things that have come up in my life that I have no idea how to handle. It weighs heavy on my heart. I know you are the answer. If I ask for wisdom, your Word tells me you will give it to me. So, Father, give me the wisdom I need to navigate through this recent set of circumstances in my life. Thank you.

Father Speaks

Wisdom, pray for wisdom in this season of choices. There are things I want you to take hold of and things to let go of. The things that take you away from me must be released. Many things demand your attention, and you must choose what you listen to. To do according to my will in excellence, you must focus on me. Ask ME! I have equipped you; come walk with me.

Scripture

It is for freedom that Christ has set us free. Stand firm, then, and do not let yourselves be burdened again by a yoke of slavery. (Galatians 5:1, NIV)

A wise man will hear and increase in learning, and a man of understanding will acquire wise counsel. (Proverbs 1:5, NASB)

If any of you lacks wisdom, you should ask God, who gives generously to all without finding fault, and it will be given to you. But when you ask, you must believe and not doubt, because the one who doubts is like a wave of the sea, blown and tossed by the wind. That person should not expect to receive anything from the Lord. (James 1:5–7, NIV)

So let's keep focused on that goal, those of us who want everything God has for us. If any of you have something else in mind, something less than total commitment, God will clear your blurred vision-you'll see it yet! (Philippians 3:15, MSG)

Let's Make It Personal

1. When you've prayed in the past to seek Father's wisdom, were you able to come boldly to him, or did you feel unworthy to approach him like that?
2. Do you remember a time in your life when you asked Father for a specific answer, and he gave it to you? How did it affect you when you realized that he actually answered you with the wisdom you had asked for?
3. What do you need to know from the Father right now? Have you asked him with confidence, knowing he will direct you?
4. Grab your journal and make a list of things you need to know from the Father and present it to him in prayer.

Scripture

My son, if you accept my words and store up my commands within you, turning your ear to wisdom and applying your heart to understanding, and if you call out for insight and cry aloud for understanding, and if you look for it as for silver and search for it as for hidden treasure, then you will understand the fear of the Lord and find the knowledge of God. For the Lord gives wisdom and from his mouth come knowledge and understanding. (Proverbs 2:1–6, NIV)

And since we know he hears us when we make our requests, we also know that he will give us what we ask for. (1 John 5:15, NLT)

Confession

Nothing I desire can compare with my longing to have wisdom for it is more precious that rubies. I have assurance that when I lack wisdom, I can ask God and he will generously give it to me. (Scripture references: Proverbs 3:15, NLT; James 1:5, NIV)

Wounded

Offended or upset by what someone has said or done. (*Cambridge English Dictionary*)

Heart's Cry

Come to me, Father, heal my wounded heart. Your Word tells me that Jesus died on the cross to not only heal my physical wounds, but to heal my emotional wounds as well. I am sure as I call out to you and seek you with all my heart you will hear my pleas and answer me swiftly. Come, Father, with healing in your wings. Touch my wounded heart, and it will be healed.

Father Speaks

Peace is yours, my daughter. These times of trial are for a purpose. I will use every wound to strengthen you, to make you pliable for my use. I have built a hedge of protection around you, my child. You are mine. I have your name inscribed in the palm of my hands. You are mine. I love you. You will not be destroyed. You will be strengthened and upheld by my righteous right hand. Come rest you head upon my chest. Breathe deeply, child, I am with you. I will never leave you. Hold on, daughter, your redemption draws nigh; only wait and trust your father. Trust your daddy, child. Trust me.

Scripture

And after you have suffered a little while, the God of all grace, who has called you to his eternal glory in Christ, will himself restore, confirm, strengthen, and establish you. (1 Peter 5:10, ESV)

Not only that, but we rejoice in our suffering, knowing that suffering produces endurance, and endurance produces character, and character produces hope, and hope does not put us to shame, because God's love has been poured into our hearts through the Holy Spirit who has been given to us. (Romans 5:3–5, ESV)

Count it all joy, my brothers, when you meet trials of various kinds, for you know that the testing of your faith produces steadfastness. And let steadfastness have its full effect, that you may be perfect and complete, lacking nothing. Blessed is the man who remains steadfast under trial, for when he has stood the test he will receive the crown of life, which God has promised to those who love him. (James 1:2–4,12, ESV)

And when these things begin to come to pass, then look up, and lift up your heads; for your redemption draweth nigh. (Luke 21:28, KJV)

The angel of the Lord encamps around those who fear him, and delivers them. (Psalm 34:7, ESV)

Let's Make It Personal

1. Why does God allow trials in your life? This is a difficult question. Can you journal your thoughts about this?
2. One would think if God loved you so much, he would stop all the pain, take it all away. However, that is not what scripture says.
3. The Word teaches that God loves his children and he "works all things together for good" for us (Romans 8:28).
4. Trials and tribulation must have a divine purpose. God's desire is that you grow more and more into the image of his Son. All things in life, including trials, are designed to help you reach that goal.

Scripture

But God demonstrates his own love for us in this: While we were still sinners, Christ died for us. (Romans 5:8, NIV)
And we know that for those who love God all things work together for good, for those who are called according to his purpose. For those whom he foreknew he also predestined to be confirmed to the image of his Son in order that he might be the firstborn among many brothers. (Romans 8:28–29, ESV)
I can do all things through him who strengthens me. (Philippians 4:13, ESV)

Confession

I will rejoice in hope; I will be patient in tribulation; and I will be constant in prayer. For I am to count it all joy when I meet trials of various kinds. I will be silent because my Lord is fighting for me. (Scripture references: Romans 12:12, ESV; James 1:2, ESV; Exodus 14:14, ESV)

Yearning

Have an intense feeling of longing for something, typically something that one has lost or been separated from. (*Oxford Dictionary*)

Heart's Cry

During the night hours, my soul yearns for you. When I awake I am yearning for you. You are the one and only God. You are my Father in heaven. I love you, Father! I want to be used by you as never before. You are my God in whom I trust. Speak to me, and I will listen. Guide me, lead me, and I will follow.

Father Speaks

Child, oh, how I love you! How I rejoice in you, your love for me. Cling to me, child. Draw from me, child. For I delight in filling you up with me. You asked for more, more you shall have. It has begun. Have you not sensed it? My hand is upon you, daughter, my hand of love, protection development. For I want to develop you. I want you for myself, my tool, my gift to you is ME! Abide in me; I shall abide in you. We have many adventures ahead of us, child. Oh, I delight in you. You are mine, and I am yours. Tell me, child, what is it I can do for you? So be it.

Scripture

Oh, that I might have my request, that God would grant me the things that I long for! (Job 6:8)

For He satisfies the longing soul, and fills the hungry soul with goodness. (Psalm 107:9)

You, Lord, are all I have, and you give me all I need; my future is in your hands. How wonderful are your gifts to me; how good they are! I praise the Lord, because he guides me, and in the night my conscience warns me. I am always aware of the Lord's presence; he is near, and nothing can shake me. And so I am thankful and glad, and I feel completely secure. (Psalm 16:5–9, GNT)

Let's Make It Personal

1. How aware are you of the Father's presence in your life? Do you yearn for him? Journal about that; pray about it and write down what the Holy Spirit has to say to you. Don't forget to find scriptures to support the Word you feel was given to you.
2. You will not be able to live your life sold out to God if your heart does not love and cherish him.
3. Ask him to fill you up with more of his love. There is nothing you have to do for that; he desires to love you; to fill you to overflowing with his love. All you need to do is desire it and allow it.
4. He can become your ultimate treasure, one you seek to commune with every day, to sit at his feet receive his love.

Scripture

And it is my prayer that your love may abound more and more, with knowledge and discernment, so that you may approve what is excellent, and so be pure and blameless for the day of Christ, filled with the fruit of righteousness that comes through Jesus Christ, to the glory and praise of God. (Philippians 1:9–11, ESV)
I love you, LORD, my strength. The LORD is my rock, my fortress and my deliverer; my God is my rock, in whom I take refuge, my shield and the horn of my salvation, my stronghold. I called to the LORD, who is worthy of praise, and I have been saved from my enemies. (Psalm 18:1–3, NIV)

Confession

I love the Lord my God with all my heart and with all my soul and with all my might. I will not grow weary in doing good, and I will not lose heart. When the time is right, I will reap what I have sown. (Scripture references: Deuteronomy 6:5, ESV; Galatians 6:9, RSV)

Beautiful

Of very high standard; excellent. Pleasing the senses or mind. (*Online Dictionary*)

Heart's Cry

My Father, my heart swells with love for you. I know I do not love you enough. I want to be consumed by your love. I must move, breathe, and exist because of you. I desire for your power to move through me. Let everything I touch be moved, healed, prayers answered because of you in me. May I bring glory to your name, my Father. May I serve you with abandon. Let me move and live with sublime audacity.

Father Speaks

My beautiful one. My beautiful daughter. You bring me such joy! Oh, how I am moved by you. Just one glance of your eye and I and all of heaven are at attention. What is it that you desire of me, my beautiful one? What can I do for you? Who would you like for me to be to you this day? Come reason with me. Let me fill you to overflowing with my goodness and love. For I love you with an everlasting eternal love. You are my diamond. You have many facets to you. Each one cleverly created by me, the one who loves you. You brighten heaven with your beauty. You fill heaven with your fragrance. Heaven rejoices over you.

Scripture

The LORD appeared to us in the past saying: "I have loved you with an everlasting love; I have drawn you with unfailing kindness." (Jeremiah 31:3, NIV)

You are altogether beautiful, my darling, beautiful in every way. (Song of Songs 4:7, NLT)

Blessed are those you choose and bring near to live in your courts! We are filled with the good things of your house, of your holy temple. (Psalm 65:4, NIV)

And walk in love, as Christ loved us and gave himself up for us, a fragrant offering and sacrifice to God. (Ephesians 5:2, ESV)

I praise you because I am fearfully and wonderfully made; your works are wonderful, I know that full well. (Psalm 139:14, NIV)

How beautiful upon the mountains are the feet of him who brings good news, who publishes peace, who brings good news of happiness, who publishes salvation, who says to Zion, "Your God reigns." (Isaiah 52:7, ESV)

Let's Make It Personal

1. What is it you would like God to do for you? Is that so you can serve others better?
2. When God sees you serving others cheerfully, he will give you more of the things you desire. You are blessed to be a blessing.
3. When you say that God works for you because you cannot do it yourself, you are glorifying him. He gets all the praise.
4. Read John 14:13 in your favorite translation. Then take a moment to reflect on the following. What if the Lord was telling you, "If you will ask anything in my name, I'll make it happen for you"?

Scripture

And he is not served by human hands, as if he needed anything. Rather, he himself gives everyone life and breath and everything else. (Acts 17:25, NIV)

For we are God's masterpiece. He has created us anew in Christ Jesus, so we can do the good things he planned for us long ago. (Ephesians 2:10, NLT)

Confession

My God supplies every need I have because of his riches in Christ Jesus. I will delight myself in the Lord, and he will give me my heart's desires. (Scripture references: Philippians 4:19, ESV; Psalm 37:4, ESV)

Epilogue

It is my prayer that in these pages you have found solace and peace for your soul, peace that can come only from him. For in him we live, breathe, and have our being.

Confession

Father, I pray that by your grace and love for me that utterance may be given to me, that I may open my mouth boldly to make known the mystery of the gospel. For since the beginning of time, men have not heard nor has any ear perceived nor has any eye seen any God beside you, Father! You are the one and only God who acts in behalf of the one who waits for you. Then it shall come to pass for those who wait; before we call upon your name you will answer for you know our hearts cry. Even yet while we are still speaking you will hear! I will remember, God is faithful, by whose name I am called into the fellowship of his Son, Jesus Christ, my Lord and my Savior! (Scripture references: Ephesians 6:1–9, Isaiah 64:4, 65:24, NKJV)

What I tell you in the darkness, speak in the light; and what you hear whispered in your ear proclaim upon the housetops. (Matthew 10:27, NKJV)

Appendix

Basic Bible English (BBE)
Berean Study Bible (BSB)
Common English Bible (CEB)
Contemporary English Version (CEV)
Christian Standard Bible (CSB)
English Standard Version (ESV)
Good News Translation (GNT)
God's Word Translation (GW)
King James Version (KJV)
Message Bible (MSG)
New American Standard Bible (NASB)
New International Reader's Version (NIRV)
New International Version (NIV)
New Living Translation (NLT)
New Revised Standard (NRS)
New King James Version (NKJV)
Revised Standard Version (RSV)
The Passion Translation (TPT)